Generals of the Army

AMERICAN WARRIORS

Throughout the nation's history, numerous men and women of all ranks and branches of the U.S. military have served their country with honor and distinction. During times of war and peace, there are individuals whose exemplary achievements embody the highest standards of the U.S. armed forces. The aim of the American Warriors series is to examine the unique historical contributions of these individuals, whose legacies serve as enduring examples for soldiers and citizens alike. The series will promote a deeper and more comprehensive understanding of the U.S. armed forces.

SERIES EDITOR: Roger Cirillo

An AUSA Book

GENERALS
OF THE
ARMY

Marshall, MacArthur, Eisenhower, Arnold, Bradley

Edited by
James H. Willbanks

Foreword by
General Gordon R. Sullivan, USA (Ret.)

UNIVERSITY PRESS OF KENTUCKY

Copyright © 2013 by the Command and General Staff College Foundation, Inc.

Published by The University Press of Kentucky,
scholarly publisher for the Commonwealth,
serving Bellarmine University, Berea College, Centre College of Kentucky, Eastern
Kentucky University, The Filson Historical Society, Georgetown College, Kentucky
Historical Society, Kentucky State University, Morehead State University, Murray State
University, Northern Kentucky University, Transylvania University, University of
Kentucky, University of Louisville, and Western Kentucky University.
All rights reserved.

Editorial and Sales Offices: The University Press of Kentucky
663 South Limestone Street, Lexington, Kentucky 40508-4008
www.kentuckypress.com

17 16 15 14 13   5 4 3 2 1

Maps are courtesy of the U.S. Army Center of Military History.

Library of Congress Cataloging-in-Publication Data

Generals of the Army : Marshall, MacArthur, Eisenhower, Arnold, Bradley / edited by
James H. Willbanks ; foreword by General Gordon R. Sullivan, USA (Ret.).
    pages cm. — (American warriors series)
  Includes bibliographical references and index.
  ISBN 978-0-8131-4213-5 (hbk : alk. paper) —
  ISBN 978-0-8131-4214-2 (epub) — ISBN 978-0-8131-4212-8 (pdf)
  1. Generals—United States—Biography. 2. Fort Leavenworth (Kan.)—Influence.
3. Marshall, George C. (George Catlett), 1880-1959. 4. MacArthur, Douglas, 1880-1964
5. Eisenhower, Dwight D. (Dwight David), 1890-1969 6. Arnold, Henry Harley, 1886-
1950. 7. Generals—United States—History—20th century. I. Willbanks, James H., 1947-
II. Title: Marshall, MacArthur, Eisenhower, Arnold, Bradley.
  D736.G46 2013
  940.54'12730922—dc23   2013000346

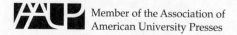

To all those who have served
at Fort Leavenworth, Kansas—
the intellectual center of the U.S. Army

Contents

Maps and Illustrations

Maps

Illustrations

Foreword

The eminent British historian John Keegan once referred to Fort Leavenworth as one of the United States Army's "most sacred places."* Fort Leavenworth was established in 1827 to support the opening of the West. In 1881 it became the Army's schoolhouse to capitalize on the lessons learned from the American Civil War. Today the U.S. Army Command and General Staff College is the Army's leader-development center, standing on the frontier of knowledge and learning in the military arts. Officers educated at Leavenworth have served the nation with distinction in every conflict since the Indian Wars. In particular, Leavenworth left an indelible impression on the Army's conduct in World War II, when Leavenworth graduates filled the great majority of higher-level command and staff positions. Five officers, educated at Fort Leavenworth, who served with distinction in World War II attained the highest military rank that this nation bestows—General of the Army. Though Leavenworth graduates have served with distinction in every conflict since its founding, this book is a tribute to Generals of the Army George C. Marshall, Douglas MacArthur, Dwight D. Eisenhower, Henry H. "Hap" Arnold, and Omar N. Bradley; to the venerable military post that molded and shaped them; and to every officer who ever has served or ever will serve at Fort Leavenworth. The Leavenworth legacy continues.

Gordon R. Sullivan
General, U.S. Army (Ret.)
CGSC Class of 1969
CGSC Deputy Commandant, 1987–88
Thirty-first Chief of Staff, U.S. Army
President, Association of the U.S. Army

* John Keegan, *Six Armies in Normandy* (New York: Viking Press, 1982), 24.

Introduction

James H. Willbanks

Five-star flag rank is the highest rank awarded within the U.S. military establishment in modern times. There were four five-star fleet admirals and five five-star Generals of the Army named during World War II and the years immediately after. To put those promotions in the proper context, it is appropriate to review the evolution of the highest ranks in the U.S. military establishment.

The highest rank ever conferred in the U.S. military is General of the Armies of the United States. Only two officers in our history have been awarded that rank, George Washington and John J. Pershing, although only General Pershing actually held the rank. During the Civil War, Congress conferred the rank of General of the Army on Lieutenant General Ulysses S. Grant, who would eventually wear four stars as the insignia of his new rank. Lieutenant General William T. Sherman, Grant's successor as Commanding General of the Army after the war, was also appointed General of the Army on March 4, 1869. After Sherman's death in 1891, however, the title ceased to exist as a military rank.

Sherman's successor was Lieutenant General Philip H. Sheridan. In June 1888, shortly before Sheridan's death, Congress enacted legislation that discontinued the grade of lieutenant general and merged it with that of General of the Army. This rank was conferred on Sheridan and was discontinued when he died, while still on active duty, on August 5, 1888.

Congress revived the rank of General of the Armies of the United States (which had never before been bestowed) by Public Law 66-45, approved on September 3, 1919, and awarded the title to General John J. Pershing for his wartime service. Pershing continued to wear four stars as the insignia of his rank. No other person held this rank until 1976, when President Gerald Ford posthumously appointed George Washington General of the Armies of the United States and specified that he would rank first among all officers of the Army, past and present.

On December 14, 1944, the temporary rank of General of the Army was reestablished by the passage of Public Law 78-482. Army

Regulation 600-35 specified that Generals of the Army would wear five stars arranged in a pentagonal pattern, their points touching. The rank of General of the Army was created in wartime to give the most senior American commanders parity of rank with their British counterparts holding the rank of field marshal. The temporary rank was declared permanent on March 23, 1946, by Public Law 333, passed by the Seventy-ninth Congress. The law also created a comparable rank of Fleet Admiral for the Navy.

The five five-star Generals of the Army were George C. Marshall (appointed December 16, 1944), Douglas MacArthur (appointed December 18, 1944), Dwight D. Eisenhower (appointed December 20, 1944), Henry H. Arnold (appointed December 21, 1944), and Omar N. Bradley (appointed September 20, 1950). Arnold was redesignated General of the Air Force on May 7, 1949. The first three five-star Fleet Admirals were William D. Leahy (December 15, 1944), Ernest J. King (December 17, 1944), and Chester W. Nimitz (December 19, 1944). William F. Halsey was promoted to Fleet Admiral on December 11, 1945.

During the course of their careers, all the Army five-star generals served and studied at Fort Leavenworth, Kansas. This experience had a seminal influence on the development of their careers. Marshall, for example, observed that "Leavenworth was immensely instructive; not so much because the course was perfect—because it was not—but the associations with the officers, the reading and discussion that we did and the leadership . . . of a man like Morrison [one of his Leavenworth instructors], had a tremendous effect on me."[1] Eisenhower called his time at the Staff College "a watershed" in his career.[2] Not surprisingly, Marshall, Eisenhower, and the other Army five-star generals have been enshrined in the Leavenworth Hall of Fame for their contributions in the service of the nation.

In 2010, following a two-year campaign, the Command and General Staff College Foundation at Fort Leavenworth succeeded in shepherding a bill through Congress to authorize the minting of commemorative coins to honor the Army five-star generals who led U.S. forces to victory in World War II and to recognize the institution they all attended. President Barack Obama signed the bill into law on October 8, 2010.

The book that follows is meant to be a companion piece to the issuance of the special commemorative coins by providing a brief look at the lives of these remarkable men and the contributions they made to the defense of the nation. Since each of these officers worked and studied at Fort Leavenworth and was shaped by the "Leavenworth experience," it is appropriate to begin with a discussion of officer education and the Leavenworth Army schools during the period when these men served and studied at the installation. Following that discussion are separate chapters on Marshall, MacArthur, Eisenhower, Arnold, and Bradley that focus on their early upbringing, their entrance into military service, the evolution of their careers, and their wartime and postwar contributions. What is intended is not hagiography, but rather an objective examination of five men who stand tall in the history of this nation. The book will conclude with an afterword that addresses the Command and General Staff College and its evolution from the days of Marshall, MacArthur, Eisenhower, Arnold, and Bradley to the institution that it is today.

Notes

1. Larry I. Bland, ed., *George C. Marshall: Interviews and Reminiscences for Forrest C. Pogue, Transcripts and Notes, 1956–57* (Lexington, Va.: George C. Marshall Research Foundation, 1986), 134.

2. Dwight D. Eisenhower, *At Ease: Stories I Tell to Friends* (Garden City, N.Y.: Doubleday, 1967), 200.

1

Officer Education and the Fort Leavenworth Schools, 1881–1940

Jonathan M. House

For many people, the term *Army education* refers to the various institutions by which men and women first enter the Army—the military academy at West Point, the Reserve Officers Training Corps, or perhaps basic combat training. In fact, however, these schools are only the first steps in military education. Like any other profession, being a soldier and especially an officer requires lifelong study as well as the study of complex concepts and procedures. Advances in rank bring new responsibilities and constant increases in the intricacies of military operations. If anything, the armed services invest more time and resources in educating their members than do many civilian businesses and institutions because officers can't practice their profession fully in peacetime. Thus, quite apart from acquiring technical skills such as piloting or parachute training, more than 10 percent of a typical Army officer's career is spent in the classroom.

School of Application

The officer education system began in 1881, when General William Tecumseh Sherman created the School of Application for Infantry and Cavalry at Fort Leavenworth, Kansas. Thoughtful observers had sought such a school for years because of the poor state of education in the officer corps. Many Army officers had gained their commissions as Civil War volunteers or by promotion from the ranks, and they needed grounding in general education, military administration, and tactics. Even graduates of West Point tended to stagnate intellectually when scattered among the tiny garrisons on the fron-

5

tier. These officers were highly proficient in small unit operations but not in the complexities of modern warfare involving hundreds of thousands of soldiers in various types of units. There were a few specialized courses, such as an artillery school at Fortress Monroe, Virginia, or an engineer school at Willet's Point in New York; the latter was moved to Washington, D.C., in 1901. For the bulk of the officer corps, however, there was no formal postgraduate education.

Initially, therefore, Sherman directed that each regiment of Infantry or Cavalry send one officer each year to the new school. Given the slow rate of promotion in the peacetime Army, virtually all these students were lieutenants. Over the next several years, the Army assembled four Infantry companies, four Cavalry companies, and an Artillery battery at Fort Leavenworth so that students could actually observe and maneuver a significant-sized force of the various combat arms. Fort Leavenworth was large enough to accommodate such a force, while sitting near the junction of multiple railroads that connected it to points throughout the country. Thus, this garrison provided a central reserve for an Army that still had to plan for possible war against the Native American tribes.[1]

During the first decade of its existence, the School of Application gradually evolved from a remedial class for poorly educated officers into a model institution that taught its students to command and administer tactical units of various sizes and types. Much of the initial instruction was based on that of the German Army, which dominated European military thought in the later 1800s. Over time, however, Fort Leavenworth developed both its own faculty and a body of distinctive American military doctrine. Colonel Arthur L. Wagner, for example, analyzed the U.S. Army's own historical experience to encourage simplified tactics that emphasized the individual initiative of soldiers at every level.

The Root Reforms and the Army Schools

Still, the School of Application focused on units of a few hundred to a few thousand men, not on the higher-level aspects of warfare. When the United States emerged as a world power in the late 1800s, its military institutions proved woefully inadequate in comparison to the professional military forces of Europe. In retrospect, it seems obvious that we needed to produce officers who could analyze the larger issues of national strategy and direct the Army in accomplishing more modern, complex missions. At the time, however, the very idea of American involvement in such wars on the European continent or elsewhere was almost inconceivable to most civilians and soldiers in this country.

The Spanish-American War of 1898 highlighted the absence of such a professionally educated officer corps. On the one hand, the United States suddenly acquired new territories in the Philippines and Puerto Rico, with all the attendant problems of guerrilla warfare, nation building, and colonial administration. On the other, the war revealed a variety of problems involved in fighting a modern conflict, problems ranging from poor sanitation to a lack of effective planning at every level of command. To fight a counterinsurgency campaign in the Philippines, the regular Army grew from 28,000 in 1897 to 81,000 in 1902 and 85,000 in 1908. Similarly, the officer corps almost doubled in size, from 2,179 in 1897 to 4,049 by 1902.[2] This expansion meant that older officers, veterans of the frontier conflicts, advanced rapidly in rank, so that almost all of them needed more military education for their new positions. During an era when politicians of both parties believed in government efficiency, the U.S. Army was a prime candidate for reform.

In 1899 President William McKinley chose an unlikely reformer to be secretary of War—Elihu Root, a prominent corporate attorney whose physical frailty had limited his own military service to a few months in the New York State militia. By his own admission, Root knew nothing about the military or about national security. He reluctantly accepted the position only because McKinley convinced him that the country needed a lawyer to establish military governments in the newly acquired territories. Very quickly, however, both the president and the new secretary realized that administering these territories required reorganizing the archaic structure of the War Department. Over the next five years Root did just that, creating the first American General Staff to plan for the Army and overcoming the entrenched resistance of various civilian and military functionaries. He even began converting the traditional state militia into the modern National Guard, providing standardized organization, equipment, and training to the states.[3]

Like any good attorney, Root researched his new assignment, reviewing decades of proposals to improve the Army. Eventually, he turned to Major William G. H. Carter (later a major general), a scholarly staff officer, to develop a plan for a hierarchy of schools that would train and educate officers throughout their careers. The result was General Order No. 155, dated November 27, 1901, which prescribed four stages of officer education after commissioning.[4] First, each military post was to conduct part-time classes that would train junior officers in the basic requirements of peacetime administration and wartime tactics. Next, additional schools were added to the existing ones so that every officer would have a place to learn about his branch—Coast Artillery (Fort Monroe, Virginia), Engineers (Washington Barracks, which is now Fort McNair, D.C.), Cavalry and Field Artillery (Fort Riley, Kansas), and so on. The top level of Carter's hierarchy was the Army War College, a combination of school and think tank in Washington, D.C., intended to help plan the Army's mobilization for future conflicts.

Yet the key to the new system lay in the third level of military education, between the branch schools and the War College. Based on Carter's original design, this third step in education was established at Fort Leavenworth, although turmoil in the Philippines and elsewhere delayed the start of instruction until mid-1902. The existing School of Application became an expanded one-year course eventually relabeled the School of the Line, teaching Infantry and Cavalry officers and a handful of artillerymen, engineers, and other specialists. Although initially many students were lieutenants, as the education system developed, more men attended as captains. The first classes, like those of the 1880s, were composed of inadequately educated young officers, but gradually the quality of both candidates and instruction improved. The most successful graduates from this school then attended a second year of classes, the General Staff College. This was the army's first attempt to produce the kinds of educated officers that increasingly dominated European armies, capable of planning and maneuvering larger military organizations when the country mobilized for war. Within a few years, the post also hosted schools in signal communications (1904) and field engineering (1910), creating an unequaled concentration of military students and innovation.

A number of talented instructors taught at the Leavenworth schools during this period, most notably Major John F. Morrison, who tried to teach his students how to apply military principles in the confusion and uncertainty of battle. To do this, he adapted a French methodology involving planning for a tactical situation on a map. Many of his students, the generation of staff officers who held the Army together during World War I, proudly called themselves "Morrison men."

Yet the overall catalyst for change was undoubtedly General J. Franklin Bell, commandant from 1903 to 1906. After a meteoric rise in rank during the Philippine insurrection, Bell was the ideal man to organize and energize the new educational system. Well educated himself, in the Philippines he had witnessed the problems of inadequately trained and undereducated leaders attempting to deal with a wide variety of complex tactical and administrative challenges. Bell lobbied passionately to get better-qualified students as well as better instructors assigned to Leavenworth. Perhaps most significantly, he strove to change perceptions about the nature of military education. At a time when most colonels and generals had learned their profession solely by practical experience on the frontier, it was difficult to convince these officers of the need for and value of formal military schooling. The younger officers educated at Fort Leavenworth between 1904 and 1916 did not rise to the top of their profession until the 1930s. Still, Bell made major strides in changing expectations so that commanders sent their best, rather than their worst, officers to school. Beginning in 1908, the Staff College also ran a number of short "Get Rich Quick" courses to give higher com-

United States Infantry and Cavalry School, Class of 1907. First Lieutenant George C. Marshall is in the third row, fifth from left. (U.S. Army, courtesy of the Combined Arms Research Library, Fort Leavenworth, Kansas)

manders, as well as a few National Guardsmen and U.S. Marines, the basics of the new tactics and problem-solving procedures.[5]

This early instruction was far from perfect, especially with regard to the devastating increase in artillery destructiveness that produced a bloody stalemate during World War I. Nevertheless, the almost seven hundred graduates of the School of the Line and the Staff College proved critical to America's performance in that conflict. They shared a common terminology and approach to problem solving that were essential to maneuvering and supplying huge numbers of soldiers and weapons effectively.

The Test of World War

In 1916 the Fort Leavenworth schools closed down when the garrison units, instructors, and students went south to participate in the punitive expedition pursuing Pancho Villa into Mexico. No sooner had the U.S. Army finished this frustrating mission than it had to conduct an unprecedented projection of power, mobilizing the country to participate in World War I. From a 1916 strength of 108,000 men, by 1918 the Army had grown to almost 2.4 million, of whom more than a million were overseas.[6] To further complicate this expansion, the new Army had to learn the deadly lessons of modern warfare, in which huge armies struggled using unprecedented weapons such as tanks, aircraft, and poison gas. Our British and French allies were frankly skeptical about the ability of Americans to do this, arguing that President Wilson should simply turn over this huge supply of half-trained troops to be used as replacements for their own, more experienced units.

The American expeditionary commander, General John J. Pershing, resisted these arguments, determined that his army would operate as a separate American force with its own tactics and organization. The graduates of Leavenworth were the key men who helped Pershing create this army from nothing.[7]

During the war, eight of the twelve officers who served as Pershing's chief of staff, deputy chief of staff, or head of primary staff sections were Leavenworth graduates; seven had attended both the School of the Line and the Staff College. Graduates also provided a disproportionate number of staff officers and commanders in the American Expeditionary Forces' corps, divisions, brigades, and regiments. Some of the historical studies at the prewar schools had focused on the Franco-German battles of 1870, which by sheer coincidence occurred in the same region of France that the Army fought over in 1918. Thus, the trained staff officers were already familiar with the terrain of the Meuse-Argonne region. Eventually, Pershing directed that, as each army unit arrived in France, its "Leavenworth men" would be detached from that unit and redistributed to satisfy the most urgent needs.

When the supply of such peacetime graduates proved inadequate for the ballooning American forces, in November 1917, Pershing established a shorter, three-month version of the Staff College in Langres, France. To save time, students were trained to work in only one particular staff section—personnel, intelligence, operations, or logistics—rather than all possible staff positions. At first, the French and British provided the instructors for the Langres course, but by the end of the war the faculty was almost completely American, primarily peacetime graduates of the Fort Leavenworth schools. At Pershing's insistence, the doctrine and concepts taught at Langres were also echoes of those at the prewar schools. The Langres course graduated a total of five hundred students in 1918. This course also institutionalized the heavy French influence on American staff organization and doctrine between the world wars.

Leavenworth between the Wars

Elihu Root's school system for officers had clearly proven its worth. Most professional army officers came out of World War I convinced that they needed to do a better job of preparing for a possible future conflict on the same scale, and that peacetime education was the key to such preparation. As the size and budget of the U.S. Army dwindled during the 1920s and 1930s, maintaining large, combat-ready units proved increasingly impractical. Leaders had few opportunities to actually maneuver troops, and thus the only way to prepare for the future was to invest in the intellectual development of the officer corps. Attending branch courses and especially the Leavenworth schools became a key component of a successful career.

Small wonder, then, that reestablishing the officer education system was a high priority in 1919. For the first four years of peace (1919–23), the restored schools followed the pre-1916 model, albeit with a wealth of new information derived from the recent war.

Thus, the yearlong School of the Line taught officers how to operate a division of up to 28,000 men, but only selected graduates of this course attended the General Staff School itself, which focused on corps and higher-level organizations. Ninety-nine officers began the School of the Line in 1919, but only forty-nine attended the second year.

From 1923 to 1928 this structure was condensed into a single-year course known as the Command and General Staff School. This change allowed Leavenworth to teach as many as 250 students per year, accommodating the large number of officers who had entered the service before and during World War I. In 1928 the War Department resumed a two-year program of study, but virtually all students attended both years of the course. Beginning in 1935, however, the looming prospect of a new world war prompted the Army to revert to a one-year course in order to generate more staff officers in anticipation of mobilization.[8]

In addition to the regular courses of one and two years' duration, a Special Command and General Staff Course, three months in length, provided the rudiments of the Leavenworth doctrine and methodology to as many as fifty National Guard and Reserve officers each spring. A separate organization conducted a three-year correspondence version of the course for other officers who could not attend in person. Although this latter program did not produce fully qualified staff officers, it did familiarize reservists and other officers with the terminology and procedures found in the resident courses.

The faculty adjusted the curriculum frequently to accommodate changes in doctrine and technology, especially during the first few years, when prewar texts proved to be largely outdated. The school's basic approach to warfare, however, remained unchanged throughout the interwar period.[9] The classes and doctrinal publications incorporated various lessons learned during the recent world war, but instructors frequently marked down students who applied the slow, grinding, attritional concepts of the trenches. Instead, the Leavenworth school in all its different incarnations consistently emphasized mobile, maneuver warfare in open country.

The instruction sought to equip student officers, as future commanders and staff officers, to adjust quickly to changing situations to gain and maintain the initiative, developing simple solutions to maneuver whether they were attacking or defending. To do this, the first portion of the course focused on combining the different combat arms—Infantry, Coast and Field Artillery, and Cavalry—as well as the principles of tactics, decision making, supply, and staff operations. Historical examples from the Civil War to World War I emphasized that frontal attacks were usually costly and often ineffective, whereas a maneuver to bypass or outflank the enemy often brought more success and less bloodshed. This emphasis on flanks represented the assumption that the World War I stalemate, where no flanks existed, was unlikely to recur. As the course progressed, the faculty introduced more complicated forms of maneuver, such as the difficult task of crossing a river defended by the enemy.

The educational methodology was equally practical. Mornings began with short lectures and discussions, and tactical problems consumed the remainder of the day. The school taught a systematic, logical procedure for evaluating and then solving such problems. Some of these exercises were completed in the classroom, using maps; others were conducted as field trips to envision operations on the terrain near the fort; and still others were actually field exercises to maneuver real units (within the constraints of the shrunken peacetime army). In most instances the student had to produce oral or written orders to execute his plan. Leavenworth students also went on staff rides, studying the actual terrain and leadership decisions of Civil War and other historical operations, or using that same terrain as the basis for fictional problems of modern tactics. As the course progressed, larger units and more complicated tactical problems, often drawn from recent history, were introduced that taxed the students' abilities. For example, after examining the failure of the German offensive in northern France in September 1914, students had to produce an evaluation and an operations order to support the decisions of the First German Army commander in that battle.

The brigade (6,000 to 8,000 men) and the division were the most common units studied in particular situations. During the first year of the two-year courses, student results were graded against a fixed standard, a rubric often referred to as the "Leavenworth solution." Critics at the time and since have argued that this approach stifled student creativity and encouraged stereotyped, predictable tactics in the field. Still, this grading at least permitted an objective means of comparing the performance of different students. In addition, using a fixed set of criteria also helped ensure that graduates would approach real-world problems from the same perspective, which facilitated cooperation between wartime units. At least some of the tactical problems used in the second half of the course did not have such fixed rubrics for evaluating student achievement, demanding more innovative solutions.

Both at the time and in retrospect, some observers also criticized the limitations of this very practical, tactically oriented curriculum. Leavenworth students learned little about strategy or mobilization, subjects taught only to the relatively few men sent to the Army War College. Advocates of airpower and mechanized warfare complained, with some justification, that these aspects of warfare received less emphasis than conventional Infantry-Artillery operations. To some extent, the neglect of aviation was inevitable, because the Army permitted the Air Corps Tactical School to emphasize the concept of independent, strategic bombardment with air units commanded by aviators, which reduced the number of air units available to support ground operations.[10] Still, in the course of the 1930s the school did incorporate increasingly sophisticated problems involving observation, ground attack, and pursuit fighters as well as entire mechanized divisions, at a time when the U.S. Army had few aircraft and even fewer tanks. Moreover, despite the addition of the words "Command and" to the title of the school, relatively little instruction was devoted to the problems of leadership or command; the assumption was that, by making students both technically proficient and self-confident, the intellectual content of the course would equip them to serve effectively as commanders and staff officers in positions far above their ranks at that time.

This instruction was by no means easy on those who attended Leavenworth. First, the increased number of student officers, and especially married officers, strained the physical facilities of the post during the early 1920s. Even after additional buildings were adapted for instruction and housing for married couples, the varied experience of these students made standardized instruction difficult. Some had commanded large units in combat during 1918, while others had remained in the states to train the expanding army; some had completed the School of the Line, whereas others had attended only the abbreviated Langres course or in some instances had no formal military education since commissioning. As the world war receded in time and the peacetime military school system took hold, the student body became more homogeneous. Regardless of when the student attended the Command and General Staff School, he faced a demanding course of instruction that often required many hours of evening and weekend study to prepare for exercises and examinations. Competition was fierce because graduates were ranked strictly according to their class averages, rankings that were often important factors in determining the students' future assignments and promotions. Among other things, class standing determined the students' subsequent standing on the list of officers eligible for positions in higher-level staffs. Despite the attractive scenery and lack of troop responsibilities, attending Leavenworth was rarely an easy assignment. Still, the majority of students considered the school a positive experience; for many of them, attendance at Fort Leavenworth proved to be the single most important developmental experience of their careers. Others grumbled about what they perceived as the rigidity and artificiality of the school environment, but they all benefited from learning standardized concepts, formats, and procedures.

Because of the glacial rate of promotion in the peacetime Army, many students were middle-aged by the time they attended. Of the 258 graduates in the class of 1925, almost 90 percent held the rank of major, and the class averaged over forty years of age. During the 1930s, many students were only captains.[11]

Between the two world wars, Leavenworth graduated a total of 3,677 officers, of whom 2,602 completed the one-year course and 1,075 attended for two years. Most of these graduates were U.S. Army officers of the Infantry, Cavalry, or Field or Coast Artillery. Strict quotas limited the numbers of students from other branches, such as Engineers, Signal Corps, Air Corps, and Quartermaster. Still, this Leavenworth experience provided some leavening throughout the interwar Army. In addition, forty-five Marines and eighteen foreign officers attended, but the classes were far more homogeneous than those of the current era.[12] After the last peacetime class graduated on an accelerated schedule in February 1940, the post shifted to shorter wartime courses, often three months in length, to produce additional temporary staff officers for wartime duty or to train division headquarters staffs as a group.

The large interwar classes did more than provide a quantity of key personnel for the huge Army of World War II. They also ensured that these graduates had a common vocabulary and approach to problems, and in many instances actually had known each other

World War II mobilization class for staff officers. (U.S. Army, courtesy of the Combined Arms Research Library, Fort Leavenworth, Kansas)

as students even when they came from disparate branches of the service. These common approaches and personal relationships were essential when the tiny interwar officer corps—fewer than 15,000 men, including Air Corps officers, in 1939—had to lead a wartime ground force of 8.5 million men. Thus, the class of 1934 included the future head of the Selective Service, Lewis B. Hershey, as well as two men who went on to be division commanders and three who later commanded corps in combat. Of the thirty-four U.S. corps commanders during the war, only one had not attended Leavenworth. Thirty-two were graduates of the regular one- or two-year courses, and Raymond McClain, the only National Guard officer to command a corps during World War II, attended the three-month short course in 1938.[13]

For all its shortcomings, the interwar Command and General Staff School provided the essential glue of concepts and staff procedures that held the U.S. Army and Army Air Force together during the massive expansion that began in 1940 and accelerated after the Pearl Harbor attack. Even more than in the previous world conflict, the Leavenworth schools were an essential component of victory, playing a key role in the education of many of the senior leaders like Generals Marshall, MacArthur, Eisenhower, Arnold, and Bradley, who would guide the nation's armed forces to victory.

Notes

1. Timothy Nenninger, *The Leavenworth Schools and the Old Army: Education, Professionalism, and the Officer Corps of the United States Army, 1881–1918* (Westport, Conn.: Greenwood Press, 1978), 21–24; Todd R. Brereton, *Educating the U.S. Army: Arthur L. Wagner and Reform, 1875–1905* (Lincoln: University of Nebraska Press, 2000), 12–14; Boyd L. Dastrup, *The U.S. Army Command and General Staff College: A Centennial History* (Manhattan, Kans.: Sunflower University Press, 1982), 13–15.

2. Russell F. Weigley, *History of the United States Army* (New York: Macmillan, 1967), 568. Although Congress authorized the Army expansion in 1901, it took seven more years to implement this growth completely.

3. Philip C. Jessup, *Elihu Root*, vol. 1, *1845–1909* (New York: Dodd, Mead, 1938), 48–49, 215–76.

4. William H. Carter, "Personal Narrative of the General Staff System of the American Army," U.S. Senate publication (Washington, D.C.: Government Printing Office, 1924), esp. 11–14.

5. Nenninger, *The Leavenworth Schools and the Old Army*, 68–79, 122–24.

6. Weigley, *History of the United States Army*, 568.

7. This assessment of the role of Leavenworth graduates in the American Expeditionary Forces is based on Nenninger, *The Leavenworth Schools and the Old Army*, 135–42, and Peter J. Schifferle, *America's School for War: Fort Leavenworth, Officer Education, and Victory in World War II* (Lawrence: University Press of Kansas, 2010), esp. 9–17.

8. This discussion of the four interwar periods at CGSS is based on Philip C. Cockrell, "Brown Shoes and Mortar Boards: U.S. Army Officer Professional Education at the Command and General Staff School, Fort Leavenworth, Kansas, 1919–1940" (Ph.D. diss., University of South Carolina, 1991), 75–78.

9. This summary of the curriculum comes from ibid., 80–90, Schifferle, *America's School for War*, esp. 68–78, and Timothy Nenninger, "Leavenworth and Its Critics: The U.S. Army Command and General

Staff School, 1920–1940," *Journal of Military History* 58.2 (April 1994): 199–231.

10. Gary C. Cox, *Beyond the Battle Line: U.S. Air Attack Theory and Doctrine, 1919–1941* (Maxwell Air Force Base, Ala.: U.S. Air Force School of Advanced Aerospace Studies, 1996).

11. Schifferle, *America's School for War*, 124–25.

12. Nenninger, "Leavenworth and Its Critics," 201.

13. The class of 1934 is described in Schifferle, *America's School for War*, 132–33; Charles H. Gerhardt commanded the 29th Division and Eugene M. Landrum commanded the 90th. The three corps commanders in the class were J. Lawton Collins (VII Corps), Frank M. Milburn (XII Corps), and Ernest N. Harmon (XXII Corps). For higher commanders who attended Leavenworth, see Robert H. Berlin, *U.S. Army World War II Corps Commanders: A Composite Biography* (Fort Leavenworth, Kans.: Combat Studies Institute, 1989).

References

Berlin, Robert H. *U.S. Army World War II Corps Commanders: A Composite Biography* (Fort Leavenworth, Kans.: Combat Studies Institute, 1989.

Cockrell, Philip C. "Brown Shoes and Mortar Boards: U.S. Army Officer Professional Education at the Command and General Staff School, Fort Leavenworth, Kansas, 1919–1940." Ph.D. diss., University of South Carolina, 1991.

Dastrup, Boyd L. *The U.S. Army Command and General Staff College: A Centennial History*. Manhattan, Kans.: Sunflower University Press, 1982.

Jessup, Philip C. *Elihu Root*, vol. 1, *1845–1909*. New York: Dodd, Mead, 1938.

Nenninger, Timothy. "Leavenworth and Its Critics: The U.S. Army Command and General Staff School, 1920–1940," *Journal of Military History* 58.2 (April 1994): 199–231.

———. *The Leavenworth Schools and the Old Army: Education, Professionalism, and the Officer Corps of the United States Army, 1881–1918*. Westport, Conn.: Greenwood Press, 1978.

Schifferle, Peter J. *America's School for War: Fort Leavenworth, Officer Education, and Victory in World War II*. Lawrence: University Press of Kansas, 2010.

2

George Catlett Marshall

Christopher R. Gabel

Among those individuals who have risen to the top of the military profession, George C. Marshall stands out as one of the most remarkable. As the leader of the U.S. Army and Army Air Forces in World War II, a senior military adviser to the president, and the chief American representative in the Allied coalition, he was perhaps the most powerful and influential soldier in American history. After the war Marshall stepped directly from military service into the highest echelons of government, serving as both secretary of State and secretary of Defense. The European Recovery Program that bore his name had an effect on global affairs equivalent to that of his military accomplishments. Marshall was the embodiment of the model professional officer and servant of the state.

Born on December 31, 1880, Marshall was the son of Laura Bradford Marshall and George Catlett Marshall Sr. Both his parents were from Kentucky, where the Bradfords and the Marshalls were families of prominence, tracing their roots back to the aristocracy of old Virginia. Chief Justice John Marshall was a distant relative. George Jr. was born in Uniontown, Pennsylvania, on the western slopes of the Allegheny Mountains, where his father had established residence in pursuit of business interests. George was the youngest of four children—a brother, William, had died in infancy, and a brother, Stuart, and sister, Marie, were five and four years older than George, respectively. Owing perhaps to the greater age of his siblings and to his father's austere, reserved character, young George was most closely attached to his vivacious mother, whom he described as having a wonderful sense of humor.

Affairs in the Marshall household took a turn for the worse when young George was ten years old. His father, an entrepreneur in the coke business, was wiped out in the financial crash of 1890. Although the family was able to subsist without considerable hardship, much of the gentility went out of George's life. As the family learned to economize, George came to recognize that he could not rely on social status or family tradition—he would have to make his own way in the world and stand on his own merits. Illustrious ancestors were all well and good, but "it was time for somebody to swim for the family again."[1]

Marshall's hometown environment was wholesome and democratic. The Marshall house was literally the last residence on the edge of town, so that the woods and countryside of rural Pennsylvania were as much a part of George's childhood as the town itself. George and his friends played in field and stream and dabbled in various youthful business enterprises, most notably horticulture. This spawned a lifelong interest in gardening—in later years, Marshall's greatest desire was to retire to the seclusion of his garden. In one respect, Uniontown left something to be desired. By his own admission, Marshall's education was mediocre at best. An indifferent student, young George was embarrassed by his poor academic performance even at the time. Nonetheless, in later years he asserted that every boy in a democracy should attend a public school, if not for the education received, then for the preparation for life acquired by associating with a cross section of society.[2]

As he neared maturity, Marshall developed the rather strange ambition to embark on a military career. There was no strong martial tradition in his family. The elder Marshall had served briefly with Union militia forces in Kentucky during the Civil War, but his only noteworthy experience consisted of being captured and paroled by Confederate cavalry raiders. Nor was service in the sleepy constabulary Army of the 1890s much to be desired. Perhaps young George's military ambitions stemmed from his interest in history, which was one of the few academic endeavors in which he displayed much aptitude. In any event, Marshall's chances of ever becoming an Army officer appeared to be vanishingly small. To win a commission meant to graduate from the U.S. Military Academy at West Point. Marshall's mediocre academic record, coupled with the fact that his father was a Democrat in a Republican district, effectively precluded his nomination to the academy.

Instead, young Marshall elected to attend the Virginia Military Institute, from which his older brother, Stuart, had recently graduated. But even this choice met with familial resistance. He overheard his brother telling their father that if George attended VMI, he

George C. Marshall in dress blues.
(Courtesy of the Virginia Military
Institute Archives)

would disgrace the family. Understandably, this bit of eavesdropping only stiffened George's resolve. "It had quite a psychological effect on my career," he later observed.[3]

In September 1897 Marshall arrived at VMI, a gangly, rather awkward, poorly educated boy with a northern accent in one of the bastions of southern heritage. Despite his unlikely prospects, he was determined to succeed. Quickly he discerned the qualities that it would take to excel at VMI, and it is perhaps fortunate that academic performance was not at the top of the list. Instead, the qualities looked for in a cadet were performance in drill, military bearing, obedience, and leadership. With these criteria in mind, Marshall set out to make himself the model cadet. The challenges were considerable. Doubtless he came in for more than his fair share of hazing because of his accent. Shortly after his arrival a hazing episode resulted in an injury that could have been quite serious, yet Marshall

Marshall in his VMI senior picture. (Courtesy of the Virginia Military Institute Archives)

kept silent rather than betray his tormenters. Thus he began to earn the grudging respect of his peers. Gradually, the natural shyness and reserve of the boy metamorphosed into the austere, disciplined, and rather distant character of the cadet. Eventually entrusted with leadership positions within the corps of cadets, Marshall excelled, demonstrating that he possessed what his foremost biographer called "the power to command."[4] By acclamation he was selected to the top post of first captain in his senior year.

Upon his graduation from VMI in 1901, Marshall accepted the position of commandant at the Danville Military Institute in Virginia. This foray into academia would be short-lived, for Marshall's old dream of gaining an Army commission had suddenly come within his grasp. While he was a student at VMI the United States had waged a war with Spain and acquired an empire. Almost overnight the sleepy frontier Army had been transformed into an overseas constabulary force, its units posted from the Caribbean to the Philippines. The resultant expansion of the Army led to a sudden demand for officers that the U.S. Military Academy could not meet. Accordingly, in 1901 the War Department administered a competitive exam for non–West Point graduates who desired a commission. Competition simply to be allowed to take the exam was intense. Marshall brought to bear all of the influence that he could muster to gain admission to the exam. His father lobbied intensively among Pennsylvania politicians, while Marshall himself traveled to Washington, D.C., buttonholing any person of influence who might further his cause. He even barged uninvited into the White House, gaining a brief audience with President William McKinley. Marshall won a seat in the exam, which proved to be a trying three-day ordeal. He emerged with one of the top scores, earning perfect ratings in "Physique" and "Moral character and antecedents," though his grades in academic subjects were rather lower—Marshall was still no scholar.[5]

In January 1902 Marshall was commissioned a second lieutenant in the Infantry. A month later he married Elizabeth C. "Lily" Coles, whom he had met in Lexington, Virginia, while at VMI. The nuptials represented a double triumph, for Marshall had not only won the hand of the girl he loved, but also gained a small victory over his older brother—Stuart Marshall had dated Lily when he was a cadet at VMI and George was still in public school.

In May 1902 Lieutenant Marshall departed for his first assignment—the 30th Infantry Regiment on the island of Mindoro in the Philippines. There Marshall received a thorough and none-too-gentle education in the profession he had chosen for himself. He joined an Army steeped in the traditions of frontier service, thrust into the role of an army of occupation thousands of miles from home. A cholera epidemic swept through town and garrison shortly after his arrival. Once past this crisis, the green lieutenant had to deal with bored soldiers and often uninterested superiors. He earned the respect of his men and began to establish a reputation among his peers. Sent off to a small garrison in the depths of the jungle, Marshall found himself serving as acting company commander and governor of the province for a number of weeks.[6] This was the first, and not the last, time Marshall excelled in duties far in excess of his rank.

In 1903 Marshall returned to the United States with an assignment to Fort Reno, Oklahoma, where he commanded Company G, 30th Infantry. His duties included a mapping expedition across the Southwest, which he later recalled as the most onerous work he ever did. While at Fort Reno he also took advantage of the garrison schools there, which constituted his introduction to formal military education. He later remarked that these schools "didn't amount to very much."[7] His attitude toward education, however, was about to change dramatically.

In August 1906 Marshall reported to the Infantry and Cavalry School at Fort Leavenworth, Kansas. The commandant was Brigadier General Charles B. Hall, who replaced Brigadier General J. Franklin Bell the same month Marshall arrived. The selection process for attendance at the school, at least in Marshall's case, was far from rigorous—no other officer from his post wanted to go. There existed a large contingent of officers within the Army who disparaged formal education and were particularly critical of the Leavenworth schools.[8] Marshall, however, recognized that in the new Army of the twentieth century, the path to the top ranks of the organization ran through Leavenworth and the Army War College in Washington. Hence, he volunteered to attend the Infantry and Cavalry School even though his previous academic endeavors had been less than stellar. His arrival at Leavenworth in some ways resembled his inauspicious arrival at VMI—many of his classmates were far better prepared than he. Some of them had actually been studying the tactical problems in the Leavenworth curriculum well in advance of their arrival. Some had been coached by past graduates, and many had competed vigorously for the privilege of attending. When one of his new classmates asked Marshall what he thought about a particular tactical problem, Marshall had to confess that he did not even know what a "tactical problem" was.[9]

As had been the case at VMI, Marshall quickly discerned what it would take to excel at the Infantry and Cavalry School (soon to be renamed the School of the Line). At VMI it had been discipline, bearing, and leadership. At Leavenworth it was hard studying and outstanding performance in the tactical problems. Competition was intense, for the stakes were selection to attend the second-year Staff College and ultimately to earn a shot at the War College and designation as a General Staff officer. "If you were going to compete you had to be near perfection," Marshall later observed.[10] The work itself was not particularly difficult, but the competition made it so. Although he may not have realized it at the time, the intensity of the competition itself was beneficial, for it forced students to do careful, thorough work under stress and in a limited period. The same qualities would be essential in combat.[11]

Marshall, never an enthusiastic student, may have started at a disadvantage, but he made up for lost time very quickly: "I knew I would have to study harder than I had ever dreamed of studying before in my life. I just worked day and night. . . . I finally got into the habit of study, which I never really had. . . . I taught myself to study very, very hard and I took nothing for granted. . . . It was the hardest work I ever did in my life."[12] Hard work brought forth what may not have been evident before—Marshall was a man of great intellectual ability. He graduated first in his class and was selected to attend the Staff College. He also won a promotion to the rank of first lieutenant. The commandant of the Leavenworth schools for the remainder of Marshall's tenure there was Brigadier General Frederick Funston, hero of the Philippine-American War and President Woodrow Wilson's first choice to command the American Expeditionary Forces at the time of Funston's sudden death in 1917.

The second-year school was less competitive and more academic in nature. Marshall became better acquainted with a group of faculty who, under the inspired leadership of an earlier commandant, Brigadier General J. Franklin Bell, constituted the forefront of an intellectual revolution in the Army. He was particularly impressed by Major John F. Morrison, head of the Department of Military Art, a true intellectual and a gifted instructor: "Morrison was outstanding. . . . He spoke a language that was new to us and appealed very much to our common sense."[13] Morrison was an advocate of the "applicatory method," under which students were presented with various command challenges and were required to formulate courses of action to address those challenges. These exercises included both map problems and field maneuvers. The Staff College curriculum culminated in the spring of 1908 with an extended historical staff ride, on horseback, to Civil War battlefields from the Shenandoah Valley to Gettysburg, where the students applied their newfound knowledge and insights to the battles of a past war.

The Leavenworth experience was a landmark in Marshall's professional development: "Leavenworth was immensely instructive; not so much because the course was perfect—because it was not—but the associations with the officers, the reading and discussion that we did and the leadership . . . of a man like Morrison, had a tremendous effect on me."[14] At Leavenworth, Marshall was imbued with a new sense of professionalism and a talent for study, not to mention the skills of the staff officer. He also formed acquaintances with many of the men who would lead the Army in the next war. Among these were First Lieutenant Stephen O. Fuqua, First Lieutenant Charles D. Herron, and Captains LeRoy Eltinge, Harold B. Fiske, James W. McAndrew, Campbell King, and John McAuley Palmer, all of whom Marshall would meet again as prominent staff officers in France. Captains Robert Alexander and Charles Farnsworth would command divisions in the Great War. First Lieutenant Benjamin D. Foulois, who attended the Signal School at Fort Leavenworth during Marshall's Staff College year, would become known as one of the founding fathers of American military airpower.[15] Not least, at Leavenworth young Lieutenant Marshall began to make a name for himself in the Army at large.

The Leavenworth experience did not end with Marshall's graduation from the Staff College. Upon the enthusiastic recommendation of his instructors, he was assigned to the faculty for a two-year tour in the Department of Engineering. Once again this constituted an assignment normally reserved for officers of greater rank. As a lieutenant, Marshall was one of the junior members of the faculty, outranked by almost all his students. Nonetheless, he excelled as an instructor. Doubtless he modeled himself after Morrison, couching his instruction in logical, commonsense terms that his students could embrace. Like all successful teachers, Marshall continued learning, deepening his understanding of the military art.

One of the duties of the Leavenworth instructor was to visit National Guard encampments during the summer, in an attempt to bring these citizen-soldiers closer to the standards of the Regular Army. Marshall's assignment was to assist the Pennsylvania National Guard, which "built up [a] very agreeable association for me, and also a very valuable one because I could try all these things experimentally on these Pennsylvania fellows and they didn't always know I was trying."[16] Thus began Marshall's long association with the National Guard, an association that fostered a profound understanding of, and empathy with, the citizen-soldier that few Regular Army officers possessed.

In fact, Marshall's very next assignment after Leavenworth was to serve as an inspector-instructor with the Massachusetts National Guard. Marshall's gifts as a teacher were invaluable there, as he explained the arcana of Army regulations to part-time soldiers. He came to the realization that the instruction and regulations employed by the Regular Army were too extensive and detailed for the National Guard officer who had only his weekends in which to master them. Accordingly, Marshall sought ways to reduce and simplify. During his time in Massachusetts he also had opportunities to exercise authority far beyond the level commonly associated with the rank of first lieutenant. He planned large-scale field maneuvers, demonstrating a gift for staff work. On one occasion he actually took temporary command of a regiment in the field.

In 1913 Marshall returned to the Philippines with an assignment to company command. His gifts as a staff officer became readily apparent, and he found himself planning higher-level field maneuvers just as he had with the Massachusetts National Guard. During one exercise in 1914 Marshall became the de facto commander of a 5,000-man force when the colonel in command was indisposed by alcohol and the chief of staff fell ill. A fellow lieutenant and future five-star general who witnessed the affair, Henry H. Arnold, remarked, "That man will one day be the Army Chief of Staff."[17] Marshall completed this second tour in the Philippines as the aide-de-camp to Brigadier General Hunter Liggett, commander of the Philippine Department.

Marshall returned to the United States in 1916 and won promotion to the rank of captain. In that year he also acquired one of the more remarkable officer efficiency reports ever seen. The evaluation form included a question concerning the rater's willingness to have the rated officer under his command again. Marshall's rater, Lieutenant Colonel Johnson Hagood, responded: "Yes. But I would prefer to serve *under his command*." "He should be made a Brigadier General in the Regular Army and every day this is postponed is a loss to the Army and to the Nation."[18]

In July 1916 Marshall became the aide-de-camp to Major General J. Franklin Bell, who had been commandant at Leavenworth before Marshall's tenure there. Bell commanded the Department of the East, which included several "Plattsburg Camps." Named for the town in upstate New York where one of the camps was located, the Plattsburg Camps were an outgrowth of the preparedness movement that swept the United States when Europe went to war in 1914. At these camps college students, businessmen, and professionals assembled at their own expense to learn the rudiments of officership and to gain an Army Reserve commission. The Army provided officers to run the camps, which ultimately generated 90,000 Reserve officers, at the cost of seriously impeding the Regular Army's own efforts to prepare for war. As Bell's aide, Marshall was involved with the problems engendered by the Plattsburg Camps, one of which, once again, was the need to tailor doctrine and training for citizen-soldiers.

Curiously, Marshall's sterling reputation, staff skills, and ability to function well above his rank began to work against him. Troop command, and not staff work or aide-de-camp billets, was the path to promotion. Much as he was honored by such assignments, Marshall would undoubtedly have preferred more troop time. Indeed, when the United States entered World War I in 1917 and embarked on a massive military buildup, Marshall did not receive the troop command he coveted. Instead, he was assigned to be the Operations officer for the 1st Division, the first combat element to be sent to Europe. His cabinmate on the voyage to France was Major Lesley J. McNair, who would be Marshall's chief deputy in organizing and training the Army for another world war.

The 1st Division was a division in name only. It was understrength and consisted largely of raw recruits. Weapons and equipment were similarly absent or inadequate. The division was truly an embarrassment when it arrived in war-weary France. Marshall was largely responsible for getting the division ready for war. Virtually everything involved in creating a combat division had to be improvised on the fly. The divisional structure was brand new. Trench warfare was unknown to the Americans. Most of the troops were untrained. Few of the officers had ever seen a formation larger than the regiment. Marshall secured training facilities, developed training programs, coordinated the American training efforts with those of the British and French, and did all of this with little guidance from above. In the process, it also fell to him to develop doctrine and tactics for the American divisions, which differed markedly in structure from those of the other belligerents.[19]

On one occasion Major General John J. Pershing, overall commander of the American Expeditionary Forces (AEF), inspected a 1st Division training exercise and did not like what he saw. He began to berate the division commander in front of his staff. The commander, Major General William L. Sibert, took his criticisms in silence, but when Pershing started in on the division chief of staff, who had just arrived on the job, Marshall could stand no more: "General Pershing, there's something to be said here, and I think I should say it because I've been here longer." He then proceeded to instruct the general in all the difficulties that had to be overcome in training the division, and he went so far as to point out that Pershing's headquarters had not been particularly helpful in dealing with those problems.[20]

Marshall's military career could have ended on that day. It was Marshall's good fortune that Pershing was one of those rare individuals who can accept candid, constructive criticism, regardless of its source, without animosity. "I never saw another commander that I could do that with," Marshall later observed.[21] In fact, during subsequent visits to the 1st Division, Pershing sought out Marshall and solicited his opinions. Rather than ending Marshall's career, his outburst undoubtedly fostered it.

Pershing remembered Marshall in 1918 when the time came to plan the American force's first major combat operations. Promoted to the temporary rank of colonel, Marshall joined the Operations section of Pershing's AEF headquarters in June, and he was detached to First Army to participate in the planning for the Saint-Mihiel and Meuse-Argonne offensives. The task was truly monumental. The Saint-Mihiel operation, which commenced on September 12, involved seven American and four French divisions. The Meuse-Argonne offensive, which began just two weeks later, involved fifteen divisions, including seven of those involved at Saint-Mihiel. These divisions had to travel forty miles to reach their new jump-off points. Marshall was largely responsible for the plan that successfully moved 600,000 troops into position for the latter offensive—a marvelous accomplishment for an army in its first major operation. Marshall finished the war as First Army's deputy chief of staff for Operations, with a recommendation for promotion to temporary brigadier general. The Armistice on November 11, 1918, resulted in a freeze on all promotions, however, and it would take Marshall eighteen years to get his first star. In fact, he reverted to his Regular Army rank of captain in 1920.

Undoubtedly, Marshall's great talents as a staff officer had actually retarded his career. Promotions went first to line officers. He had clearly demonstrated a mastery of tactics and logistics on a large scale, and nobody doubted his ability to lead troops, but his repeated requests to be assigned to line duty were all denied. His lack of command time would continue to plague Marshall in the postwar years, as his peers who had led troops in combat edged ahead of him in rank. Although he was never a combat commander, he was no stranger to combat. His duties as staff officer took him to the front on numerous occasions. A careful observer and shrewd analyst, he derived a wealth of insights regarding troops in combat. Among the most significant of these was that he developed a profound understanding of the importance of troop morale. He saw firsthand how the privations of frontline duty, including the violence and fatigue inherent in combat, could rapidly erode the fighting man's effectiveness if the leadership did not look closely to the welfare of the troops. To the end of his career, he never lost sight of the fact that combat calls on men to make the greatest conceivable exertions under the worst possible circumstances, and that the leader who failed to ease the burden of the frontline soldier, or added to that burden through arbitrary strictness, was negligent in his duties.

In addition, Marshall learned the art of high command through observation of a wide cross section of senior officers. He learned the difference between commanders who were stern and those who were unduly severe, recognizing that a higher commander had to be understanding of the challenges his subordinates faced. Pershing he found to be an "almost implacable executive" at work, but delightful company, "almost boyish" after hours.[22] (Marshall himself would later be an "implacable executive" at work but unlike Pershing was a private and reserved person off duty.) Marshall particularly admired Major General Charles P. Summerall, commander of V Corps, as an "iron man," and a "Jackson type," probably an allusion to Lieutenant General Thomas S. "Stonewall" Jackson of Civil War fame. Once, when his headquarters party came under artillery fire while near the front, Summerall remarked, "Every shell that comes here is one less over our devoted infantry."[23] Marshall found General Peyton C. March, the Army chief of staff whom he came to know after the war, to be a great administrator, but "very arbitrary, tactless."[24] In addition to the Americans he observed, Marshall interacted with a number of French commanders and staffs, to the extent that he picked up a working knowledge of French military vocabulary.

In May 1919 General Pershing summoned Marshall to be his aide-de-camp, an assignment that lasted five years, during which he was promoted to major and then lieutenant colonel. Although duty as an aide was not the most desirable assignment for an ambitious officer, this experience did serve to cement Marshall's standing within the Army's most important power bloc. Moreover, it brought him into contact with a wide variety of powerful individuals. While still in France, Marshall associated with a number of French political and military leaders, including Premier Georges Clemenceau and the generals Joseph Joffre, Philippe Pétain, and Maxime Weygand. When Pershing moved his headquarters to Washington, D.C., Marshall accompanied the general on tours and to congressional hearings, which afforded him a firsthand education in top-level political and military affairs. He also witnessed the damage done to Pershing's standing in the eyes of the nation when Pershing allowed his name to be mentioned in connection with the presidential election of 1920. Marshall, who had no political affiliations, became even more rigidly apolitical.

Another unfortunate episode that Marshall witnessed during this time was the Pershing-March controversy. At the heart of the dispute was a struggle over who held precedence—Pershing, the commander of field forces, or March, the chief of the General Staff. The dispute, which nearly tore the War Department apart, was not really resolved until 1921, when Pershing himself became chief of staff. (Army regulations later stipulated that the chief of staff was superior to all other officers.) The fight went public in a "battle of the books" in which the protagonists and their various supporters presented their arguments in the form of memoirs and accounts of the war. This is why Marshall himself never authored any memoirs after he retired and consented only reluctantly to having an "official" biography produced. The hero of this sad episode, in Marshall's eyes, was Secretary of War Newton D. Baker, whom Marshall credited with holding the War Department together. Marshall thought Baker "the greatest American—or, I will put it—the greatest mind—that I came into contact with in my lifetime. . . . I admired him beyond any other man that I have known."[25] Baker was a penetrating observer and a master of the English language, from whom Marshall learned to appreciate the power of communication.

The immediate issue over which Pershing and March clashed was the form that the postwar Army would assume. Clearly, the mobilization for World War I had left much to be desired. March proposed a greatly increased Regular Army as the answer to the need for better readiness. Pershing, on the other hand, promoted the proposals of Colonel John McAuley Palmer, who asserted that readiness could best be attained by establishing universal military service for all young men and by enhancing the role of the National Guard and Reserves. Marshall assisted Palmer in preparing his arguments before Congress. In the end, the National Defense Act of 1920 embodied the Palmer concept, though without universal military training. A small Regular Army would be distributed about the United States, its principal peacetime responsibility being the training of the Reserve components. The National Guard formations of the various states, organized into divisions, would be the nation's first line of defense. Reserve divisions under the control of the federal government would fill out the Army in time of war. In practice, lacking universal military training, the Reserve formations evaporated over the years as the pool of World War I veterans, enrolled in the Reserves, passed beyond the age of military duty. Nonetheless, this was essentially the framework within which Marshall spent the interwar years, and which he activated as the nation mobilized for World War II.

Understandably, many Regular Army officers were uncomfortable with the role mandated for them in the new National Defense Act. In a 1923 lecture to the Army War College, Marshall spelled out the ramifications of the new defense policy, and he warned his audience that a change in attitude was necessary. Whereas before World War I 80 percent of the Regular Army's officers had been assigned to troop duty, only 25 percent were so employed under the 1920 legislation. "By every dictum of the law and plan of the War Department we [the Regular Army] are frankly engaged in creating a citizen force to fight our battles, rather than a small, highly trained professional army," said Marshall. "If we fail in the development of a citizen army we will be impotent in the first year of a major war."[26]

Upon General Pershing's retirement from the Army in 1924, Marshall was assigned to troop duty with the 15th Infantry in Tientsin, China. There he found himself enmeshed, not for the last time, in the tortured internal affairs of that country. Warlord conflicts, incipient nationalism, and anticolonial sentiment all posed great challenges to the foreign garrisons stationed there with the mission of preserving some semblance of order and stability. Marshall found it expedient to acquire a working knowledge of Mandarin in his dealings with the various indigenous parties. His homecoming in 1927 was marred by the sudden and unexpected death of his wife, Lily, a loss that left him devastated; she died of a heart condition aggravated by a diseased thyroid gland. He sought solace by throwing himself into his next assignment, which would ultimately prove to be an unexpectedly crucial one for the future of the Army.

This posting was to Fort Benning, Georgia, where Marshall was designated the assistant commandant of the Infantry School, in which position he was given full control over the academic department. In this capacity Marshall was able to bring to bear the wealth of experience that he had acquired throughout his career. Specifically, Marshall had the sagacity to recognize that World War I was an anomaly, and that it was a mistake to base the Army's professional education exclusively on this experience. By the time the American Expeditionary Forces had arrived in France, the war had long since settled into the stalemate of trench warfare. This static fighting involved artillery in huge masses, detailed intelligence, excellent maps, ample communications, and ready supply. Such circumstances led armies to employ elaborate planning procedures and assured that green troops inserted into the front could often afford to make mistakes without disaster.[27] Marshall, however, believed that Army training and education should focus on surviving the first six months of the next war, where poor intelligence, bad maps, strange terrain, haste, and confusion would be the rule. This would be a war of movement, where brief, concise oral orders and not elaborate decision making and planning procedures would prevail.[28]

Upon his arrival at Benning, Marshall found that the instructors based their lectures on "elaborate Leavenworth training which was really based on static war."[29] Marshall quietly but firmly compelled the faculty to simplify everything—to base their instruction on the scenario of preparing a new Army for war and having little time in which to do it. The new course of instruction employed greatly simplified manuals and taught the student-officers how to make quick decisions with imperfect knowledge. Marshall ultimately forbade his instructors to use notes when they lectured, compelling the teachers themselves to demonstrate the qualities of brevity, conciseness, and simplicity that he wished to impart to the students. He himself frequently visited classes and field exercises, where he would unexpectedly interrupt the proceedings and have students make impromptu briefings on the tactical situation at hand, as a way of teaching them to think on their feet.[30] Marshall encouraged the commandant of the Command and General Staff School at Leavenworth to undertake a comparable restructuring of the curriculum there: "I insist that we must get down to the essentials, make clear the real difficulties, and expunge the bunk, complications, and ponderosities. . . . We must develop a technique and methods so simple and so brief that the citizen officer of good common sense can readily grasp the idea."[31]

To fully implement these reforms, Marshall brought to Benning what he later called "a very brilliant group of young officers" to serve on the faculty.[32] This group included many names that would become well known in the next war: James A. Van Fleet, J. Lawton Collins, Charles L. Bolté, Joseph W. Stilwell, Edwin F. Harding, Omar Bradley, and Harold R. Bull.[33]

The five years that Marshall spent at Benning had a profound effect on the Army that would soon be fighting another world war. At any given time Marshall was actively molding the minds of sixty to eighty instructors and three hundred to five hundred students.[34] By one estimate, some two hundred future general officers passed through the Infantry School on Marshall's watch.[35] Thus, the Army of World War II in large part embodied the philosophy and concepts that Marshall introduced at Benning.

The tour at Fort Benning brought another happy development into Marshall's life. There he met Katherine Tupper Brown, a widow with three children, whom he married in 1930. By all accounts, Marshall was devoted to his new wife and fell readily into the role of stepfather, and their relationship proved to be a happy and rewarding one for all concerned.

In 1932 Marshall was assigned to command a battalion of the 8th Infantry at Fort Screven, Georgia, and in 1933 he was promoted to colonel and made the regimental commander of the 8th, which was headquartered at Fort Moultrie, South Carolina. In both these assignments he became intimately involved with one of the initiatives undertaken by the new president, Franklin D. Roosevelt, to mitigate the effects of the Great Depression. This was the Civilian Conservation Corps (CCC), a program in which unemployed young men were brought together in camps and put to work on various public works projects, under the leadership and supervision of the Army. In the first three months of the program, 250,000 men were assembled in 1,468 camps.[36] The demands of this massive new program brought to a sudden halt the normal garrison routine of the Army, as officers and NCOs went off to establish and supervise the camps. Many officers found CCC duty to be onerous and distasteful, but not Marshall. As colonel of the 8th Infantry, he found himself responsible for nineteen CCC camps scattered across the southeastern United States.[37] He was prescient enough to see that the CCC experience gave the Regular Army a salutary lesson in the type of leadership that would be necessary in mobilizing an army of citizen-soldiers. He later observed, "I found the CCC the most instructive service I ever had, and the most interesting."[38]

His next assignment was less happy. At the direction of the Army chief of staff, General Douglas MacArthur, Marshall was assigned to be the senior instructor for the 33rd Infantry Division, Illinois National Guard, and his place of duty was to be the city of Chicago. Marshall, who from childhood had loved the open countryside, chafed at his confinement in this urban setting. He also recognized that this assignment was a setback to his career, as it took him away from command yet again. Some commentators have asserted that this assignment reflected malice on the part of MacArthur, but this does not appear to be substantiated—Marshall clearly was the right man to get the faltering 33rd Infantry Division up to standard. Indeed, as Marshall himself had pointedly informed the War College in 1923, such assignments reflected the Regular Army's key mission in peacetime. As MacArthur no doubt expected, Marshall brought to bear his considerable skills as a teacher and his insights into the abilities and special requirements of the part-time soldier. At the end of his tour, the 33rd Infantry Division was performing to standard.

Marshall's reward was a promotion to the long-coveted rank of brigadier general in 1936 and assignment to command the 5th Brigade, 3rd Infantry Division, at Vancouver Barracks in the state of Washington. For Marshall it was an ideal assignment—command of troops in a beautiful rural setting, responsibility for a number of CCC camps, and ample opportunities for outside recreation. His satisfaction was tempered by the realization, however, that his promotion to brigadier general had probably come too late for him to ever win a second star.[39]

Indeed, the next transfer took Marshall not to division command, but to yet another staff assignment, this time in the War Department in Washington, D.C., where in 1938 he became the assistant chief of staff, War Plans Division. Shortly thereafter he was elevated to the position of deputy chief of staff. In the latter capacity he became closely involved in laying the groundwork for mobilization in case of war, an eventuality that looked increasingly likely. Marshall's skill in the ways of bureaucracy and politics proved crucial in this assignment, for the War Department was divided into factions—Secretary of War Harry Woodring was an isolationist, whereas Assistant Secretary of War Louis Johnson was an advocate of preparedness. Marshall had to thread his way carefully through this internecine dispute, as well as another between advocates of airpower and those who sought a more conventional force.[40]

As deputy chief of staff, Marshall accompanied the chief of staff, General Malin C. Craig, to the White House for meetings with President Roosevelt. At one such meeting on November 14, 1938, Roosevelt proposed a rearmament plan that called for a massive buildup of airpower to the detriment of the ground army. Marshall himself favored a balanced buildup of all the arms. When Roosevelt asked Marshall for his opinion, Marshall replied, "Mr. President, I am sorry, but I don't agree with you at all."[41] As had been the case when he confronted General Pershing twenty-one years earlier, Marshall escaped the encounter with his career intact—and perhaps even enhanced. Like Pershing, Roosevelt was able to accept candid observations even when they clashed with his own views.

Marshall had one last chance to attain the pinnacle of his profession. General Craig, the Army chief of staff, was due to retire in 1939. Marshall was a contender for the post but was by no means the leading candidate. He had never commanded a formation larger than brigade. Moreover, there were thirty-three generals senior to Marshall. All but four of these, however, were themselves scheduled to retire before they could complete the four-year term as chief of staff.[42] The top contender was Major General Hugh A. Drum, who had been Marshall's senior in World War I and had held commands at the division and corps levels.[43] Like Marshall, he had remained a protégé of Pershing's through the postwar years. Drum took advantage of his standing with Pershing and his many political connections to launch a large-scale publicity campaign in his quest to become chief of staff.

Marshall, on the other hand, dissuaded supporters who wished to lobby in his behalf: "My strength with the army has rested on the well known fact that I attended strictly to business and enlisted no influence of any sort at any time. . . . Therefore, it seems to me that at this time the complete absence of any publicity about me would be my greatest asset, particularly with the President." He went on to add, "The National Guard knows me now. The Reserve Corps know me well. The ROTC people, including many college presidents, know me. And the Regular Army know me. It is not time for the public to be brought to a view of my picture."[44]

In the end, Drum's lobbying and publicity failed to impress Roosevelt, and it may well have actually hurt his cause. In any event, one day in the spring of 1939 Roosevelt summoned Marshall to the White House and informed him that he would be the next chief of staff. Marshall told the president that he reserved the right "to say what I think and it would often be unpleasing."[45] Roosevelt found this to be acceptable, and on April 27 he announced Marshall's appointment. On July 1 Marshall assumed the position of acting chief of staff when General Craig departed on terminal leave.

The date of September 1, 1939, was a momentous one for George C. Marshall and, indeed, for the world. On that date the United States awoke to the news that Germany had invaded Poland, inaugurating World War II in Europe. Later that morning Marshall was promoted to the rank of major general, and shortly thereafter he was sworn in as the fifteenth Army chief of staff, an assignment that carried with it the temporary rank of four-star general. Both Marshall and the Army adjutant general, who administered the oath of office, wore civilian clothes, for Marshall did not want to have "a lot of uniforms plastered around Washington" in peacetime, and he encouraged officers in the War Department to do likewise.[46] By noon that day Marshall was in the White House discussing the implications of the new war for the United States.

As chief of staff, Marshall wielded more power than any American officer before or since. Under Army regulations dated 1936, Marshall was both head of the General Staff in Washington and commander of all field forces, responsible for their training in peacetime and serving as expeditionary force commander in war, unless and until the president designated a separate combat commander.[47] His

George C. Marshall, chief of staff, 1940. (Library of Congress)

authority extended over not only the ground forces, but also the Army Air Corps. Marshall reported directly to the secretary of War and, often, directly to the president.

With the outbreak of war in Europe, and growing tensions in the Pacific, it was increasingly likely that the United States would eventually be embroiled in war. Marshall was absolutely determined that the Army and the nation not find themselves in a state of unpreparedness if and when that occurred. The task of mobilizing an army would be a monumental one, given the state of decrepitude into which the Army had fallen since the end of World War I. As a first step, President Roosevelt declared a state of "Limited National Emergency" on September 8, and he directed a modest expansion of all the military services. This was the first stage in a process that would increase the Army (including the Army Air Corps) from 190,000 officers and enlisted men on the day Marshall became chief of staff to a force of over 8 million by 1945. From the outset, Marshall was determined that the buildup would proceed methodically, step by step, rather than the "single plunge" that had characterized the mobilization for World War I.[48] In the process, the politically astute Marshall took care not to invite accusations of warmongering, and to avoid swamping the small peacetime Army with excessively rapid growth and change.

In many ways the situation Marshall found himself in as chief of staff was analogous to that he had experienced in taking the incomplete and unprepared 1st Division to France in 1917: "There wasn't anything. We had a terrible time getting ourselves together."[49] Fortunately, Marshall's determination to expand methodically meshed with President Roosevelt's intent to proceed cautiously in pursuing rearmament. Roosevelt was determined to follow, rather than lead, public opinion. He saw that he could garner more support for a military buildup (and for assistance to Britain) if he allowed events to precipitate action, rather than trying to whip up public opinion on his own.[50] Perhaps Marshall's greatest problem was that Roosevelt, Congress, and the public did not fully understand the need for conventional ground forces—Marshall found himself competing for resources with the Navy, Marshall's own Air Corps, and Lend-Lease aid to Britain. In particular, he repeatedly had to deflect Roosevelt's calls for a massive buildup of airpower without a commensurate increase of ground forces. Even so, he refused to force the president's hand by going public with his case for ground troops, recognizing that he needed to retain the administration's trust and confidence. Marshall said he "tried to do [his] convincing within that team."[51] He was, however, more than willing to speak bluntly to the president. In May 1940, when Roosevelt balked at sending a rather modest but essential appropriation request to Congress, Marshall told him pointedly that "you have got to do something and you've got to do it today. . . . I know you can get them to accept it. They can't evade it."[52]

American preparedness efforts received a major boost in June 1940 when Roosevelt appointed two Republicans, Henry L. Stimson and Franklin Knox, to be secretary of War and secretary of the Navy, respectively. Stimson's long record of public service included previous appointments as secretary of War under William H. Taft and secretary of State in Herbert C. Hoover's administration. He had served in World War I, attaining the rank of colonel in the American Expeditionary Forces, where Marshall and he had met. He shared Marshall's attitude toward selfless public service. The two men developed a very close and highly effective relationship.

Marshall also developed a good reputation and healthy relationship with Congress. Thanks to his considerable experience as a staff officer, he was a talented briefer, thoroughly versed in his subject, and a candid, forceful, and succinct speaker. His lack of political affiliation promoted his image as an apolitical proponent of the nation's best interests. Marshall's efforts to build up the Army brought him before congressional committees five times between January and April 1940.[53] Over the succeeding five months, he spent twenty-one days testifying before Congress.[54]

The floodgates of congressional appropriations broke open in May 1940, when the German military stunned the world with its rapid conquest of France. The French Vichy government's subsequent alignment with Nazi Germany suddenly opened the prospect of German forces occupying French holdings in Africa and perhaps even the Western Hemisphere. On May 29 Marshall testified in support of a $2.5 billion appropriation that equaled the total military expenditure of the preceding five years.[55] A year later, in June 1941, Congress passed a record-breaking $9.8 billion appropriation that included a $25 million discretionary fund placed at the disposal of the chief of staff—a testament to the high regard in which Marshall was held.[56] "For almost twenty years we had all of the time and almost none of the money," he observed, "today we have all of the money and no time."[57]

Given the new sense of urgency toward preparedness measures, in June 1941 Marshall for the first time spoke openly about the need for mobilizing the National Guard and implementing selective service. Marshall, long a proponent of universal military training, clearly favored the implementation of conscription before the nation's declaration of war. He recognized, however, that an influx of draftees would inundate the small Regular Army and interrupt other modernization programs. Moreover, he was well aware of the widespread isolationist sentiment that would oppose such an unprecedented measure as peacetime conscription. Accordingly, Marshall himself declined to take the lead in the push for conscription, leaving it to preparedness-minded legislators to serve as the front men. He did, however, detail several officers from the War Department to assist in drafting the eventual legislation.[58] Meanwhile, Marshall also supported a move to bring the National Guard on active duty, in large part because the understrength Guard units would serve as ready receptacles for an influx of draftees. Throughout, Marshall cast all this expansion in terms of hemispheric defense and not intervention in Europe. On August 27, 1940, a joint resolution of Congress authorized the federalization of the National Guard, and on September 16 President Roosevelt signed the nation's first peacetime selective service bill. Marshall remarked, "The National Defense Act of 1920, the lesson of our lack of preparation in 1917 and 1918, is being put into effect in a progressive, businesslike manner."[59]

One preparedness measure that Marshall resisted was the revival of the Plattsburg Camp movement. This was one of the few direct clashes he ever had with Stimson, who was a strong proponent of the idea. With conscription a reality, the Army could not spare officers to train Plattsburg volunteers. Moreover, Marshall preferred the early implementation of Officer Candidate Schools for qualified enlisted men as a way to boost morale and make conscription more palatable.[60] After a pointed dispute with Stimson, during which Marshall allegedly threatened to resign, the chief of staff prevailed over the secretary of War.

As funding and manpower became available, Marshall was able not only to expand the force, but also to modernize it. One of his first measures as chief of staff was to force through the adoption of a new organization for the infantry division that had been under study for years. The new division structure was oriented toward a mobile war of maneuver, rather than trench warfare. He also brought to completion a program to replace all the Army's draft animals with motor vehicles (though the Cavalry kept their horses for three more years). Through the winter of 1939–40 Marshall brought the Regular Army formations up to strength and inaugurated a program of large unit training.

In addition to restructuring the infantry division, Marshall established entirely new combat arms formations. Dissatisfied with the slow pace of tank development that had been displayed over previous years, in July 1940 Marshall summarily removed all tanks from the Infantry and Cavalry branches and assigned them to a new Armored Force. Similarly, when the Army's efforts to create an antitank capability foundered on interbranch squabbling over proponency, Marshall simply assigned antitank development to the War Department Operations Division. These episodes reflect one of Marshall's great challenges—getting the Army to stop thinking and acting like a business-as-usual peacetime force. He practically had to force the officer corps to move out and get things done, rather than endlessly debating decisions and accounting for every penny.[61]

One of the more dramatic such moves that Marshall made was to grant the air service virtual autonomy. In June 1941 the War Department established the Army Air Forces, with its own chief, Major General Henry H. "Hap" Arnold, who continued to report to Marshall and Stimson. Marshall, although a supporter of airpower, did not believe that air alone could win wars. "You've got to get down and hold things," he later observed.[62] Nor did he feel that the air service was ready for complete independence. Relatively few air officers had attended the Command and General Staff School or the Army War College in the interwar period, and so there were not sufficient qualified General Staff officers to establish a fully independent entity. Marshall did, however, grant Arnold a large degree of latitude in all matters related to military aviation.[63]

As part of the push to modernize the Army, Marshall often became involved in questions of technological innovation. He found that there was no shortage of ideas for new weapons and equipment, but that few of these proposals were practicable. On occasion, though, Marshall did override his staff in support of some new item of equipment. It is part of Army lore that Marshall personally supported the adoption of the one-quarter-ton four-by-four truck, better known as the jeep. When it came to innovation, Marshall believed that the "Ordnance [branch] was conservative, I would say, but at the same time it had to insist on a certain precision that the line officers objected to as too prolonged."[64]

Modernization reached the intellectual sphere as well as the technical. Marshall's old associate from his 1st Division days, Brigadier General Lesley J. McNair, was commandant at Fort Leavenworth in 1939. Marshall encouraged him to modernize the curriculum there, and he applauded his success in doing so: "You apparently . . . have vitalized the place and yet in a most harmonious manner. . . . Anything I can do to assist, you command me, but I want you to feel perfectly free to act, and we all have complete confidence in your judgment, your leadership, and your integrity."[65]

The immediate objective that Marshall worked toward in the period 1939–41 was the creation of the Protective Mobilization Plan (PMP) Army. Laid out in mobilization plans drafted in the 1930s, the PMP Army was intended to provide security for the Western Hemisphere while the nation geared up for war. It consisted principally of the existing Regular Army divisions brought up to full strength, plus the National Guard divisions under federal control. With the mobilization of the Guard and the inauguration of Selective Service in 1940, the PMP Army became a reality. By July 1941 the Army consisted of 1.4 million men. Marshall directed that the elements of the PMP Army embark on a systematic, progressive training program starting at the small unit level and carrying through to higher and higher echelons. Throughout, Marshall continually had to defend the existence of this force and the need to train it: "Well, the hardest thing in the world to train is a ground army of infantry and artillery."[66] The foot soldier has to make the utmost exertions when he is tired, wet, and cold: "The moment when his high courage was necessary was, as a rule, at dawn when he woke up half-frozen to deal with an enemy he couldn't see . . . all of which required a very high state of training, higher than that of any other force that I know of."[67]

In the summer of 1941, just as Marshall's program of progressive training had reached the stage of division, corps, and army maneuvers, the PMP Army stood on the verge of disintegration. The National Guardsmen and draftees inducted in the fall of 1940 were nearing the end of their twelve-month obligation. Efforts to extend the term of service touched off a surge of opposition among isolationists and anti-administration political factions and, unfortunately, within the Army itself. Disgruntled troops adopted the slogan "OHIO"—"over the hill in October." Marshall argued long and hard in support of the extension. He called it a "struggle for survival," and he feared that failure to extend the servicemen's obligation would lead to "the complete destruction . . . of the fabric of the army that we had built up."[68] In the end, Congress approved the extension of service from twelve months to two and one-half years. The measure cleared the House of Representatives by a single vote.[69]

With the future of the PMP Army assured for the time being, Marshall directed that the force embark on the largest and most ambitious training exercises in the Army's history—the famous Louisiana Maneuvers. Marshall announced that "the present maneuvers are the closest peacetime approximation to actual fighting conditions that have ever been undertaken in this country."[70] Not only did the maneuvers provide an opportunity to train troops, practice movement and supply, and test new concepts, but they also afforded Marshall an opportunity to gauge the abilities of the higher commanders. Following the Louisiana Maneuvers and a comparable set of exercises in the Carolinas, Marshall began to remove a number of senior officers who had passed their prime. Only eleven of the forty-two generals who commanded divisions, corps, or armies in the Louisiana and Carolinas maneuvers went on to hold significant combat commands in World War II.[71]

For the first time in the nation's history, mobilization and training had preceded the initiation of hostilities. The PMP Army was not entirely combat-ready, by any means, but the contrast with earlier conflicts in this regard was dramatic. As Marshall told Congress in April 1941, compared to the 1917 experience, "there has been an opportunity to organize on a very much better basis. There has been more uniformity, more careful inspection, more education, and more logical development."[72] The moving force behind this accomplishment was Marshall himself.

Even as the great maneuvers were in progress, the General Staff began drafting plans to release the National Guard divisions upon the completion of the training season. President Roosevelt, apparently still unconvinced of the need for a large ground force and, perhaps, unappreciative of the difficulties in training such a force, wished to divert resources into other channels. The American entry into World War II forestalled this drawdown.

Through the late autumn of 1941 it became obvious that hostilities with Japan were imminent. American cryptographers had broken a secret Japanese communications code, affording Marshall and other top civilian and military leaders an indication of Japanese intentions. By the end of November there was clear evidence that Japanese military might was massing in the direction of Southeast Asia. There was no such unmistakable indicator that the Japanese planned any operations in the central Pacific. On November 27 Marshall warned the Army commanders in the Pacific region that negotiations with Japan had essentially terminated, and that war was imminent. The chief of naval operations, Admiral Harold R. Stark, sent an even stronger message to his subordinates in the Pacific, containing the phrase "war warning."[73] And yet on the morning of December 7 a task force of six Japanese aircraft carriers caught the defenders of Hawaii, both Army and Navy, by surprise. In later years certain authors asserted that Marshall and the high command in Washington knew that the attack was coming and deliberately withheld that knowledge from the field commanders, to ensure the American entry into World War II. Responsible historians have refuted this conspiracy theory. The worst that can be said of Marshall and his naval counterpart is that they were negligent in following up on the actual defense measures taken by their subordinates. In any event, the attack on Pearl Harbor meant that the Army would not be drawn down, but would instead embark on a new phase of expansion.

Among the first wartime measures that Marshall undertook was a thorough reorganization of the General Staff. "This is the poorest command post in the Army and we must do something about it," he remarked.[74] No fewer than sixty-one officers and War Department officials had, in theory, direct access to the chief of staff. A multiplicity of offices and branches complicated and delayed measures that needed to be executed with urgency. Accordingly, in March 1942 Marshall was authorized to sweep away the existing structure and implement a more streamlined, centralized organization that served to enhance his own ability to control Army affairs. He eliminated the branch chiefs (Infantry, Cavalry, Field Artillery, Coast Artillery) and established a new agency, Army Ground Forces (AGF), to supervise the doctrine, training, manning, and equipping of all the combat arms. He placed his old associate Lieutenant General Lesley J. McNair in charge. Major General "Hap" Arnold headed Army Air Forces, which performed similar duties for the air arm, in addition to planning and executing air strategy in the combat theaters. Services of Supply (later redesignated Army Service Forces), under Lieutenant General Brehon B. Somervell, managed logistical and transportation matters. Operations Division (OPD) became Marshall's command post for supervising combat operations on a global scale. Marshall remained the military adviser to both the secretary of War and the president.[75]

Even as the wreckage of Pearl Harbor still smoldered and America's Pacific garrisons fell one by one, Marshall guided the War Department into a new expansion program. Just as in 1940, when Marshall used the Regular Army as seed corn for the Protective Mobilization Plan force, so in 1942 the PMP Army provided the nucleus for what would become the ninety-division wartime Army. The 1.6 million men in uniform at the time of Pearl Harbor would ultimately expand to over 8 million in 1945, including the Army Air Forces. Whereas the Victory Program, an early projection of wartime requirements, called for more than two hundred divisions to defeat the Axis, Marshall preferred having fewer full-strength, fully trained divisions rather than a larger number of "watered-down" formations.[76] Under the direction of General McNair, Army Ground Forces developed a template for establishing new divisions, starting with a commander, 172 officers, and 1,190 enlisted men as a cadre, and culminating, in as little as thirty-five weeks, in a division of 14,000 ready to deploy into combat.[77] Above all, Marshall insisted that divisions be fully trained before shipment overseas. He had no intention of revisiting the embarrassment of 1917, when the incomplete and untrained 1st Division arrived in France.

Among the formations raised were three divisions of African American troops, as well as a large number of similarly constituted combat and support units. Marshall's staff urged him to establish training bases for these forces in the northern United States, but Marshall refused, on the grounds that construction costs for barracks would be higher and the training season shorter in the colder regions. Unfortunately, these African American units faced harassment and discrimination in some of the southern states where they ended up training. "I failed to visualize what was going to happen," Marshall later commented, "and it caused us all sorts of difficulties, and I regard it as one of the most important mistakes I made in the mobilization of the army."[78] Although not a civil rights activist per se, Marshall held deep convictions about citizenship that applied to all races: "When you are calling on a man to risk his life in the service of the country, he had every right, it would certainly seem, to demand the same rights [as] the other fellow who was risking his life."[79] Later in the war, when heavy casualties caused a shortage of infantrymen in frontline units, Marshall supported General Dwight D. Eisenhower's decision to integrate African American replacements directly into previously all-white formations.[80] Similarly, the demands of all-out mobilization caused Marshall to lend his personal support to the formation of the Women's Army Auxiliary Corps. "Women must certainly be employed in the 'over-all' effort of this nation," he asserted.[81]

One of the greatest challenges that Marshall faced in mobilizing the wartime Army was the selection of senior leaders. Marshall personally reviewed and approved every appointment to division, corps, and field army command: "Every bit of data we receive from the fighting fronts clearly shows that this is a young man's war. . . . We have to be absolutely firm on the question of age for command."[82] In a process that began well before the attack on Pearl Harbor, Marshall persuaded the War Department to lower the retirement age for senior officers, set upper age limits for officers in command of troops, and establish a policy allowing for temporary promotions regardless of seniority. Under these measures, the average age of a new division commander dropped from fifty-nine years in 1939 to forty-nine in 1943.[83] The process of moving out the officers who were too old to lead in combat was a painful and difficult one for Marshall, for many of these men were peers, if not friends. He was unsparing, however, noting that the officer corps suffered from "arteriosclerosis," because most individuals began to lose their "fine qualities" when in their fifties. Few men past the age of sixty were usable.[84] He even offered to resign (though several years short of mandatory retirement age) by way of setting an example to the rest of the officer corps.[85]

Marshall did not, however, simply discard the men too old to command in combat. Although lacking the vigor and resiliency demanded by frontline duty, they possessed a wealth of experience and administrative skills. He kept many of them in their higher-command positions to supervise mobilization and training. Meanwhile, the younger officers destined to lead in combat passed through a series of developmental assignments, often on higher-level staffs, to broaden their perspectives and prepare them for command. Many of the men Marshall tapped for this track toward high command were young officers whom he knew personally. One of the most prominent of these individuals was Dwight D. Eisenhower, whom he had known by reputation for years. Eisenhower was a protégé of Major General Fox Conner, who, like Marshall himself, was a member of Pershing's inner circle. Marshall saw through Eisenhower's unassuming, amiable persona and discerned the logical thinker and natural leader beneath.

Even as the wartime ninety-division army was taking form, Marshall was called on to participate in strategic decisions at the highest levels. He was largely responsible for establishing principles of strategy that guided not just the American but also the Allied war effort. Foremost among these was the concept of unity of command. He saw clearly that to wage global coalition warfare involving all the armed services, traditional lines of authority had to be replaced. At the first wartime conference with the British leaders held in Washington, D.C., Marshall advocated establishing a single headquarters to command all the arms of all Allied nations in the hard-pressed southwest Pacific. Overcoming resistance from Prime Minister Winston Churchill, Marshall persuaded the British to assign Field Marshal Archibald Wavell to command the American-British-Dutch-Australian Command (ABDACOM), a headquarters established to defend the Dutch East Indies and Malaysia, which had authority over ground, sea, and air forces from the member countries.[86] Although ABDACOM went down to rapid defeat, the precedent of unified joint and combined command was established.

A second principle of strategy took much longer to achieve. Marshall recognized that the far-flung global conflict offered endless opportunities for the Allies to dissipate their strength in nondecisive operations. He sought to resist such a dispersal of force and instead concentrate the preponderance of Allied power where it would do the most good. In a June 1942 message to President Roosevelt he wrote, "You are familiar with my view that the decisive theater is Western Europe. That is the only place where the concerted effort of our own and the British forces can be brought to bear on the Germans."[87] In this Marshall had the concurrence of the United States Navy—as early as May 1941 the Joint Board, consisting of the Army chief of staff and the chief of naval operations and their key subordinates, approved the concept of "Germany First."[88] Churchill and the British planners, however, held a different interpretation of "Germany First." To Marshall it meant an assault across the English Channel into occupied France at the earliest possible date. To the British it meant weakening Germany through blockade, aerial bombardment, and Resistance activities, the cross-Channel assault being the coup de grâce against a tottering Nazi regime. Not until 1944 would Marshall's views entirely prevail.

No matter which direction Allied strategy might go, Marshall understood that the critical factor in success or failure would be the strength of the Allied coalition. He was perhaps the critical figure in forging that coalition. But before Marshall could establish ties with the British military, he needed to build a coalition among the American services—the Joint Chiefs of Staff (JCS). The first order of business was to establish a working relationship with Admiral Ernest J. King, the chief of naval operations appointed after Pearl Harbor. King was difficult and short-tempered, but he and Marshall recognized that they had to work together. Their relationship was never close, but it was effective. King supported Marshall's ideas pertaining to the war in Europe, and, in turn, Marshall backed King in the Navy's strategy for the Pacific war. Marshall gave "Hap" Arnold the de facto status of chief of staff and added him to the JCS on his own initiative, thus including the air service in all joint deliberations. Marshall suggested that Admiral William D. Leahy act as chairman of the JCS, thus balancing the two Army generals with two Navy admirals. Leahy, however, acted more as military aide to Roosevelt than as true chairman of the JCS, leaving Marshall as the first among equals. The American JCS joined with its British counterpart to form the Combined Chiefs of Staff (CCS), which constituted the highest-level military body for the direction of the war, and which was answerable only to Roosevelt and Churchill.

Forging a coalition with the British proved to be more difficult than establishing joint relationships with the Navy and Army Air Forces. Marshall discovered that there was considerable anti-British sentiment within the War Department—he later stated that the Americans were more anti-British than the British were anti-American.[89] Beyond that, his greatest difficulty early in the war was that Roosevelt and Churchill tended to make strategic decisions between the two of them, informing their military staffs after the fact. Roosevelt in particular tended to side with Churchill against the advice of Marshall. The head of the British military mission to Washington, D.C., Field Marshal John Dill, salvaged the situation. He took advantage of his close personal relationship with Marshall (one of the few such relationships that Marshall ever formed) to keep the Americans informed about what Churchill and Roosevelt were up to.[90]

The most contentious of these strategic decisions in 1942 had to do with a British proposal for the Allies to invade North Africa. Marshall perceived this as being exactly the type of dissipation that he sought to avoid. He preferred an early invasion of France, to relieve pressure on the Soviet Union and to keep the Allied effort focused on a decisive theater. Roosevelt, however, sided with the British. It is most likely that the president saw the operation as a vote of confidence in the British and as a means of maintaining domestic American support for the war.[91] In later years Marshall observed that the military "failed to see that the leader in a democracy has to keep the people entertained. That may sound like the wrong word, but it conveys the thought. . . . People demand action. We couldn't wait to be completely ready."[92] "Both Churchill and Roosevelt suffered because they had to take action. Public can't sit around and wait. What can you do that won't ruin you?"[93] Marshall could take some consolation from the fact that the commander named for the invasion was Dwight Eisenhower. Code-named Operation Torch, the invasion took place in November 1942.

In early 1943 the Allied leaders met at Casablanca in Morocco to hammer out the next strategic move. The British pushed hard for a continuation of Mediterranean operations, with invasions of Sicily and then Italy. Once again, Roosevelt sided with the British. Additionally, the heads of state approved Admiral King's proposal for offensive operations in the Pacific, further diluting Marshall's cherished principle of "Germany First." This was to be the last inter-Allied conference that Marshall attended without first informing himself fully about the political pressures operating on military strategy. It was also the last conference at which the American JCS arrived without first establishing a common agenda. Marshall thereafter saw to it that the Americans, including the president, went in with a unified position.

The next such meeting was the Trident Conference, held in Washington, D.C., in May 1943. Here the Americans acceded to a continuation of Mediterranean operations only with a British guarantee that there would be a cross-Channel assault in 1944. When Churchill resisted, Roosevelt sided with his JCS. The same was true at the Quadrant Conference, held three months later in Quebec.

Roosevelt, Churchill (both seated), and other leaders on board HMS *Prince of Wales* during the Atlantic Charter Conference, 1941. (Naval History and Heritage Command)

Again the Americans spoke with one voice, and a firm date for the cross-Channel assault, code-named Overlord, was set.

The final great conference of 1943 involved the British, Americans, and Soviets. This conference took place late in the year in Tehran, Iran. Joseph Stalin, leader of the Soviet Union, supported Operation Overlord and promised that the Red Army would launch a summer offensive in 1944 to facilitate the cross-Channel assault. He went on to pledge Soviet participation in the war against Japan once Germany was defeated. At long last Marshall could see his campaign for a coordinated Allied strategy, focused in the decisive theater, bear fruit. Marshall had emerged as the dominant military voice in the Allied coalition.

The next top-level conference bringing together all three powers took place in Yalta in February 1945. Here the three great leaders laid the groundwork for the postwar world. Of equal importance, the conference ensured that the coalition would remain intact through the end of hostilities, thus robbing Germany and Japan of their last chance to escape overwhelming defeat. By this time Marshall was more than a military strategist. He had risen into the realm of statesmanship.

In addition to his obligations in the fields of strategy and coalition building, Marshall was responsible for directing the operations of Army forces in all theaters of the war. In keeping with the decisions of the JCS and CCS, Marshall gave priority to theaters and supervised the conduct of campaigns. He often had to contend with a condition he called "localitis"—the tendency of each theater commander to assume that his domain should be the main effort of the war.[94] Marshall did not, however, attempt to run battles from Washington, D.C. It was his practice to delegate authority readily to the commanders on the ground, and to allow them considerable latitude, even when he might disagree with some of their decisions. On February 16, 1943, in the midst of the Kasserine Pass debacle in Tunisia, Marshall sent the following words of reassurance to Eisenhower: "You can concentrate on this battle with the feeling that it is our business to support you and not harass you and I'll use all my influence to see that you are supported."[95]

In one respect Marshall was willing to exert his influence over operations. He sometimes found it necessary to press commanders into action. After the war he remarked: "Everybody wanted things we couldn't give them. And you had to press them to accomplish the thing without all of the means that might later become available."[96]

Some of Marshall's greatest challenges in this regard were his dealings with General Douglas MacArthur, commander of forces in the Philippines at the onset of war and the head of the southwest Pacific theater after his evacuation from the Philippines. MacArthur was, in terms of personality and character, the antithesis of Marshall. Marshall diplomatically noted MacArthur's "very independent nature" and his tendency to be suspicious of everything Marshall did.[97] Although he was less than a year older than Marshall, MacArthur had been the senior of the two until 1939. He had ended World War I as a division commander and had been Army chief of staff when Marshall was a lieutenant colonel. During World War II MacArthur undoubtedly had the worst case of "localitis" in the Army. He opposed the cross-Channel invasion of Europe and never saw the merit of the Navy's "island hopping" campaign in the central Pacific. Accused of being hostile toward MacArthur, Mar-

From left: Lieutenant General Krueger, General MacArthur, and General Marshall at a field headquarters, late 1943. (U.S. Army Signal Corps)

shall responded: "In the first place, it is damn nonsense. I did everything in the world I could for him."[98] Marshall personally wrote the citation for the Medal of Honor that MacArthur received in 1942. Marshall clearly perceived that President Roosevelt had to keep MacArthur prominently active in the war for political reasons if for no other. MacArthur was closely linked to the most conservative elements of the Republican Party; thus, his prominent stature in the military was a crucial means of maintaining bipartisan support for the war effort.

As the Army's overall director of global operations, Marshall made some key decisions that had a significant influence on the course of the war. One of these was his adherence to the cross-Channel attack that culminated in the invasion of Normandy in June 1944. Another was his refusal to countenance operations in the Balkans. In the spring of 1945 he supported Eisenhower's decision not to race the Soviets to Berlin. As he told Eisenhower, "Personally, I should be loath to hazard American lives for purely political purposes."[99] Postwar critics seized on this remark as an indication that

Marshall and indeed all the American leaders were politically naive in their dealings with the Soviet Union. In fact, Marshall was fully attuned to the political ramifications of this and all his decisions. He recognized that it was not within his purview to overturn the agreements forged at Yalta regarding the postwar world. Moreover, the war was still in progress, and he recognized the folly of risking coalition unity before the last German soldier had laid down his arms. Following Germany's defeat, Marshall staunchly advocated an invasion of the Japanese home islands, even when the Army Air Forces and Navy argued that an invasion would not be necessary. Finally, Marshall supported the use of the atomic bomb against Japan. He had used his personal influence in Congress to secure funding for the Manhattan Project, which developed the bomb, even though he could not tell Congress what the funds were for.[100]

Marshall's greatest failure as a director of strategy was China. Roosevelt and Marshall hoped that, with sufficient Allied aid, the Nationalist forces under Chiang Kai-shek could mount a serious challenge to Japanese forces on the Asian mainland. Despite mountains of aid, committed over the objections of the British, Chiang's forces failed to fulfill the role Marshall envisioned for them. Marshall compounded the problem with one of his least successful appointments to high position. Lieutenant General Joseph W. Stilwell, one of Marshall's contacts from his days at Fort Benning, proved to be unsuited to the complex and delicate task of nurturing the Chinese Nationalist forces. After the war Marshall conceded that the British had been right all along: "You can see how hopeless the whole thing was."[101]

Other than the failure of his China strategy, the greatest disappointment to befall Marshall during World War II was his inability to secure a major operational command for himself. Just as in World War I, his talents as a staff officer precluded his assignment to command. In 1942 and 1943 it was generally assumed that Marshall himself would become the overall Allied commander for Operation Overlord. Following the Tehran Conference, where Stalin pressed the Western Allies to name the commander, Roosevelt remarked to Marshall, "I could not sleep at night with you out of the country."[102] Eisenhower got the Overlord command, and Marshall remained in the Pentagon. On December 16, 1944, in recognition of his selfless service, Marshall was the first man promoted to the rank of five-star general and accorded the title General of the Army.

By 1945 Marshall was probably Roosevelt's closest adviser, often drafting messages for the president's signature. With the death of Roosevelt in April 1945, Harry S. Truman became president. Truman, who had chaired a Senate special committee charged with investigating national defense, had acquired an enormous respect for the general. Marshall later remarked that President Truman would approve anything that Marshall proposed, which worried Marshall: "There were other facets of the affair that I might not understand."[103]

Despite all his strategic-level responsibilities, throughout the war Marshall maintained a close interest in the well-being of the common soldier. In World War I he had witnessed the vital importance of morale and the way in which unnecessary hardships could degrade the combat performance of the soldier. On his own initiative, Marshall arranged for the Hollywood director Frank Capra to produce the *Why We Fight* film series. He personally intervened to make sure that frontline soldiers received all possible creature comforts, as well as access to entertainment, reading material, and PX facilities. He was the chief advocate for the establishment of campaign medals and overseas service ribbons. He stifled proposals to ban alcohol on or near military posts, remarking, "It is no time to inflict experiments on this great army."[104] After the war Marshall spoke of the importance of maintaining the morale of the combat soldier: "I was for supplying everything we could and then requiring him to fight to the death when the time came. You had to put these two things together. . . . I thought it was quite essential—quite essential—that the soldier be convinced that so far as we were concerned in the Pentagon . . . we were doing everything in our power to help him."[105]

Marshall also took time to think of the families on the home front, particularly those who lost a relative in the war. Early in the conflict, Marshall attempted to write a personal note to the family of every soldier killed in action. When the increasing number of casualties made this impossible, he paid close attention to the wording of the letter of condolence sent out by the War Department, and he took great pains to ensure that the president was fully aware of the conflict's human cost.[106] The full effect of the war struck his own household in May 1944, when Marshall's stepson Allen Brown was killed in action in Italy, fighting in a campaign that Marshall had opposed.

As the end of the war drew near, the tributes to Marshall began to pour in. He was named *Time* magazine's man of the year for 1944. On May 8, 1945, Victory in Europe Day, Secretary of War Stimson gathered a group of top War Department officials to mark the end of the war with Germany. Of Marshall he said, "I have never seen a task of such magnitude performed by man." To Marshall he said, "I have seen a great many soldiers in my lifetime and you, sir, are the finest soldier I have ever known."[107]

On November 26, 1945, Marshall retired from military service. President Truman personally awarded him the second oak-leaf cluster to the Distinguished Service Medal he had earned in World War I. (This was the only military decoration that Marshall accepted during his six-year term as chief of staff.) Truman himself read the citation: "In a war unparalleled in magnitude and horror, millions of Americans gave their country outstanding service. General of the Army George C. Marshall gave it victory."[108]

Marshall's retirement from the Army was by no means the end of his public service. One day later President Truman summoned him to head up a special mission to China, with the task of resolving the civil war between Chiang Kai-shek's Nationalists and the Communist People's Liberation Army under Mao Tse-tung. The task was probably hopeless from the outset—there was nothing that an external power could do to reconcile the contending factions. Marshall's inability to impose an American solution on China, and Mao's defeat of the Nationalists in 1949, later provided Senator Joseph McCarthy with all the evidence he needed to fabricate the incredible charge that George Marshall was pro-Communist.

Early in 1947 Truman recalled Marshall to the United States only to give him a new and even larger job—that of secretary of State. During his two years in that office, Marshall implemented an organizational reform of the department, just as he had reconfigured the War Department in 1942. He brought in a team of brilliant, forward-thinking younger men, not unlike what he had done when he restructured the faculty at Fort Benning in the 1930s, and when he selected younger commanders in World War II. By far the most significant accomplishment of his tenure as secretary of State, if not the most important of his life, was the formulation and passage of the Economic Recovery Act for the reconstruction of war-torn Europe. Better known as the Marshall Plan, this program was formulated by a small group of individuals within the State Department, with the full approval of the president. Marshall announced the plan at the

Harvard commencement exercise in June 1947 and then embarked on a campaign to secure its approval. "I worked on that as hard as though I was running for the Senate or the presidency," he later recalled.[109] He succeeded in building a broad base of foreign and domestic support for the policy, attracting adherents from both political parties and all economic sectors. Just as General Marshall's military strategy saved Europe from Axis domination, Secretary Marshall's recovery plan secured Europe's future peace and prosperity. In 1948 he was again named *Time* magazine's man of the year.

Marshall resigned as secretary of State in early 1949, only to be recalled by President Truman yet again in September 1950, this time to serve as secretary of Defense. His main task was to oversee the buildup of military forces for the Korean War. This marked the third occasion that Marshall confronted the problems of mobilizing for war. His one-year tenure as secretary of Defense also occasioned one of the most unpleasant and controversial incidents of his long career—the relief of General MacArthur as commander in Korea and the Far East. MacArthur had attempted to circumvent the national policy in Korea as laid down by the president—an act of insubordination that was anathema to Marshall. He sided with the Joint Chiefs of Staff in recommending MacArthur's removal, which occurred in April 1951.

Finally, in September 1951, Marshall retired for the last time. He withdrew to the seclusion of his home and garden for eight years of peaceful retirement. In December 1953 he reemerged in the public eye to receive the Nobel Peace Prize for his European Recovery Act. Marshall was the first professional soldier to be so honored.

George Marshall died at Walter Reed Army Hospital on October 16, 1959, and was interred at Arlington National Cemetery. He was two months short of his seventy-ninth birthday. His life of public service spanned forty-nine of those years, during forty-three of which he wore the uniform of the United States Army. A model officer, dedicated professional, and true soldier-statesman, George C. Marshall left an indelible mark on the Army, the nation, and the world.

Notes

1. Larry I. Bland, ed., *George C. Marshall: Interviews and Reminiscences for Forrest C. Pogue, Transcripts and Notes, 1956–57* (Lexington, Va.: George C. Marshall Research Foundation, 1986), 68.

2. Ibid., 25.

3. Ibid., 21.

4. Forrest C. Pogue, *George C. Marshall: Education of a General, 1880–1939* (New York: Viking Press, 1963), 54.

5. Ibid., 66.

6. Ibid., 76–77.

7. Bland, *George C. Marshall*, 123.

8. Ibid., 131, 136.

9. Ibid., 129.

10. Ibid., 138.

11. Ibid., 131, 138.

12. Ibid., 135.

13. Ibid., 130, 138.

14. Ibid., 134.

15. *Annual Report of the Commandant, U.S. Infantry and Cavalry School, U.S. Signal School, and Army Staff College, for the School Year Ending Aug. 31, 1907* (Fort Leavenworth, Kans.: Staff College Press, 1907). See also the *Annual Reports* for 1908, 1909, 1910, all in the archives of the Combined Arms Research Library, Fort Leavenworth, Kans.

16. Bland, *George C. Marshall*, 137.

17. Thomas M. Coffey, *Hap: The Story of the U.S. Air Force and the Man Who Built It, General Henry H. "Hap" Arnold* (New York: Viking Press, 1982), 80.

18. George C. Marshall, *The Papers of George Catlett Marshall*, vol. 1, *"The Soldierly Spirit," December 1880–June 1939*, ed. Larry I. Bland and Sharon R. Ritenour (Baltimore: Johns Hopkins University Press, 1981), 103n; emphasis in original.

19. Ibid., 150–51.

20. Bland, *George C. Marshall*, 175–76.

21. Ibid.

22. Ibid., 228.

23. Ibid., 220.

24. Ibid., 226.

25. Ibid., 246.

26. Marshall, *Papers of George Catlett Marshall*, 1:241.

27. Ibid., 335.

28. Ibid., 335, 338.

29. Bland, *George C. Marshall*, 508.

30. Marshall, *Papers of George Catlett Marshall*, 1:320.

31. Ibid., 409–13.

32. Bland, *George C. Marshall*, 508.

33. Marshall, *Papers of George Catlett Marshall*, 1:320.

34. Ibid.

35. Mark A. Stoler, *George C. Marshall: Soldier-Statesman of the American Century* (New York: Twayne Publishers, 1989), 56.

36. Marshall, *Papers of George Catlett Marshall*, 1:392.

37. Pogue, *George C. Marshall: Education*, 227.

38. Marshall, *Papers of George Catlett Marshall*, 1:659.

39. Pogue, *George C. Marshall: Education*, 299.

40. Stoler, *George C. Marshall: Soldier-Statesman*, 63.

41. Marshall, *Papers of George Catlett Marshall*, 1:650–51.

42. Pogue, *George C. Marshall: Education*, 327.

43. Ibid., 328.

44. Marshall, *Papers of George Catlett Marshall*, 1:641–42.

45. Pogue, *George C. Marshall: Education*, 330.

46. George C. Marshall, *The Papers of George Catlett Marshall*, vol. 2, *"We Cannot Delay," July 1, 1939–December 6, 1941*, ed. Larry I. Bland, Sharon R. Ritenour, and Clarence E. Wunderlin Jr. (Baltimore: Johns Hopkins University Press, 1986), 452n.

47. Ibid., 3.

48. Ibid., 195.

49. Bland, *George C. Marshall*, 183.

50. Eric Larrabee, *Commander in Chief: Franklin Delano Roosevelt, His Lieutenants, and Their War* (New York: Harper and Row, 1987), 62.

51. Bland, *George C. Marshall*, 271.

52. Ibid., 302.

53. Marshall, *Papers of George Catlett Marshall*, 2:133.

54. Stoler, *George C. Marshall: Soldier-Statesman*, 76.

55. Marshall, *Papers of George Catlett Marshall*, 2:231.

56. Mark S. Watson, *Chief of Staff: Prewar Plans and Preparations* (1950; repr., Washington, D.C.: Center of Military History, 1985), 217.

57. Marshall, *Papers of George Catlett Marshall*, 2:274.

58. Bland, *George C. Marshall*, 279.

59. Marshall, *Papers of George Catlett Marshall*, 2:311.

60. Bland, *George C. Marshall*, 282.

61. Ibid., 477.

62. Ibid., 266.

63. Ibid., 283–84, 287, 400–401.

64. Ibid., 245.

65. Marshall, *Papers of George Catlett Marshall*, 2:30–31.

66. Bland, *George C. Marshall*, 237–38.

67. Ibid.

68. Ibid., 262.

69. Forrest C. Pogue, *George C. Marshall: Ordeal and Hope, 1939–1942* (New York: Viking Press, 1965), 152–54.

70. Marshall, *Papers of George Catlett Marshall*, 2:606–10.

71. Christopher R. Gabel, *The U.S. Army GHQ Maneuvers of 1941* (Washington, D.C.: United States Army Center of Military History, 1992), 187.

72. Marshall, *Papers of George Catlett Marshall,* 2:487.

73. Pogue, *George C. Marshall: Ordeal and Hope,* 204–18.

74. Marshall, *Papers of George Catlett Marshall,* 2:687–88n.

75. George C. Marshall, *The Papers of George Catlett Marshall,* vol. 3, *"The Right Man for the Job," December 7, 1941–May 31, 1943,* ed. Larry I. Bland and Sharon Ritenour Stevens (Baltimore: Johns Hopkins University Press, 1991), 128.

76. Bland, *George C. Marshall,* 504.

77. Robert R. Palmer, Bell I. Wiley, and William R. Keast, *The Procurement and Training of Ground Combat Troops* (Washington, D.C.: Historical Division, United States Army, 1948), 37.

78. Bland, *George C. Marshall,* 422–23.

79. Ibid., 463–64.

80. Ibid., 465.

81. Marshall, *Papers of George Catlett Marshall,* 3:99.

82. Ibid., 152–53.

83. Christopher R. Gabel and Matthew C. Gabel, "A Matter of Age: Division Command in the U.S. Army of World War II," *Global War Studies* 8.1 (2011): 57–73.

84. Bland, *George C. Marshall,* 498.

85. Ibid., 441–43.

86. Ibid., 327–28.

87. Marshall, *Papers of George Catlett Marshall,* 3:249.

88. Ibid., 2:517.

89. Bland, *George C. Marshall,* 572.

90. Ibid., 379–80.

91. Larrabee, *Commander in Chief,* 138–39.

92. Bland, *George C. Marshall,* 586.

93. Ibid., 578.

94. Ibid., 549.

95. Marshall, *Papers of George Catlett Marshall,* 3:553–54.

96. Bland, *George C. Marshall,* 339.

97. Ibid., 573.

98. Ibid., 221.

99. Ibid., 381.

100. Ibid., 388–89.

101. Ibid., 580.

102. Stoler, *George C. Marshall: Soldier-Statesman,* 108.

103. Bland, *George C. Marshall,* 303.

104. Marshall, *Papers of George Catlett Marshall,* 3:257–58.

105. Bland, *George C. Marshall*, 446.
106. Ibid., 494.
107. Stoler, *George C. Marshall: Soldier-Statesman*, 130.
108. Forrest C. Pogue, *George C. Marshall: Statesman, 1945–1959* (New York: Viking Penguin, 1987), 1.
109. Bland, *George C. Marshall*, 520–21.

References

Bland, Larry I., ed. *George C. Marshall: Interviews and Reminiscences for Forrest C. Pogue, Transcripts and Notes, 1956–57*. Lexington, Va.: George C. Marshall Research Foundation, 1986.

Cray, Ed. *General of the Army George C. Marshall: Soldier and Statesman*. New York: W. W. Norton, 1990.

Larrabee, Eric. *Commander in Chief: Franklin Delano Roosevelt, His Lieutenants, and Their War*. New York: Harper and Row, 1987.

Marshall, George C. *The Papers of George Catlett Marshall*. 5 vols. Edited by Larry I. Bland, Sharon Ritenour Stevens, and Clarence E. Wunderlin Jr. Baltimore: Johns Hopkins University Press, 1981–2003.

Palmer, Robert R., Bell I. Wiley, and William R. Keast. *The Procurement and Training of Ground Combat Troops*. Washington, D.C.: Historical Division, United States Army, 1948.

Pogue, Forrest C. *George C. Marshall: Education of a General, 1880–1939*. New York: Viking Press, 1963.

———. *George C. Marshall: Ordeal and Hope, 1939–1942*. New York: Viking Press, 1965.

———. *George C. Marshall: Organizer of Victory, 1943–1945*. New York: Viking Press, 1973.

———. *George C. Marshall: Statesman, 1945–1959*. New York: Viking Penguin, 1987.

Stoler, Mark A. *George C. Marshall: Soldier-Statesman of the American Century*. New York: Twayne Publishers, 1989.

Watson, Mark S. *Chief of Staff: Prewar Plans and Preparations*. 1950. Reprint, Washington, D.C.: Center of Military History, 1985.

3

Douglas MacArthur

Tony R. Mullis

Douglas MacArthur was undoubtedly the most polarizing of America's five-star generals. General George C. Kenney, MacArthur's World War II air commander, remarked: "Very few people really know Douglas MacArthur. Those who do, or think they do, either admire him or dislike him. They are never neutral on the subject." General George E. Stratemeyer was an admirer. He described MacArthur as "the greatest leader, the greatest commander, the greatest hero in American history." General Robert L. Eichelberger, MacArthur's Eighth Army commander, was less flattering. "We have difficulty in following the satellites of MacArthur," Eichelberger concluded, "for like those of Jupiter, we cannot see the moons on account of the brilliance of the planet. . . . Even the gods were alleged to have their weaknesses."[1] Regardless of how MacArthur's subordinates, peers, and superiors saw him, his significant accomplishments over a fifty-two-year military career justify his presence in the pantheon of outstanding American military leaders and strategists.

Few could equal Douglas MacArthur's contributions to American military history. He served in key leadership positions during both world wars and the Korean War. His peacetime assignments were equally significant. As a junior officer, he was an aide to his father, General Arthur MacArthur, and to President Theodore Roosevelt. Following World War I, he returned to West Point as its superintendent. He also held key commands in the Philippines and headed the IV Corps area in Atlanta, the III Corps area in Baltimore, and the IX Corps area in San Francisco during the 1920s. He became the Army's chief of staff in 1930. MacArthur returned to the Philippines in 1935 and retired in 1937. He became the military adviser to the Philippines and held the rank of field marshal in the Filipino military. He was recalled to active duty in 1941 as commander of the U.S. Army Forces Far East. After Japan's surrender, he held the position of supreme commander of the Allied Powers and oversaw Japan's occupation. When the Korean War began in 1950, MacArthur became the commander in chief of the United Nations Command. His brilliant amphibious envelopment at Inchon in September 1950 highlighted his strategic genius, but his relief for insubordination in April terminated his long and distinguished career. Despite this abrupt end, MacArthur's contributions to American history and his legacy as an exceptional leader and strategist are without comparison.

Before Douglas MacArthur made a name for himself, he lived in the shadow of his famous father and grandfather. Both elder Mac-Arthurs were accomplished individuals. His grandfather, Arthur MacArthur, emigrated from Scotland in 1825. He established a law practice in Springfield, Massachusetts. His first son, Arthur Jr., was born in 1845. He moved to Milwaukee, Wisconsin, in 1849 and became the city attorney two years later. He was elected lieutenant governor, and in 1856, he served five days as governor during an electoral controversy. He completed his term as lieutenant governor in 1857. After he won two terms as a judge for the Second Judicial District, President Ulysses S. Grant appointed MacArthur to the Supreme Court of the District of Columbia in 1870.[2] His appointment and access to Washington society allowed the senior MacArthur to influence the careers of both his son Arthur and his grandson Douglas.

Arthur MacArthur Jr. had a tremendous influence on Douglas. A Civil War hero and Medal of Honor recipient, he established a high standard of military accomplishment for his sons to emulate. Although he was only sixteen when the Civil War began, Arthur MacArthur Jr. volunteered to fight with the 24th Wisconsin Volunteer Infantry. West Point had accepted him for the class beginning in 1862, but he volunteered and became the regiment's adjutant in August. He received a brevet to captain after the battle of Perryville in October 1862. MacArthur's bravery and leadership at Missionary Ridge in November 1863 garnered the Medal of Honor and made him famous. He received a brevet promotion to colonel in 1864 at age nineteen, which earned him a nickname: "the Boy Colonel."[3] His speedy rise through the ranks foreshadowed his son's rapid advance.

Following the Civil War, Arthur MacArthur Jr. practiced law, but the military was his passion. He received a Regular Army commission as a lieutenant in 1866 and was soon elevated to captain because of his extraordinary Civil War accomplishments. He remained a captain for the next twenty-three years. MacArthur spent most of his early career in the West. While posted at Jackson Barracks in New Orleans, he met Mary Pinkney "Pinky" Hardy of Norfolk, Virginia. They fell in love and married in 1875. Their first son, Arthur III, was born in 1876; he was followed by a second son, named Malcolm, in 1878. Douglas, the couple's third son, was born at Arsenal Barracks in Little Rock, Arkansas, on January 26, 1880. Malcolm died of measles in 1883 and Arthur III would die prematurely of appendicitis in 1923.[4]

As a youth, Douglas MacArthur flourished in the American West. Assigned to Fort Wingate and Fort Selden, New Mexico, and other small frontier outposts, Arthur MacArthur Jr. participated in Native American pacification campaigns. Douglas MacArthur developed his own passion for the military during these formative years. Like most frontier youth, MacArthur learned to ride and shoot before he could read or write.[5]

In 1886 Arthur MacArthur Jr. and his young family transferred to Fort Leavenworth, Kansas. The move allowed young Douglas to attend formal public schooling for the first time. This initial Leavenworth experience shaped the youngest MacArthur's views of himself and his future. Although he was a poor student, the pomp and ceremony of the drill field mesmerized him. At one point during his time at Leavenworth, his father went to Oklahoma and young Douglas wanted to go with him. Arthur insisted that he stay behind and focus on his education.[6] Douglas later learned the value of education as his father earned promotions and relocated to new assignments.

Major Arthur MacArthur moved to Washington, D.C., in 1889 to become an assistant adjutant general. His father's assignment exposed Douglas to a completely new world. He attended Force Public School on Massachusetts Avenue. Young Douglas saw firsthand the "whirlpool of glitter and pomp . . . of statesmanship and intrigue." The allure of Washington would never really appeal to MacArthur. He preferred the openness of the frontier. After four years in Washington, Major MacArthur relocated to Fort Sam Houston in San Antonio, Texas. While there, young Douglas developed a deep appreciation of and commitment to learning. As a student at the West Texas Military Academy, MacArthur found purpose and meaning in education. "My studies enveloped me," MacArthur recalled, "my marks went higher, and many of the school medals came my way. But I also learned how little such honors mean after one wins them." MacArthur also developed a passion for sports. He possessed limited athletic abilities, but his lust for success on the playing field overcame many of his physical and talent limitations. His four years in San Antonio were MacArthur's happiest.[7]

In 1896 Lieutenant Colonel Arthur MacArthur moved to St. Paul, Minnesota. The family, however, went to Milwaukee. By this point young Douglas had decided to seek an appointment to the U.S. Military Academy at West Point, New York. His father and grandfather unsuccessfully sought a presidential appointment from Presidents Grover Cleveland and William McKinley. Unable to get a presidential appointment, MacArthur continued his studies at West Side High School in Milwaukee and sought an appointment from Milwaukee's fourth congressional district. During these preparatory years, he learned a valuable life lesson. Pinky told her son that he could win at anything if he did not lose his nerve: "You must believe in yourself, my son, or no one else will believe in you. Be confident, self-reliant, and even if you don't make it, you will know you have done your best. Now, go to it." MacArthur did. He scored a 93.9 on his entrance exam. "Preparedness," MacArthur learned, is "the key to success and victory."[8]

Douglas MacArthur entered West Point on June 13, 1899. As a cadet, MacArthur "worked hard and played hard." While her husband was off fighting the Spanish-American War, Pinky moved to a hotel near the military academy to be close to her son. Her timely advice and motivation kept MacArthur focused. She was not the only famous mother to go to West Point. Ulysses S. Grant III's mother stayed at the same hotel, and the two mothers seemed to compete for power and influence as much as their famous sons did.[9]

MacArthur's peers scrutinized him more than they scrutinized the average cadet because of his famous father. Nonetheless, he not only withstood this intense attention; he excelled. Cadet Mac-Arthur thrived under the rigid discipline system, and he relished the challenge of the academy's athletic program. As a cadet leader, he became a senior corporal as a yearling, first sergeant as a second classman, and the first captain of the corps as a first classman. Moreover, he achieved a higher scholastic record than anyone else had in twenty-five years. On the sports field "Dauntless Doug" was extremely proud of his contributions to the Academy's baseball and football teams. Throughout the remainder of his life, he wore his varsity letter "A" on his bathrobe with pride.[10]

His greatest test as a cadet brought him before a congressional committee in January 1901. The committee summoned MacArthur to appear as a "so-called victim" of hazing in response to the death of a cadet who had resigned. MacArthur refused to divulge the names of any cadet alleged to have committed hazing against him. He risked his military future if he did not cooperate fully. His parents had taught MacArthur never to lie, but they had also emphasized that he should never tattle, either. Fortunately for MacArthur, the committee gathered the names it needed without forcing MacArthur to make the difficult choice of adhering to his principles or "ratting" on his comrades.[11]

MacArthur's four years at West Point tested his self-confidence and leadership. In the end, he proved he had the necessary skills and talents to succeed. On June 11, 1903, he graduated as a second lieutenant of Engineers.[12] With all his academic rigor, his athletic challenges, and his moral and ethical tests, MacArthur had not yet experienced combat—the ultimate test of a military leader. West Point had given him something much more valuable and useful to a future five-star general—a bedrock commitment to the Academy's motto, "Duty, Honor, Country."

His father's example, his mother's motivation, and West Point's education set Lieutenant MacArthur on a firm foundation. None of these factors, however, guaranteed MacArthur's success. Like all newly minted officers, he had to prove himself in the crucible of command. From his commissioning in 1903 until his relief in 1951, MacArthur served the American or the Filipino government in some official military capacity. MacArthur began this forty-eight-year span as an engineer in his beloved Philippines, which would become the symbol of his greatest success. After his arrival in Manila, MacArthur conducted routine engineering duties that took him to locations that would become famous in World War II.[13] In 1903, however, thoughts of global conflagration were far from MacArthur's mind.

In April 1904 MacArthur left the Philippines for San Francisco. He performed harbor defense duties for a short time before he was reassigned to Japan in October 1905. In Japan he served as his father's aide-de-camp, which gave the younger MacArthur a unique opportunity to observe the Far East and to meet key Japanese military leaders. During his tour MacArthur "encountered the boldness and courage" of the Japanese soldier for the first time. MacArthur was impressed with the Japanese soldier's "almost fanatical belief in and reverence for his Emperor." This experience left a lasting impression on the young MacArthur. More important, MacArthur developed a lifelong appreciation of Asia and its importance to the United States and its national interests. MacArthur never altered his views on the importance of Asia to America's future, but he would not return to the Far East for another sixteen years.[14]

In 1906–7 MacArthur was an engineering student at Washington Barracks. He spent a short time as an aide to President Theodore Roosevelt, which allowed him the opportunity to observe the highest levels of decision making and formulation of strategic policy. Roosevelt also reinforced MacArthur's Asian focus. "I greatly admired Theodore Roosevelt. His prophetic vision of Asian politics," MacArthur observed, "marked him as a statesman of brilliant imagination."[15] This, of course, was an example of confirmation bias, but it certainly strengthened MacArthur's predisposition toward Asia and perhaps affected how he viewed the presidency.

After working for the president, MacArthur returned to engineering duties in Milwaukee. Once again, he was responsible for rivers and harbors, but MacArthur did not have his heart in his duties. Major William V. Judson penned one of the few negative remarks found in MacArthur's impeccable record. "I am of the opinion," Judson concluded, "that Lieutenant MacArthur, while on duty under my immediate orders, did not conduct himself in a way to meet commendation, and that his duties were not performed in a satisfactory manner."[16] This pejorative remark had the potential to ruin MacArthur's career. MacArthur protested Judson's evaluation, but his attempts to remove the offending remarks were unsuccessful. If nothing else, the remarks taught MacArthur a poignant, albeit brief, lesson in humility.

MacArthur left Milwaukee in 1908 after he received orders for Fort Leavenworth and the 3rd Engineer Battalion. During his time in Kansas, the young MacArthur reestablished his slightly tarnished reputation and proved himself a dynamic and capable leader. Although he did not attend any of the Army Service Schools as a student while at Leavenworth, he lectured at the General Services School and at the Cavalry School at Fort Riley. Lieutenant MacAr-

Lieutenant Douglas MacArthur (seated on handrail) at Fort Leavenworth, Kansas, 1909. (Courtesy of the Frontier Army Museum, Fort Leavenworth, Kansas)

thur contributed a special lecture and pamphlet on military demolition for the Department of Engineering during the 1908–9 academic year. His lecture supplemented a curriculum that dealt with surveying, map reproduction, fortification problems, sketching, and fortress warfare. His was one of six lectures that augmented the regular engineering course offerings. The other lectures were focused largely on issues related to the Franco-Prussian War and the more recent Russo-Japanese War. MacArthur presented his special lecture to the Mounted Service School at Fort Riley in November 1908 and to the Staff College at Fort Leavenworth the following month. He gave his last lecture on military demolition to the School of the Line in January 1909.[17] Although MacArthur's contributions to the Leavenworth schools were minimal, the opportunity exposed the young lieutenant to the engineering aspects of the various curricula while enhancing his technical and professional skills as a junior officer.

More important, MacArthur received his first command while at Fort Leavenworth. As the junior company commander, he received command of Company "K," the lowest rated of twenty-one companies on post. MacArthur turned that situation around and made Company "K" the best through determined direction and hard work. He ultimately demonstrated his leadership when he became the 3rd Battalion's adjutant. MacArthur later recalled that his assignment at Fort Leavenworth completed his "military education as a combat engineer." Before he departed Leavenworth, MacArthur had completed career-enhancing temporary duty assignments to San Antonio in 1911 and to Panama in 1912.[18]

MacArthur's Leavenworth assignment also brought him into contact with Robert L. Eichelberger and Walter Krueger. Both served as MacArthur's Army commanders during World War II. George C. Marshall, who was a faculty member of the Engineering Department, was also at Leavenworth. According to William Manchester, however, the two future generals already "rubbed each other the wrong way." Others commented on MacArthur's abilities as a poker player and his enthusiastic participation on the post's polo and baseball teams. Perhaps his most significant achievement was his ability to devise clever strategies to outwit his opponents. Heavily feeding his opponents before a baseball game was one such strategy. Another involved the payment of two Texas professionals to play for the post team. He identified them as West Point graduates to justify their participation.[19] Both tacks achieved the desired end, although the means were questionable. These creative approaches to winning informed MacArthur's strategy formulation during World War II. Winning, from MacArthur's perspective, was the only option in sports and in war.

MacArthur became a captain in February 1911. Two years earlier, his famous father had retired to Milwaukee. While the elder MacArthur was speaking at the fiftieth reunion of the 24th Wisconsin Regiment on September 5, 1912, the hero of Missionary Ridge fell dead. Upon hearing the news, Douglas MacArthur remembered, "My whole world changed that night. Never have I been able to heal the wound in my heart."[20] His father had been a significant influence on his life and career, but his mother remained to encourage and guide MacArthur. Pinky moved to Fort Leavenworth after her husband's death, and she followed her son to Washington with his assignment to the Office of the Chief of Staff in 1912.

As a junior officer on the General Staff, MacArthur saw military matters in a different light. Once again, he experienced the highest levels of Army bureaucracy normally not seen until one was a more senior officer. While he was in Washington, General Leonard Wood ordered him to Mexico to "study the land." Tensions with Mexico had risen again in 1914, and Wood wanted MacArthur to analyze the situation and to provide an assessment. As part of his experience, MacArthur managed to escape an ambush while conducting his reconnaissance duties. He received a recommendation for the Medal of Honor for his actions behind Mexican lines and for his capture of three locomotives. The award was denied because MacArthur's heroic activities "lacked proper prior authorization."[21] Regardless, he was promoted to major in December 1915. He was clearly on the fast track, but his proximity to key leadership coupled with the entry of the United States into World War I in 1917 provided an opportunity to soar even higher.

Major MacArthur had an unusual opportunity to influence American military policy in two key ways. On June 30, 1916, he became military assistant to the secretary of War. Newton Baker placed MacArthur in charge of the department's Bureau of Information. Within a week, he became the Army's first press secretary. "I was expected to explain our national military policy to the country," MacArthur recalled, "and to shatter the prevailing delusion of a world living in security." This experience provided insight few officers enjoyed; he used this knowledge of the media quite effectively

Major MacArthur. (Library of Congress)

throughout his career. MacArthur also affected policy regarding the National Guard. He advocated the use of the National Guard in combat. When asked how to employ these Guard units, MacArthur suggested that units from different states form a division. The resultant 42nd Division, which drew Guardsmen from twenty-six states, became the famous Rainbow Division.[22]

Major General William A. Mann became the division's commander, but he had no chief of staff. MacArthur assumed the position despite his junior rank. Secretary Baker remedied the situation by promoting him to colonel. Asked if he wanted the rank in the Engineer branch, MacArthur chose the Infantry. The new colonel influenced the selection of the overall American Expeditionary Forces (AEF) commander after news of General Frederick Funston's premature death reached Washington. Baker asked MacArthur for his recommendation. MacArthur suggested John J. Pershing.[23] His endorsement may have been a restatement of the obvious, but the fact that Baker sought his advice was indicative of the trust, power, and influence MacArthur had acquired.

By the time MacArthur and the Rainbow Division arrived in Europe, Major General Charles Menoher had replaced Mann.[24] Colonel MacArthur sailed on October 18, 1917, and deployed with his division to training areas in eastern France. One of MacArthur's first challenges was the possible dissolution of the division. The American headquarters at Chaumont considered using the 42nd for replacements to strengthen other divisions. As the division's chief of staff and staunch proponent of maintaining the unit's cohesion, MacArthur went to Pershing's chief of staff to get the order revoked. It worked. "My action was probably not in strict accord with normal procedure," MacArthur admitted, "and it created resentment against me among certain members of Pershing's staff."[25] This was not the last time MacArthur circumvented the chain of command. It was also the genesis of MacArthur's distrust and personal hatred for higher headquarters and the so-called Chaumont gang.

As soon as the 42nd made its way to the Luneville Sector in February 1918, Colonel MacArthur displayed the same courage and daring he had in the Philippines and in Mexico. There is always a fine line between inspired leadership and stupidity, but MacArthur's daredevil actions were more of the former. As a leader and strategist, he preferred firsthand observation of the battlefield. This preference took him to the front lines more often than was typical of

World War I commanders. MacArthur believed that an operation's plan must consider the troop's quality, the nature of the terrain, and the enemy's intent and capability. Even with solid preparation, MacArthur understood that a plan would become "confused and fail."[26]

His gutsy leadership style led to recognition for several meritorious actions during his deployment to Europe. MacArthur, for example, received the Croix de Guerre and the Silver Star for his "extraordinary heroism and gallantry in action" near Réchicourt in February 1918. He later earned the Distinguished Service Cross (DSC) in March 1918 for "coolness and conspicuous courage."[27] These were the first of many medals MacArthur earned for leadership and bravery. MacArthur's reputation as a great combat leader was also reflected in the nicknames he acquired. With colorful sobriquets from "the d'Artagnan of the AEF" to the "fighting Dude," his men willingly paid homage to his leadership.[28]

On June 26, 1918, MacArthur became the youngest brigadier general in the AEF. Barely fifteen years after his commissioning, MacArthur had outpaced his famous father. With the promotion came additional responsibility and new opportunities to prove his worth. The 42nd turned westward to join the French Fourth Army north of Suippes in early July. This position placed the unit on the primary road to Châlons-en-Champagne—the German offensive's objective. The French conducted a defense in depth that repulsed the German assault. MacArthur received a second Silver Star for his heroic efforts that helped halt the German advance.[29]

On July 25, 1918, the 42nd Division relieved the 26th Division near Château Thierry. MacArthur described the next six days as "the bitterest days and nights of the war for the Rainbow." The fighting was brutal. "Crawling forward in twos and threes against each stubborn nest of enemy guns," MacArthur recollected, "we closed in with the bayonet and the hand grenade. It was savage and there was no quarter asked or given. It seemed to be endless."[30] By this point MacArthur had proven his mettle, but the thirty-eight-year-old one-star was destined for even greater accomplishments.

On July 31, 1918, General Menoher relieved the 42nd Division's 84th Brigade commander and replaced him with MacArthur. By mid-October he had prepared his brigade for the Meuse-Argonne offensive. In conjunction with the assault, General Charles Summerall demanded that the 84th secure a gap in the German lines near

Brigadier General MacArthur in France, September 1918. (Courtesy of the National Archives, 111-SC-23921)

Côte de Châtillon. MacArthur led the assault; he was wounded and garnered his second DSC.[31] Generals Menoher and Summerall cited MacArthur's heroism. Summerall also nominated MacArthur for the Medal of Honor and recommended his promotion to major general. As had happened after his first nomination, for his actions in

Mexico, the award was disapproved. The Chaumont Awards Board action further alienated MacArthur from the General Headquarters and played to his growing paranoia regarding higher headquarters in general.[32]

Whether MacArthur's distrust of the Chaumont gang was justified is debatable, but his commitment to professional excellence and victory in Europe was unquestioned. In the war's last major operation, MacArthur led part of the Allied movement that pressed toward Sedan in early November. Just before the Armistice, Menoher became the VI Corps commander, vacating the 42nd Division commander's position. MacArthur took command, but the war's end resulted in the suspension of all pending promotions. His brief tenure as division commander ended when he and other brigadier generals returned to their earlier positions. Brigadier General MacArthur and the 84th Brigade remained in Europe for occupation duty until April 1919. Upon their return stateside, MacArthur was disappointed with the lackluster greeting the 42nd received: "We reached New York on the 25th [April 1919] but where-oh-where was that welcome they told us of?"[33] Despite his disappointment, MacArthur made the transition from wartime commander to peacetime leader with zeal and persistence.

MacArthur's postwar assignment took him back to West Point. It had been sixteen years since he had graduated, but he was now a brigadier general and superintendent. His immediate concerns centered on the Academy's curriculum and the Army's need for high-quality junior officers. "West Point is forty years behind the times," General Peyton March informed MacArthur; "West Point would have to be revitalized, the curriculum re-established."[34] March's assessment was correct, but the challenge placed before MacArthur would prove virtually impossible to resolve completely during his tenure.

In addition to the curriculum, MacArthur also noted other impediments to improving West Point. One obstacle was the American tendency to "ignore security needs in the pleasanter times of peace." Why maintain a military academy at all if there were to be no more wars? Moreover, if war did come, many felt that the Reserve Officer Training Corps would meet the nation's military leadership needs. MacArthur disagreed. He understood the need for a professional officer base that West Point produced. The other challenge was economic. He was adamant that Congress fund the Academy and the larger Army properly to meet the nation's security needs. He used an insurance metaphor to make his point: "Premiums must be paid to correspond with the needs of our country in peace or war."[35] His emphasis on preparedness was clear, but MacArthur could not control the antimilitary forces that dominated American society during the interwar period.

One of MacArthur's primary goals as superintendent was to develop a new type of officer. This new officer must retain "all of the cardinal military virtues as of yore," and he must also possess "an intense understanding of his fellows, a comprehensive grasp of world and national affairs, and a liberalization of conception which amounts to a change in his psychology of command." These were lofty yet appropriate goals for the changed strategic environment of the interwar period. To maintain traditional virtues, MacArthur stressed duty, honor, and country. The new superintendent also deemphasized hazing and demanded that the cadet leadership enforce the honor code. The prohibition on lying, cheating, and stealing dated back to West Point's early years, but its enforcement was left to the tactical officers. According to Geoffrey Perret, the Corps of Cadets was not pleased with MacArthur's changes, but MacArthur's actions altered existing hazing practices and forced the cadets to take ownership of the honor code. To enlarge the students' appreciation of the wider world, he actively sought to deemphasize the cloistering of the cadets and got them involved beyond the Academy's walls. His last action stressed athletics. He believed that sports were a great venue for cadets to learn how to perform as individuals, but they also allowed cadets to teach others. Under MacArthur's tenure, every cadet participated in sports.[36] It is difficult to evaluate fully the success of MacArthur's measures to improve West Point, but he was proud of his efforts.

MacArthur returned to the Philippines as commander of the Military District of Manila in October 1922. By this time his old Filipino friend Manuel Quezon was playing a prominent role in Filipino independence initiatives. As speaker of the Philippine House of Representatives, Quezon impressed MacArthur greatly. His relationship with Quezon would prove critical for MacArthur when he returned in 1935.[37]

He became a major general in January 1925 and served as commander of the 23rd Infantry Brigade before his return to the United States.[38] He also served in various regional commands in the United

States and completed another assignment in the Philippines. One of MacArthur's most unpleasant duties during this period was serving as a member of Billy Mitchell's court-martial board. He described the duty as "distasteful," and he found it difficult to be objective. MacArthur believed Mitchell's message, but the latter was not convicted for his beliefs; he was on trial for insubordination. Ironically, he concluded "that a senior officer should not be silenced for being at variance with his superior in rank and with accepted doctrine. I have always felt that a country's interest was paramount, and that when a ranking officer, out of purely patriotic motives, risked his own personal future in such opposition, he should not be summarily suppressed. Superior authority can, of course, do so if it wishes, but the one thing in this world that cannot be stopped is a sound idea." MacArthur foreshadowed his own future when he concluded, "The individual may be martyred, but his thoughts live on."[39]

Following the Mitchell court-martial, MacArthur headed the 1928 U.S. Olympic Team. It was an unusual assignment, but MacArthur approached it as he would any major military operation. Given his personal emphasis on athletics, MacArthur was a great choice. He was determined not only to win, but to win decisively. The U.S. team led the medal count. General Summerall applauded MacArthur's accomplishment.[40] After his success in Amsterdam, MacArthur returned to Manila. As department commander, he argued for stronger Filipino defenses, but Washington was unresponsive. On the positive side, MacArthur became friends with Henry Stimson, the governor general. He also renewed his contact with the future Filipino president Manual Quezon during this short tour.[41]

In July 1929 President Herbert Hoover offered MacArthur the position of chief of Engineers. MacArthur was flattered, but he declined because accepting the position would have taken him out of the line. The following year MacArthur succeeded Summerall as chief of staff. His patience had paid off, but MacArthur preferred to stay in the field. His mother, however, convinced him to take the job. Douglas MacArthur became Army chief of staff on November 21, 1930.[42]

MacArthur and the Army faced significant challenges in the early 1930s. The most substantial was the failing national economy. The Great Depression restricted funding for the near future. Despite MacArthur's persistent attempts to squeeze more national defense dollars from Congress, he was largely unsuccessful. MacArthur,

From left: General Douglas MacArthur, Mamie Eisenhower, President Quezon, and Lieutenant Colonel Eisenhower. (U.S. Army, 64-484)

"usually assessed by historians as one of the few senior leaders who had the courage to take Congress to task for lack of resources, . . . came very close to insubordination in at least one speech before he became chief of staff."[43] Courage and persistence could not overcome financial shortfalls. MacArthur had hoped to make a broad plan for American defense, but he could not fund his vision.[44] Following significant post closures and congressional threats to reduce the officer corps, MacArthur's best efforts could do little to fulfill the security aims he envisioned. Although he stopped the proposed officer reduction, created a General Headquarters for the Air Force, and opened the Command and General Staff College to lieutenants, MacArthur lacked the means to achieve his broad security goals.[45]

According to MacArthur, the "most poignant episode" of his tour as chief of staff was the infamous Bonus March of 1932, spearheaded by World War I veterans (many of them disabled and nearly all down on their luck) hoping to redeem early their $1,000 bonus certificates that were not due to be paid until 1945. From his perspective, the Bonus Marchers constituted an "army of disillusioned and lost men."[46] MacArthur ultimately blamed Communists and pacifists for the incident. As tensions increased over the summer, Mac-

Arthur advised against Army intervention into what he saw as a domestic affair. On July 28, 1932, however, the Bonus March reached a critical moment. A mob 5,000 to 7,000 strong engaged local law enforcement. Gunfire ensued, and the situation went beyond police control. A request for federal troops went to the president. Hoover placed Secretary of War Patrick Hurley in charge. Hurley issued orders to MacArthur to use 600 soldiers under Brigadier General Perry Miles to clear Pennsylvania Avenue of the marchers. MacArthur accompanied Miles, along with Majors Dwight D. Eisenhower and George Patton. Unfortunately for MacArthur, press reports of his association with the Bonus Marcher dispersal were not always flattering, and they did not see the threat the same way he did. The accounts that appeared in the newspapers were, from MacArthur's perspective, "the most extravagant of distortions of what happened."[47] Regardless of the means employed, the Bonus March episode came to an abrupt albeit controversial end after troops evicted the marchers and used tear gas to force stragglers across the Eleventh Street Bridge.[48]

In 1934 President Franklin D. Roosevelt extended MacArthur's tenure as chief of staff. By 1935 MacArthur had completed five years, and he was ready to move on. The Commonwealth of the Philippines achieved semi-independent status that same year. The Filipino president, Manuel Quezon, then asked MacArthur if he would lead the establishment of a national army. MacArthur became a field marshal in the Filipino military in 1936 while serving as the chief military adviser to the Philippines as a U.S. Army officer. By law MacArthur had reverted from his four-star rank to his permanent rank of major general when he left the chief of staff position. The dual assignment was a highly unusual arrangement, but it served both the American and Filipino needs. Accompanied by his ailing mother, a thirty-seven-year-old socialite named Jean Marie Faircloth, and a small staff that included Eisenhower, MacArthur sailed from San Francisco and began his fifth tour in the Philippines in late 1935.[49]

His return to the Philippines began an extraordinary sixteen-year journey that saw MacArthur's greatest accomplishments as a commander and military strategist. Unfortunately, it began with personal tragedy. Two months after he arrived, his beloved mother passed away. Pinky MacArthur had supported her son well beyond the call of duty. Her death left a huge void that would soon be filled by Jean Faircloth. The couple married in New York on April 30, 1937. The following February the MacArthurs had their first and only child, a son named Arthur IV.[50]

MacArthur served as military adviser until 1937, when he retired from active service. After thirty-eight years as a professional soldier, MacArthur had done as much as any American could in the early twentieth-century American Army. He had held every officer rank with the exception of lieutenant colonel, which he skipped during World War I, and lieutenant general, which he would hold briefly at the outbreak of World War II. He had attained the one position that eluded his famous father, Army chief of staff. The fifty-seven-year-old general had little left to prove as a professional soldier.

As military adviser, MacArthur inherited a simple Filipino defense plan. The Swiss citizen-soldier system of conscription was the organizational model. Unfortunately, the Filipino military budget was too small to develop, equip, and sustain an adequate Filipino defense force. The plan's goal was to train 40,000 men per year, but only about 20,000 Filipinos were ready by 1937. That same year, MacArthur and President Quezon traveled to Japan, Mexico, and the United States to assess the strategic environment and to bolster island defenses. Their efforts to get the War Department and Congress to increase funding and support for the Filipino defenses were unsuccessful. Their only success came from the Navy Department, which offered to develop a new naval vessel that became the famous PT boat. When MacArthur retired on December 31, 1937, he remained Quezon's adviser. His trusty aide, Eisenhower, returned to the States in 1939. Lieutenant Colonel Richard K. Sutherland became MacArthur's new chief of staff and remained at the general's side throughout World War II.[51]

The Nazi invasion of Poland in September 1939 marked the beginning of World War II in Europe. The Japanese invasion of China in 1937 triggered hostilities in Asia. Most Western nations, however, remained aloof from the challenges presented by Japanese aggression. The mounting threat from Germany after the ill-fated Munich Conference was a greater menace to European peace and security. MacArthur and Quezon were well aware of the potential Japanese threat to the Philippines, but they could do little to prepare for a possible invasion, given the resource limitations and the low security priority afforded the islands.

In late May 1941 the Army's chief of staff, General George C. Marshall, provided guidance to MacArthur regarding the growing Asian security concerns. Because of MacArthur's Philippine experience, Marshall and Secretary of War Henry Stimson believed he was "the logical choice for Army Commander for the Far East should the situation approach a crisis." On July 27, 1941, MacArthur became the commanding general of U.S. Army Forces in the Far East. He was recalled to active duty as a lieutenant general.[52] Once in command, MacArthur immediately expedited the strengthening of the forces available to defend the islands. MacArthur would have to accelerate his original ten-year defense program.

MacArthur had insufficient assets to repel any Japanese invasion, and his situation did not improve significantly before the Japanese assault on the Philippines on December 8, 1941. Airpower was one concern. There was an overwhelming need for light and heavy bombers and protective fighters. He also appreciated airpower doctrine's demand for a strong bomber force and the importance of air's operational reach, given the Pacific theater's geography.[53]

MacArthur also understood the Philippines' strategic significance. The supply lines to sustain any Japanese expansion radiated from the Home Islands to Australia, the Dutch East Indies, Malaya, Mindanao, and Manila.[54] The greatest strategic challenge was how to exploit time and space. If the Japanese delayed their attack, he might be able to shift from a defensive posture to an offensive one. This offensive mindset guided MacArthur's planning and strategy throughout the war. Unfortunately, he simply could not consider offensive operations without adequate defensive capabilities. These did not exist in 1941, and even with Washington's promises of support, there was not enough to save the islands when the Japanese attacked late in the year.

By December the available operational air forces in the Philippines consisted of only thirty-five bombers and seventy-two pursuit planes. The defense plan called for twice the number of each. Moreover, MacArthur lacked sufficient airfields, accessories, and munitions to support the planes he did have. His ground component was equally insufficient. MacArthur possessed about 12,000 U.S. troops, 12,000 Filipino Scouts, and 110,000 members of the Citizens National Army. Equipage and training were major concerns. Naval assets were available, but they were not under MacArthur's control. The naval element contained a regiment of Marines, three cruisers, thirteen destroyers, eighteen submarines, and six PT boats. If MacArthur could somehow gain more time and strengthen his forces, he believed the Philippines represented the "single hope of effective resistance in Southeast Asia, and, given time and resources, the Philippine Defense Plan would accomplish its long range objective of making them too costly in men and dollars to attack."[55] The Japanese did not give MacArthur the time he desired; the Japanese timeline mandated a quick and decisive assault in December 1941.

The total complement of Filipino defense forces was grossly insufficient. MacArthur's command, however, did not simply wait for the Japanese attack. He was aware of the likelihood of a Japanese attack and took appropriate actions. MacArthur's air chief, Major General Lewis Brereton, recommended moving the bomber force beyond Japanese bomber range, to Mindanao. In one of the war's great mysteries, only about half were relocated. MacArthur later remarked, "I never learned why these orders were not promptly implemented." Washington also forbade any offensive action against Japan. It was essential that Japan commit the first overt act of armed hostilities. A preemptive assault on Japanese forces was politically unacceptable. The Army commenced night air patrols on December 4, 1941. These initial sorties reported Japanese air activity twenty to fifty miles beyond Filipino air space. These were clear indicators of Japanese intentions. By December 7 MacArthur believed that "every disposition had been made, every man, gun, and plane was on the alert."[56]

It was not enough. At 0340 on December 8, 1941, MacArthur learned of the Japanese attack on Pearl Harbor. Ever the optimist, he hoped that the Japanese might have suffered a setback. He later learned of the Japanese success, but by then he was also under attack. At 1145, MacArthur received the first of many reports of Japanese bomber formations approaching the Philippines and Clark Field. The lack of resources and the failure to disperse their air assets led to heated debate among MacArthur's staff regarding who was responsible. There was plenty of blame to go around, but most focused on Brereton's actions or inactions. MacArthur defended Brereton to a certain degree. "The force was in the process of integration, radar defenses were not yet operative, and the personnel was raw and inexperienced. They were hopelessly outnumbered," MacArthur stressed, "and never had a chance of winning." MacArthur refused to accept responsibility, and he did not blame his chief

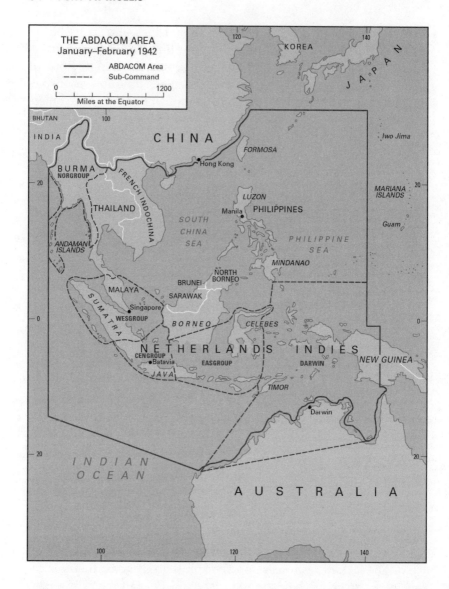

of staff, Major General Richard K. Sutherland.[57] Regardless of American shortfalls, one must give the Japanese their due. They identified and eliminated American and Filipino strongholds and set the stage for a successful Japanese occupation of the Philippines.

War Plan Orange, the Rainbow Plan associated with Japan, detailed the general defense approach regarding a Japanese invasion.

THE PHILIPPINES
1942

0   150
Miles

BABUYAN IS.

S O U T H

C H I N A

S E A

L U Z O N

Manila

P H I L I P P I N E

S E A

MINDORO

MASBATE   *SAMAR*

VISAYAN ISLANDS

PANAY   *LEYTE*

CEBU

PALAWAN   *BOHOL*

NEGROS

S U L U   S E A

M I N D A N A O

N O R T H
B O R N E O   *Sulu Archipelago*   *C E L E B E S   S E A*

It called for the U.S. Navy to keep the Philippines' supply lines open to sustain the forces until massive reinforcements arrived. The plan called for the ground forces to hold out for four to six months. After Pearl Harbor, this was impossible. In MacArthur's words, "Our sky defense died with our battleships in the waves off of Ford Island. It cancelled Rainbow 5, and sealed our doom." This was true, but MacArthur always believed that the Navy could have rescued his forces. MacArthur assumed that the "Navy deprecated its own strength and might have cut through to relieve our hard-pressed forces."[58] Regardless of the Navy's capabilities and intent, time and space worked against MacArthur and those forces that remained.

After the Japanese secured a beachhead at Lingayen on December 21, 1941, they marched toward Manila. The retreat to Bataan and Corregidor soon symbolized American pluck. MacArthur had no plans to surrender and instilled hope in his troops on the basis of Washington's promises of aid and resupply that would never arrive. MacArthur, as he usually did, blamed Washington. "No one will ever know how much could have been done to aid the Philippines," MacArthur reasoned, "if there had been a determined will-to-win."[59] Military necessity clouded MacArthur's understanding of geopolitical realities.

This was not the last time MacArthur questioned Washington's political will, but without immediate reinforcements he knew he and his forces could not hold out indefinitely. He was prepared to die if necessary, but Roosevelt ordered him to Australia in February 1942. There he would lead the Allied effort to halt the Japanese advance and liberate occupied territories. Australia must hold. It was the last major land mass between India and the United States. Without its resources, ports, and manpower, Japan's defeat might prove unattainable. In a Hollywood-esque escape from Corregidor, MacArthur departed with his family along with select members of his staff on PT-41. They made it to Mindanao and flew to Batchelor Field, forty miles south of Darwin, on St. Patrick's Day. While there, MacArthur made one of his famous wartime statements: "The President of the United States ordered me to break through the Japanese lines and proceed from Corregidor to Australia for the purpose, as I understand it, of organizing the American offensive against Japan, a primary objective of which is the relief of the Philippines. I came through and I shall return." MacArthur later described the context and intent of his famous promise. "I spoke casually enough,"

MacArthur remembered, "but the phrase 'I shall return' seemed a promise of magic to the Filipinos."[60]

From Batchelor Field MacArthur flew to Alice Springs. General Jonathan Wainwright assumed command of Corregidor. Bataan held until May 6, 1942. After its surrender, MacArthur agonized over the details of the subsequent Bataan Death March. He had directed the issuance of the story to the press, but Washington "forbade the release of any details of the prisoner-of-war atrocities." Perhaps, MacArthur speculated, it was because of the Europe-first strategy. The American government did not want to arouse American public opinion to the point that it would demand more action in the Pacific at the expense of operations against Nazi Germany. Regardless of America's grand strategy, MacArthur would always focus on his theater's needs and requirements. He was also driven by his need to fulfill his promise to the Filipino people. The Philippines were and would always be his "obsession—and his redemption."[61]

MacArthur received the Medal of Honor for his actions. It was the first time in American history a father and son had received the award. Though medals and ribbons were important to MacArthur, he believed that they meant little in the absence of commensurate results. He knew the road back to Manila would be difficult, but he hoped it would be short. He was right on the first count but wrong on the second. Before he could liberate the Philippines, he had to defend Australia. MacArthur did not like the existing plan; it was too defensively oriented. He decided to abandon the plan and focus on the Owen Stanley Mountains in New Guinea. He believed the only way to save Australia was to go on the offensive.[62] In his quest for operational maneuver, he faced the same obstacles all theater commanders encountered—too little time, limited resources, and vast spaces. To compensate, MacArthur needed airfields within range of New Guinea to supply and reinforce any offensive efforts there. He needed the cooperation of the indigenous peoples, and he had to overcome Japan's command of the sea.

To surmount these challenges, MacArthur relied on all three components of his Allied forces. Unfortunately, his air, land, and sea elements were all inadequate. Fortunately, MacArthur had capable component commanders. MacArthur became supreme commander of Allied Forces in the Southwest Pacific Area (SWPA) on April 18, 1942. His land component commander was an Australian, General Sir Thomas Blamey. His initial naval component commander was

Vice Admiral Herbert F. Leary. Vice Admiral Arthur S. Carpender took control of the Allied Naval Forces SWPA in September 1942. Carpender's command became the vaunted Seventh Fleet in March 1943 and functioned as MacArthur's navy.[63]

His original air commander was Lieutenant General George H. Brett. A capable airman, Brett had arrived in Australia before MacArthur. Because of Brett's rank, his recommendations to cut off reinforcements to the Philippines, and his close working relationship with the Australian leadership, MacArthur probably saw Brett as a potential rival to his command. "Brett's relief," moreover, "was also the result of his 'complete failure to accommodate' MacArthur's wishes."[64] Brett had to go. Brett's replacement, Major General George C. Kenney, was an exceptional choice. From MacArthur's perspective, none surpassed Kenney in "those three great essentials of combat leadership: aggressive vision, mastery of air tactics and strategy, and the ability to exact the maximum in fighting qualities from both men and equipment."[65] Kenney did not disappoint.

Though Kenney was the consummate air commander, MacArthur did not always act as the ideal joint force commander. He was successful, but he often had to be reminded that military operations in his area of responsibility were multinational. Marshall chided MacArthur for the apparent lack of Allied officers on his staff. The Allies contributed, especially General Blamey and his Australians, but MacArthur limited Allied participation in key positions and he favored the use of American troops over Allied forces. MacArthur's Sixth Army commander, Lieutenant General Walter Krueger, "suspected that MacArthur and his staff designed it [Sixth Army] to prevent General Blamey, the Australian in charge of the Allied Forces, from controlling American combat forces."[66]

The greater concern for MacArthur and Admiral Chester Nimitz, the Pacific Ocean Areas commander, was how much manpower and matériel they would have to prosecute the war. The Europe-first strategy initially limited what Pacific commanders would receive and when they would get it. Moreover, there was no overall commander identified for the Pacific effort. MacArthur understood the importance of unity of command, and he recommended the selection of an overall commander. Although MacArthur was the senior ranking officer, he was "willing to accept a subordinate position to accomplish the general good." The role of overall commander in the Pacific, such as that Eisenhower was to play in Europe, was never filled. "The failure to do so," MacArthur determined, "cannot be defended in logic, in theory, or in common sense."[67] The decentralized command structure had its drawbacks, but it would have been extremely difficult to have a single Pacific commander, given the personalities involved and the theater's geography.

The first changes in the strategic situation occurred in the Coral Sea in May 1942 and then most decisively at Midway in June. Those American victories altered the strategic balance. They halted the Japanese advance and forced the Japanese to reestablish a smaller defensive perimeter. Australian defensive operations in Papua and New Guinea in July, coupled with the Guadalcanal effort in August 1942, marked the beginning of a coordinated campaign to isolate or destroy the Japanese stronghold of Rabaul, on New Britain island. After Midway, the Japanese turned their attention toward Milne Bay off the far southeastern corner of New Guinea. The Japanese needed to control this strategic location to protect their advance on the Australian-controlled city of Port Moresby. In anticipation of the Japanese action, MacArthur built air, land, and sea bases at the head of Milne Bay. Besides the sea approach, the Japanese could also use the Kokoda Trail to launch an overland assault against Moresby from their stronghold at Buna. As the Japanese advanced over the Owen Stanley Mountains toward Moresby, a contingent of Australians stopped them at Imita. The Japanese advance having been halted, the Allied strategic plan took shape. MacArthur saw an opportunity to attack the enemy, and he rushed as many forces as he could to the area. General Blamey served as the commander, and Lieutenant General Robert L. Eichelberger led the U.S. I Corps. To reinforce the effort, MacArthur had two regiments from the 32nd Division transported by air. "This was the first large scale airborne troop movement by the United States forces in any theater of operations," he observed.[68] By the end of October 1942, close to five divisions were available to press the initiative.

While conducting these operations in New Guinea, MacArthur supported the South Pacific Command's efforts at Guadalcanal. He supported Guadalcanal with bombers while using short-range aircraft to promote operations in New Guinea. Japanese resistance and Allied logistical challenges limited the offensive's speed and effectiveness. MacArthur's ground force lacked covering artillery and possessed insufficient small landing craft for an amphibious assault at Buna. The Navy was unwilling to risk its destroyers and smaller craft in uncharted and dangerous waters. MacArthur reverted to infiltration tactics he had experienced in World War I. Without additional forces, the situation stalemated. MacArthur finally sent Eichelberger in with the last reserves and the Allied forces took Buna on December 14, 1942.[69] By late January 1943 this phase of the New Guinea campaign had ended.

This campaign provided MacArthur with valuable insights on modern war. The use of integrated and coordinated air, land, and sea capabilities had created a new type of warfare. MacArthur referred to this as "triphibious warfare." It also guided his strategic thought. MacArthur determined that he had to avoid frontal attacks, bypass Japanese strong points, and neutralize them by cutting their supply lines to isolate and starve them on the battlefield. He referred to this strategic approach as "leapfrogging," as opposed to the "island hopping" associated with the central Pacific campaigns. This was not an original concept. He simply adapted the classic strategy of envelopment to modern conditions. MacArthur clearly understood the need for joint operations even though his staff lacked a joint presence. He understood that one service or branch was not going to defeat the Japanese without the support of the other. His approach was also the "ideal method for success by inferior but faster-moving forces. The paucity of the resources at my command," MacArthur concluded, "made me adopt this method of campaign as the only hope of accomplishing my task."[70] The lack of aircraft carriers was the most critical shortfall. Without land-based airpower, carriers were critical. Unfortunately, he rarely had command of the carrier forces he required.

The New Guinea campaign opened the way for the drive up the northern coast. The primary goal of 1943 was to cut off Japanese means to sustain the war. MacArthur knew direct pressure would take time, but his isolation strategy offered a viable solution. MacArthur planned to apply his envelop, incapacitate, and "'hit 'em where they ain't—let them die on the vine' philosophy."[71]

The U.S. Sixth Army headquarters arrived in early 1943. MacArthur wanted Walter Krueger as the commanding general "because of [his] long and intimate association with him." By mid-February 1943 all American combat troops serving under MacArthur were assigned to the Sixth Army. This allowed MacArthur to keep American forces away from General Blamey. MacArthur chose wisely. Krueger "became to the Sixth Army what George Kenney was to

General Douglas MacArthur (right) with Major General Jonathan Wainwright, 1943. (Library of Congress)

the Fifth Air Force."[72] The relationship between the two would not always be cordial, but each general respected the other.

The Joint Chiefs of Staff (JCS) approved the plan (Operation Cartwheel) to secure the remainder of New Guinea in March 1943. Krueger's Alamo Force initiated the offensive. The Third Fleet attacked New Georgia, in the Solomon Islands, and controlled it by

October 7. MacArthur's primary target was Lae, located on the northern New Guinea coast. To distract the Japanese from Lae, Mac-Arthur used deception effectively. When the Japanese reinforced Wewak, northwest of Lae, Kenney's air force eliminated the air threat. The seizure of Lae began in September with an airborne assault at Nadzab. Lae fell on September 16.[73]

Meanwhile, MacArthur also used the Fifth Air Force to wreak havoc on Rabaul. MacArthur did not want a direct assault on the Japanese stronghold, but he did want to inflict as much damage as possible to limit Japanese operations. Kenney launched a massive raid on October 12, 1943. MacArthur was elated. "George, you broke Rabaul's back yesterday," he told Kenney, who replied, "The attack marks the turning point in the war in the Southwest Pacific."[74]

Japanese resistance on New Guinea continued after Lae fell. MacArthur's forces next secured the Admiralty Islands in February 1944. MacArthur once again decided to bypass the remaining Japanese strongpoints; he secured the weaker locations at Aitape and Hollandia. The plan was risky, but MacArthur was a risk taker. The opportunity to advance almost five hundred miles up the New Guinea coastline appealed to MacArthur's need for speed in his quest to return to the Philippines. MacArthur's push for Hollandia was indicative of his infamous impatience. He always pushed his subordinate commanders "to meet continually revised deadlines." His use of deception in conjunction with coordinated naval and air support secured the objective. Nimitz supported the operation because the timing did not interfere with his own campaign.[75] Once again, MacArthur's strategic concept and operational approach proved wildly successful.

With Hollandia and Aitape secure, MacArthur looked to the Vogelkop Peninsula. It was the last Japanese stronghold on the island. The Allied capture of Sansapor in late July ended the long and hard-fought New Guinea campaign. By August 10, 1944, all effective Japanese resistance had ceased. MacArthur's offensive had advanced 1,800 miles west and 700 miles north since 1942.[76] He had employed operational maneuver and used deception as well as any great captain in military history. He was now poised to fulfill his promise to liberate the Filipino people.

Before he could return to the Philippines, he had to confer with President Roosevelt on grand strategy. In July 1944 Roosevelt and Admiral William D. Leahy held a conference in Hawaii. Both Mac-

Arthur and Nimitz attempted to convince the president to approve their strategies to defeat Japan. This was MacArthur's first opportunity to provide direct input into American and Allied grand strategy. The key issue centered on whether to secure the Philippines or Formosa. The Navy wanted Formosa; MacArthur argued for the Philippines. MacArthur opposed the Navy's approach on strategic and psychological grounds. From his perspective, Formosa, with a hostile population, might prove useless as a base of attack against Japan. His most convincing argument, however, was moral. He stressed that the United States could not sacrifice the Philippines a second time. Roosevelt approved MacArthur's plan.[77]

The liberation of the Philippines was "the most important strategic objective in the Southwest Pacific Area," according to MacArthur. He selected Mindanao as the initial objective. MacArthur hoped to establish a foothold by November 15 and then turn toward the Leyte Gulf region by December 20, 1944. After the Third Fleet struck Mindanao in September, Admiral William F. Halsey reported weak resistance, which suggested that the path to Leyte was "wide open." If that was true, MacArthur could shift his timetable by two months and expedite the liberation.[78]

MacArthur knew the Leyte assault would be a difficult undertaking. The major risk was the lack of ground-based air support. In its absence, MacArthur had to rely on naval airpower. Leyte was the springboard from which MacArthur would seize Luzon, Manila, and then Japan. The SWPA commander departed Hollandia on October 16, 1944, aboard his flagship, the USS *Nashville.* After the first two assault waves stormed Leyte's beaches, MacArthur landed with the third. In one of the most famous moments of the Pacific war, MacArthur waded ashore with Filipino President-in-Exile Sergio Osmena. Once he completed his dramatic entrance, he broadcast the following: "People of the Philippines: I have returned. By the grace of Almighty God, our forces stand again on Philippine soil—soil consecrated in the blood of our two peoples."[79]

MacArthur had returned, but the Leyte beachhead was not firmly secured when the entire operation was almost undermined. Halsey's fleet was supposed to protect the northern approaches to Leyte Gulf. Unfortunately, he bit on a Japanese deception operation. He raced northward after Admiral Jisaburo Ozawa's fleet, while the remaining Japanese naval forces sought to isolate and annihilate the invasion force. In what became the greatest naval battle in history, the Japanese had constructed a daring but potentially highly rewarding operation to thwart Allied efforts to seize Leyte. The enemy commander, Admiral Soemu Toyoda, had divided his fleet into three distinct groups. The central force was to transit through the critical San Bernardino Straits while the southern force sailed through Mindanao Sea and Surigao Straits. The two naval elements would execute a pincer movement around Leyte and destroy the Allied invasion force. Admiral Ozawa's northern force was a decoy. The ruse worked; Halsey chased Ozawa's force far to the north and away from Leyte.[80] Without Halsey's air support, MacArthur's return would be a short one if the Japanese battleships joined forces in Leyte Gulf.

Luck, and the tenacity of Vice Admiral Thomas Kincaid's remaining Seventh Fleet elements, ultimately saved the amphibious force from disaster. The damage inflicted on the Japanese central force caused them to retreat. Halsey could not send his battleships to Leyte quickly enough to sink the retreating force. His risky chase of Ozawa had sunk four Japanese carriers, but those vessels were empty of the aircraft that had made them a real threat. Halsey's action did not endear the Navy or its promises of air support to MacArthur. Ultimately, the Japanese defeat at Leyte Gulf ensured Allied control of Leyte. It also set the stage for MacArthur's next and most important objective—the liberation of Luzon.

On December 18, 1944, MacArthur received his fifth star and assumed the newly created rank of General of the Army. His promotion occurred one day before Nimitz became a fleet admiral and two days after Marshall became a five-star general. MacArthur selected Mindoro, off the coast of Luzon, as a preliminary objective before invading Luzon, to ensure he had ground-based airpower to support his forces. There would be no need to rely on the Navy. The Japanese on Luzon, unlike those on Mindoro, offered stiff opposition to the Allied advance. MacArthur's intelligence section estimated 137,000 Japanese on the island. The Sixth Army estimated 234,000. In reality, the Japanese had more than 287,000 troops determined to defend Luzon to the last soldier.[81]

After Mindoro fell, the Japanese did not reinforce Luzon; but despite their isolation and the futility of resistance, the Japanese troops there did not surrender. They literally fought to the death to hold the island. MacArthur's plan to defeat the remaining Japanese was as risky as his earlier ones had been. Krueger's Sixth Army landed

General Douglas MacArthur, 1945. (Library of Congress)

an amphibious force on northern Luzon to divert Japanese forces from the south. Eichelberger's Eighth Army conducted an amphibious landing in the south, where it met weak Japanese resistance. MacArthur boarded his new flagship, the USS *Boise,* on January 4, 1945. The *Boise* anchored near Lingayen on January 9. The amphibious operation secured a twelve-mile-wide beachhead, and MacArthur waded ashore from his I Corps landing craft onto the soil of Luzon for the first time since his departure in 1941.[82]

As American forces advanced southward, Japanese resistance stiffened. The difficult Filipino terrain favored defensive positions. As they had done on Leyte, "every Japanese soldier fought to the death." It took twelve days to get to Tarlac, the halfway point to Manila. "The speed of our advance," MacArthur concluded, "gave the enemy little, and in some cases, no time to utilize their well-prepared defense positions." Speed and audacity overcame Japanese defensive advantages. MacArthur also had the advantage of time. Since the Japanese forces were not being reinforced, he could have waited for the Japanese to starve, but siege warfare was too slow. MacArthur moved as quickly as possible to free imprisoned Allied soldiers and to rescue imperiled Filipino civilians. As the Sixth Army pressed toward Manila from the north and the Eighth Army moved toward the capital from the south, MacArthur decided to expedite the city's liberation. In late January he ordered the 1st Cavalry Division to conduct a rapid assault. By February 3 the unit was on Manila's northern edges, but the Japanese fought fanatically over the next two weeks. MacArthur ruefully concluded that the Japanese resistance had "caused numerous unnecessary casualties and much destruction of property."[83]

With Luzon relatively secure, MacArthur focused on the occupied southern islands. He used the coordinated efforts of the Eighth Army, Seventh Fleet, and Thirteenth Air Force to free them. On June 28, 1945, MacArthur proclaimed that the "entire island of Luzon, embracing 40,420 square miles and a population of 8,000,000, is now liberated."[84] By July 4 the entire nation was free. It had not been as quick or as bloodless as MacArthur had wanted, but it served as a testament to MacArthur's leadership and strategic wisdom. Moreover, the initial success of MacArthur's operations in Luzon, combined with the capture of Iwo Jima in February, set the stage for the Ryukyus campaign in April 1945. Although the bloody fight for the Ryukyus Islands did not end until June, Okinawa, the largest of the Ryukyus, was critical to Allied invasion plans to secure air bases proximate to mainland Japan.

Before the Philippine campaign's conclusion, the American forces in the Pacific were reorganized. Once again, there was no unity of command. MacArthur received command of all ground troops and Nimitz controlled all naval units in the Pacific. Each commander controlled the organic air elements of his services with the exception of the Twentieth Air Force; General Henry H. "Hap" Arnold retained control of this strategic air element. The three air forces operated under the direction of Kenney, Nimitz, and Arnold. Although MacArthur lost command of the Seventh Fleet, he gained control of the Tenth Army.[85]

With the Philippine campaign concluded, his promise kept, and the reorganization of the Pacific forces under way, MacArthur looked to the invasion and defeat of Japan. Kyushu was the first objective. Although there were others involved in planning Japan's final defeat, MacArthur recommended and the JCS approved his suggestion to conduct a "direct attack at Kyushu" to set the conditions for the invasion of Honshu. The target date for Operation Olympic was November 1, 1945.[86]

MacArthur had primary responsibility for conduct of the entire operation. After Kyushu fell, Operation Coronet, the invasion of Honshu, would follow. The Sixth Army had primary responsibility for Olympic; the Eighth Army together with the First from Europe would lead the Coronet effort. The XXIV Corps would secure Korea "when opportunity permitted."[87] Contrary to U.S. and Allied policy regarding Soviet entry into the Pacific theater, MacArthur did not believe Russian intervention was necessary in 1945. He felt it would have been appropriate in 1941 under the strategic circumstances of the time, but not in 1945, when the United States and its Pacific Allies were on the cusp of victory.[88] No one in Washington, MacArthur lamented, seemed to want his advice on the matter of Soviet intervention.

Operation Olympic never occurred. The atomic bomb's detonation over Hiroshima on August 6 and the subsequent atomic attack over Nagasaki on August 9, in conjunction with the Soviet entry into the war and potential civilian unrest, led to Japanese capitulation. On August 15 Emperor Hirohito announced Japan's surrender. MacArthur became the supreme commander for the Allied Powers (SCAP), and by late August he exercised his authority over a prostrate Japan. The official surrender ceremony occurred aboard the USS *Missouri* on September 2, 1945. MacArthur, with General Jonathan Wainwright and British General Arthur Percival to his rear, officiated. MacArthur spent the next six years rebuilding a decimated nation. Not only did he restore Japan's economic and political infrastructure, he also led efforts to reconstitute Japanese society in accordance with Western models and values without eradicating the essence of Japanese culture. The Allies had disarmed Japan, but MacArthur insisted that the Japanese had to be spiritually demilitarized as well. Article 9 of the May 3, 1947, Japanese constitution was one manifestation of this spiritual demilitarization. The Japanese constitution outlawed belligerency as a means of state policy.[89]

MacArthur, determined to mold Japan into a democratic society, had to implement significant and difficult changes in Japanese attitudes and traditions. His handling of the emperor was one challenge. MacArthur understood the cultural imperative to maintain the emperor, but he also had to reduce if not eliminate the emperor's political influence and spiritual hold on the Japanese people. MacArthur exempted Hirohito and the imperial family from war crimes charges, and he saw no need for the emperor to abdicate, as some had suggested. His initial encounters with Hirohito went a long way in establishing MacArthur's credentials as the ruler of Japan. They also reflected his magnanimity as the Gaijin Shogun (foreign military ruler) of Japan.[90]

MacArthur was clearly in charge, but he was a benevolent yet firm ruler. He did not want to seek vengeance against the Japanese, but he insisted on harsh punishment for those military and civilian leaders associated with the rape of Nanking, the Bataan Death March, and the destruction of Manila. As SCAP, he confirmed and enforced the International Military Tribunal for the Far East judgments and sentences.[91]

To transform Japan, MacArthur relied heavily on the new constitution as the primary instrument of change. As long as U.S. forces occupied Japan and the Japanese complied with MacArthur's demands, the changes specified in the constitution altered Japanese society. Some of the more significant political and societal changes included the enfranchisement of women, the adoption of a parliamentary form of democratic government that limited the emperor's role and enhanced the power of the Parliament and the Cabinet, and the decentralization and reduction of police and local government power.[92]

Economic reforms reinforced MacArthur's political changes. MacArthur demanded changes in land ownership and distribution. Between 1947 and 1949 the Japanese government purchased approximately 38 percent of Japan's limited and valuable agricultural lands and resold them to independent farmers. Under this program

Japan's farmland was redistributed from wealthy property own-
ers to independent farmers. By 1950 almost 90 percent of Japan's
farmers owned their own land, which broke the former practice
of land tenancy. In addition to land restructuring, MacArthur also
insisted on labor reform. His initial efforts saw an amazing rise in
trade union membership. The greatest effect on Japan's economic
structure was MacArthur's disruption of the infamous *Zaibatsu*.
This tight-knit financial coalition consisting of prominent Japanese
families had virtually monopolized Japan's economy before the war.
These changes met resistance, but MacArthur's power was virtually
absolute. Until the Japanese assumed full sovereignty in 1952, the
Japanese business elite could do little to resist or alter MacArthur's
economic policies. In sum, MacArthur's actions as SCAP reflected
what the historian Samuel Eliot Morison considered to be the general's "greatest claims to fame." Ambassador William J. Sebald reinforced Morison's assertion by stating that "MacArthur became not
only the symbol of the Occupation; to the Japanese people he *was*
the Occupation."[93]

Success in occupied Japan, however, would not equate to triumph in MacArthur's next challenge—Korea. Before President Harry S. Truman fired MacArthur in April 1951, the general achieved
one of the most spectacular military victories in history. The Allied
powers had divided the peninsula at the 38th parallel in 1945 as
a temporary measure before Korea's eventual unification. Soviet
forces occupied the northern section and the Americans controlled
the south. As the Cold War intensified, the two Koreas became separate states. The Republic of Korea (ROK) had formed in 1948 and
the Democratic People's Republic of Korea (DPRK) in 1949. Both
North and South Korea sought unification, but on June 25, 1950,
the North opted for a military solution and launched an invasion of
South Korea.

The United Nations established the United Nations Command
(UNC) to restore peace and order to Korea. The U.S. JCS unanimous-
ly recommended MacArthur as the new UNC commander. While
serving as UNC commander, MacArthur retained his positions as
SCAP and as commander of the United States Army Forces in the
Far East. President Syngman Rhee placed his South Korean troops
under MacArthur. Reluctant to leave Tokyo, MacArthur commanded all three elements from his headquarters there. The North Korean
advance stalled around Pusan. The rapid deployment of the U.S.

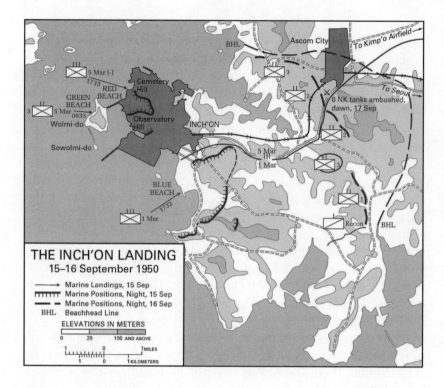

THE INCH'ON LANDING
15–16 September 1950

⟶ Marine Landings, 15 Sep
⊓⊓⊓⊓ Marine Positions, Night, 15 Sep
— – Marine Positions, Night, 16 Sep
BHL Beachhead Line

ELEVATIONS IN METERS

0   20   100 AND ABOVE

1   0   1 MILES
1   0   1 KILOMETERS

Eighth Army, combined with U.S. air and sea dominance, prevented a North Korean victory, but the crisis was not over. MacArthur devised a plan to defeat the North Koreans and restore South Korea's sovereignty. Operation Chromite was a risky, audacious amphibious assault designed to envelop the beleaguered and logistically constrained North Korean forces south of Seoul with a landing at Inchon.[94] The JCS originally opposed the plan, but MacArthur persisted. The astounding success of the operation exceeded almost everyone's expectations.

With the landing's success, U.S. forces quickly recaptured Seoul, linked with the Eighth Army, and forced the North Koreans to retreat in disorder. South Korea's liberation having been achieved and UN forces proximate to the 38th parallel, the UNC had accomplished its mission. MacArthur now faced a critical decision—should UN forces halt at the 38th parallel or continue into North Korea? With Washington's and the UN's written approval, MacArthur pushed northward. He sent the Eighth Army up the western coast and de-

MacArthur (far right) at the front lines above Suwon, Korea, accompanied by other senior officers. (Library of Congress)

ployed the X Corps to Wonsan and up the east coast.[95] Pending any unforeseen occurrence, the two forces would eliminate any North Korean resistance and reunify the entire peninsula. All went according to plan until the Communist Chinese intervened in late November 1950.

Despite indications of Chinese intervention, little had been done to prepare for a possible Communist offensive against UN forces in North Korea. MacArthur had met President Truman at Wake Island in October. Truman was concerned about possible Chinese intervention in the war. MacArthur assured the president that, despite significant indications to the contrary, the Chinese were not a threat and American troops would begin withdrawing by Christmas.[96] MacArthur was wrong. The Chinese intervention changed the calculus of the war and forced a massive U.S.–UN retreat. Inchon may have been his greatest military accomplishment, but the humiliating withdrawal from North Korea tarnished MacArthur's image. Mac-

Arthur did not give up, but he now faced an entirely different kind of war, and he seemed unsure of what to do next.

Fortunately for MacArthur and the UN, the new Eighth Army commander, Lieutenant General Matthew B. Ridgway, proved remarkably adept at reorganizing and motivating his troops. "Under Ridgway's ubiquitous battlefield leadership the Eighth Army stiffened, recaptured Seoul, and slowly pushed the enemy northward toward the thirty-eighth parallel," the historian Russell Weigley observed, "while MacArthur's excessive pessimism on the heels of his earlier excess of optimism set events in motion toward his recall from command."[97] MacArthur could not isolate the North Koreans the way he had the Japanese in New Guinea or in the Philippines. MacArthur believed that if the United States would have bombed or blockaded China, or used the atomic bomb, perhaps the war could have been won. None of MacArthur's options was viable, given the limited nature of the Korean War.

Truman refused to extend the war to China. The Soviet Union was the main threat to U.S. national security, and increased use of resources for a wider war in Asia did not support America's national security interests. As General Omar Bradley, chairman of the JCS, remarked, a war with China would be "the wrong war, at the wrong place, at the wrong time, and with the wrong enemy." MacArthur's famous response exemplified the general's concept of warfare— "There is no substitute for victory."[98] The Korean War was not World War II. The nature of warfare had not changed, but atomic weapons and a severely altered strategic environment had limited its character. Absolute victory could lead to absolute destruction. Truman grasped this concept; MacArthur did not.

The final event that led to MacArthur's relief was his letter to Representative Joseph Martin, the Republican leader in the House of Representatives. Martin read MacArthur's criticism of Truman's policies on the House floor on April 5, 1951. Truman and the JCS had had enough. Truman's order to relieve MacArthur went out on April 10 with Bradley's signature.[99] The long and distinguished military career of one of the nation's best soldiers had come to a sudden and inglorious end. General Ridgway replaced MacArthur, and the war dragged on for two more years until the belligerents signed an armistice in July 1953.

MacArthur and his family returned to the United States to parades and adulation from a grateful American public. He made his last official appearance before Congress, during which he gave his famous farewell address. His conclusion best summarizes his life and his career:

> I am closing my 52 years of military service. When I joined the Army, even before the turn of the century, it was the fulfillment of all of my boyish hopes and dreams. The world has turned over many times since I took the oath on the Plain at West Point, and the hopes and dreams have long since vanished, but I still remember the refrain of one of the most popular barrack ballads of that day which proclaimed most proudly that—"Old soldiers never die; they just fade away."
>
> And like the old soldier of that ballad, I now close my military career and just fade away—an old soldier who tried to do his duty as God gave him the light to see that duty.
>
> Good-by.[100]

Some thought MacArthur might run for president in 1952. He had considered the White House during World War II, but he never made a commitment to seek the presidency while on active duty. He hinted that he might respond to a call from the Republican Party, but that was about as far as his political aspirations went until 1952. He did not run, and his former aide Dwight D. Eisenhower received the nomination. MacArthur consulted with President Eisenhower only once during the latter's tenure in office. Meanwhile, he and his wife, Jean, lived at the famous Waldorf-Astoria Hotel. He accepted a position as chairman of the board of Remington Rand Corporation. The MacArthurs lived comfortably in New York, and the celebrated hotel proudly hosted the general's birthday party every January.[101] Poor health began to restrict the general's activities in the early 1960s. He saw Eisenhower at the White House in 1961, visited the Philippines once more, and wrote his memoirs before he died on April 5, 1964. Before he passed away, West Point honored MacArthur with the Sylvanus Thayer Award for outstanding service to the country.[102] Going back to where he began his illustrious military career and to where he had served as superintendent, MacArthur regaled the cadet corps with one last memorable speech in which he stressed the motto "Duty, Honor, Country," for which he will always be remembered.

General of the Army Douglas MacArthur received a state funeral by the direction of President Lyndon Johnson. MacArthur lay in state at the Seventh Regiment Armory and then at the nation's Capitol. On April 11 MacArthur traveled to his final resting place in the city of his beloved mother's birth—Norfolk, Virginia.[103]

Nearly fifty years have passed since MacArthur's death. Historians and military professionals still debate his actions, his decisions, and his legacy. Whether one hates him or loves him, compares him to Julius Caesar or castigates him as the most arrogant, vainglorious general in history, MacArthur was an exceptional leader and a consummate strategist. Several military institutions honor MacArthur's legacy through established and highly coveted leadership awards. The U.S. Army Command and General Staff College and the Canadian Royal Military College both recognize distinguished officers for exceptional leadership and scholarship through a MacArthur Award.[104] Though not as elaborate or extensive as Eisenhower's presidential library or the George Marshall Institute, the MacArthur Memorial in Norfolk stands as a testament to the general's vast and significant contributions to American society and to military history. The United States, Japan, the Philippines, and the world are the better for his accomplishments in war and in peace. He may not have been the most humble of military leaders, but he is among the most successful. All vanity and hubris aside, Douglas MacArthur deserves his place in the pantheon of great military leaders, and this book is a fitting tribute to the legacy of one of the nation's greatest military leaders and strategists.

Notes

1. Quotations in William Manchester, *American Caesar: Douglas MacArthur, 1880–1964* (New York: Dell, 1978), 18.

2. Douglas MacArthur, *Reminiscences: Douglas MacArthur, General of the Army* (New York: McGraw-Hill, 1964), 4–5.

3. MacArthur, *Reminiscences*, 6–10; Manchester, *American Caesar*, 26–30; and Geoffrey Perret, *Old Soldiers Never Die: The Life of Douglas MacArthur* (New York: Random House, 1996), 6–9.

4. MacArthur, *Reminiscences*, 11–14; D. Clayton James, *The Years of MacArthur*, 3 vols. (Boston: Houghton Mifflin, 1970–85), 1:23; and Perret, *Old Soldiers Never Die*, 15.

5. MacArthur, *Reminiscences*, 14–15, and Perret, *Old Soldiers Never Die*, 16.

6. MacArthur, *Reminiscences*, 16, and James, *Years of MacArthur*, 1:56.

7. James, *Years of MacArthur*, 1:59–60; Manchester, *American Caesar*, 57–58; and MacArthur, *Reminiscences*, 17.

8. Manchester, *American Caesar*, 61; MacArthur, *Reminiscences*, 18; and James, *Years of MacArthur*, 1:62–66.

9. MacArthur, *Reminiscences*, 25, and Manchester, *American Caesar*, 67.

10. Manchester, *American Caesar*, 68–69; James, *Years of MacArthur*, 1:79; and MacArthur, *Reminiscences*, 27.

11. MacArthur, *Reminiscences*, 25–26, and James, *Years of MacArthur*, 1:69–71.

12. MacArthur, *Reminiscences*, 27–28, and Manchester, *American Caesar*, 72–73.

13. James, *Years of MacArthur*, 1:87–89.

14. MacArthur, *Reminiscences*, 30–32; Manchester, *American Caesar*, 78–80; and James, *Years of MacArthur*, 1:90–94.

15. MacArthur, *Reminiscences*, 32–33, and James, *Years of MacArthur*, 1:95–97.

16. Manchester, *American Caesar*, 82.

17. MacArthur, *Reminiscences*, 30–32; Douglas MacArthur, "Military Demolition," http://usacac.army.mil/cac2/cgsc/carl/download/lectures/MacArthur.pdf (accessed February 12, 2012), and "Annual Report of Commandant, the Army Service Schools, Fort Leavenworth, Kansas, School Year Ending August 31, 1909," Army Service Schools Press, http://usacac.army.mil/cac2/cgsc/carl/download/reports/rep1909.pdf (accessed February 12, 2012), 23–24, 61–62.

18. MacArthur, *Reminiscences*, 34; Manchester, *American Caesar*, 83; and James, *Years of MacArthur*, 1:105–9.

19. Manchester, *American Caesar*, 84.

20. Ibid., 53.

21. Ibid., 88, and Richard B. Frank, *MacArthur* (New York: Palgrave, 2007), 6. For more on MacArthur's Mexico experience, see James, *Years of MacArthur*, 1:115–27.

22. MacArthur, *Reminiscences*, 44–45.

23. Manchester, *American Caesar*, 91, and MacArthur, *Reminiscences*, 46–48.

24. James, *Years of MacArthur*, 1:148.

25. MacArthur, *Reminiscences*, 53.

26. Ibid., 54–55.

27. James, *Years of MacArthur*, 1:157, and Manchester, *American Caesar*, 100–103.

28. Manchester, *American Caesar*, 103.

29. Perret, *Old Soldiers Never Die*, 94, and MacArthur, *Reminiscences*, 56–58.

30. MacArthur, *Reminiscences,* 59.

31. See citation in MacArthur, *Reminiscences,* 67.

32. Robert H. Ferrell, *The Question of MacArthur's Reputation: Côte de Châtillon, October 14–16, 1918* (Columbia: University of Missouri Press, 2008); MacArthur, *Reminiscences,* 67; and James, *Years of MacArthur,* 1:187, 223–24.

33. MacArthur, *Reminiscences,* 72.

34. Ibid., 77.

35. Ibid., 77–78.

36. Ibid., 79–82; Perret, *Old Soldiers Never Die,* 120–21; and Stephen A. Ambrose, "MacArthur as West Point Superintendent," in *MacArthur and the American Century: A Reader,* ed. William M. Leary (Lincoln: University of Nebraska Press, 2001), 20–21. As MacArthur neared the end of his USMA assignment, he married Louise Cromwell Brooks in February 1922, but they divorced in 1929.

37. James, *Years of MacArthur,* 1:295–97.

38. Ibid., 300–305, and MacArthur, *Reminiscences,* 84.

39. MacArthur, *Reminiscences,* 85.

40. Ibid., 86–87.

41. James, *Years of MacArthur,* 1:325–33, and MacArthur, *Reminiscences,* 88.

42. MacArthur, *Reminiscences,* 88–89.

43. Peter J. Schifferle, *America's School for War: Fort Leavenworth, Officer Education, and Victory in World War II* (Lawrence: University Press of Kansas, 2010), 25.

44. MacArthur, *Reminiscences,* 91–92.

45. James, *Years of MacArthur,* 1:357–71, 367, 458–60, and Perret, *Old Soldiers Never Die,* 177.

46. MacArthur, *Reminiscences,* 92.

47. Ibid., 92–95; Perret, *Old Soldiers Never Die,* 154–61; and James, *Years of MacArthur,* 1:389–414.

48. Frank, *MacArthur,* 21–25.

49. James, *Years of MacArthur,* 1:479–94, and Manchester, *American Caesar,* 177–80.

50. MacArthur, *Reminiscences,* 106–7, and James, *Years of MacArthur,* 1:494–95, 525.

51. James, *Years of MacArthur,* 1:513, and Paul P. Rogers, *The Good Years: MacArthur and Sutherland* (New York: Praeger, 1990), 39–40.

52. MacArthur, *Reminiscences,* 109, and Louis Morton, *The Fall of the Philippines* (1953; repr., Washington, D.C.: Office of the Chief of Military History, 2004), 19.

53. MacArthur, *Reminiscences,* 109.

54. Ibid., 110.

55. Ibid., 110–11.

56. Ibid., 113–14.

57. Ibid., 117–20, and Thomas E. Griffith Jr., *MacArthur's Airman: General George C. Kenney and the War in the Southwest Pacific* (Lawrence: University Press of Kansas, 1998), 49.

58. MacArthur, *Reminiscences*, 121.

59. Ibid., 127–28.

60. Ibid., 145; Perret, *Old Soldiers Never Die*, 274–75; Rogers, *The Good Years*, 190–93; and James, *Years of MacArthur*, 2:105–6.

61. See note in Kevin C. Holzimmer, "Walter Krueger, Douglas MacArthur, and the Pacific War: The Wadke-Sarmi Campaign as a Case Study," *Journal of Military History* 59.4 (October 1995): 667–68.

62. MacArthur, *Reminiscences*, 147, 152, and James, *Years of MacArthur*, 2:130–32.

63. Harry A. Gailey, *MacArthur's Victory: The War in New Guinea, 1943–1944* (New York: Presidio Press, 2004), 7–14; Samuel Eliot Morison, *History of the United States Naval Operations in World War II* (Boston: Little, Brown, 1963), 30–32; and Samuel Milner, *Victory in Papua* (Washington, D.C.: Department of the Army, 1957), 18–23.

64. Griffith, *MacArthur's Airman*, 51–52.

65. Ibid.; Wesley Frank Craven and James Lea Cate, eds., *The Army Air Forces in World War II*, vol. 1, *Plans and Early Operations* (Chicago: University of Chicago Press, 1948), 418–21; and MacArthur, *Reminiscences*, 157.

66. Griffith, *MacArthur's Airman*, 53, and Gailey, *MacArthur's Victory*, 14–18.

67. MacArthur, *Reminiscences*, 173.

68. Ibid., 159–62, and Milner, *Victory in Papua*, 77–88.

69. MacArthur, *Reminiscences*, 163–64, and Jay Luvaas, *Dear Miss Em: General Eichelberger's War in the Pacific, 1942–1945* (Westport, Conn.: Greenwood Press, 1972), 32–33.

70. MacArthur, *Reminiscences*, 165–66.

71. Ibid., 168–69.

72. Ibid., 170.

73. For more on New Guinea operations, see Stephen R. Taaffe, *MacArthur's Jungle War: The 1944 New Guinea Campaign* (Lawrence: University Press of Kansas, 1998), and John Miller Jr., *Cartwheel: The Reduction of Rabaul* (1959; repr., Washington, D.C.: U.S. Army Center for Military History, 2006).

74. MacArthur, *Reminiscences*, 180.

75. Holzimmer, "Walter Krueger, Douglas MacArthur, and the Pacific War," 668; MacArthur, *Reminiscences*, 189; and Taaffe, *MacArthur's Jungle War*, 101–3.

76. MacArthur, *Reminiscences*, 194–96.

77. James, *Years of MacArthur*, 2:521–33.

78. MacArthur, *Reminiscences*, 210–11.

79. Ibid., 212–16.

80. Ibid., 222.

81. James, *Years of MacArthur*, 2:604–10, and Edward J. Drea, *MacArthur's ULTRA: Codebreaking and the War against Japan, 1942–1945* (Lawrence: University Press of Kansas, 1992), 180–86.

82. James, *Years of MacArthur*, 2:616–22.

83. MacArthur, *Reminiscences*, 242–47.

84. Ibid., 253.

85. MacArthur, *Reminiscences*, 258, and Perret, *Old Soldiers Never Die*, 462.

86. James, *Years of MacArthur*, 2:765–71.

87. MacArthur, *Reminiscences*, 261.

88. Ibid.

89. Ibid., 265, 269–304.

90. Manchester, *American Caesar*, 545–60. For more on MacArthur's role in Japan's occupation, see Robert B. Textor, "Success in Japan—Despite Some Human Foibles and Cultural Problems," in Leary, *MacArthur and the American Century*, 258–86, and David J. Valley, *Gaijin Shogun: General Douglas MacArthur, Stepfather of Postwar Japan* (San Diego: Sektor, 2000), xi.

91. MacArthur, *Reminiscences*, 318–19.

92. James, *Years of MacArthur*, 3:119–39, and Manchester, *American Caesar*, 597–605.

93. Perret, *Old Soldiers Never Die*, 522–23; James, *Years of MacArthur*, 3:174–92; Samuel Eliot Morison, *The Oxford History of the American People* (New York: Oxford University Press, 1965), 1062; and William J. Sebald, *With MacArthur in Japan: A Personal History of the Occupation* (New York: W. W. Norton, 1965), 11. For more current assessments of the occupation, see John W. Dower, *Embracing Defeat: Japan in the Wake of World War II* (New York: W. W. Norton, 1999), and Takemae Eiji, *Inside GHQ: The Allied Occupation of Japan and Its Legacy* (New York: Continuum, 2002).

94. James, *Years of MacArthur*, 3:436–85. See also H. Pat Tomlinson, "Inchon: The General's Decision," in Leary, *MacArthur and the American Century*, 345–51.

95. Perret, *Old Soldiers Never Die*, 559–60.

96. MacArthur, *Reminiscences*, 360–63.

97. Russell Weigley, *The American Way of War: A History of United States Military Strategy and Policy* (Bloomington: Indiana University Press, 1977), 390.

98. Bradley quoted in ibid., 390; Manchester, *American Caesar*, 764; and MacArthur, *Reminiscences*, 386.

99. Clay Blair, *The Forgotten War: America in Korea, 1950–1953* (New York: Times Books, 1987), 758–61, 783–88.

100. MacArthur, *Reminiscences*, 405.

101. Perret, *Old Soldiers Never Die*, 581–83.

102. Ibid., 584–85.

103. B. C. Mossman and M. W. Stark, "General of the Army, Douglas MacArthur, State Funeral, 5 April 1964," in Mossman and Stark, *The Last Salute: Civil and Military Funerals, 1921–1969* (Washington, D.C.: Department of the Army, 1991), 216, and Manchester, *American Caesar*, 839. "General of the Army Douglas MacArthur died on 5 April 1964 in Walter Reed General Hospital at the age of eighty-four. Earlier President Kennedy had authorized a State Funeral, and President Johnson confirmed the directive when he ordered that General MacArthur be buried 'with all the honor a grateful nation can bestow on a departed hero.'" See www.macarthurmemorial.org (accessed September 21, 2012) for more information on the MacArthur Memorial in Norfolk, Va.

104. For more on the Canadian Royal Military College award, see www.rmc.ca/aca/ac-pe/ug-apc/spa-bprpa-pr-eng.asp (accessed September 21, 2012).

References

Blair, Clay. *The Forgotten War: America in Korea, 1950–1953.* New York: Times Books, 1987.

Craven, Wesley Frank, and James Lea Cate, eds. *The Army Air Forces in World War II,* vol. 1, *Plans and Early Operations.* Chicago: University of Chicago Press, 1948.

Dower, John W. *Embracing Defeat: Japan in the Wake of World War II.* New York: W. W. Norton, 1999.

Drea, Edward J. *MacArthur's ULTRA: Codebreaking and the War against Japan, 1942–1945.* Lawrence: University Press of Kansas, 1992.

Ferrell, Robert H. *The Question of MacArthur's Reputation: Côte de Châtillon, October 14–16, 1918.* Columbia: University of Missouri Press, 2008.

Frank, Richard B. *MacArthur.* New York: Palgrave, 2007.

Gailey, Harry A. *MacArthur's Victory: The War in New Guinea, 1943–1944.* New York: Presidio Press, 2004.

Griffith, Thomas E., Jr. *MacArthur's Airman: General George C. Kenney and the War in the Southwest Pacific.* Lawrence: University Press of Kansas, 1998.

Holzimmer, Kevin C. "Walter Krueger, Douglas MacArthur, and the Pacific War: The Wadke-Sarmi Campaign as a Case Study." *Journal of Military History* 59.4 (October 1995): 661–85.

James, D. Clayton. *The Years of MacArthur*, vol. 1, *1880–1941*. Boston: Houghton Mifflin, 1970.

———. *The Years of MacArthur*, vol. 2, *1941–1945*. Boston: Houghton Mifflin, 1975.

———. *The Years of MacArthur*, vol. 3, *1945–1964*. Boston: Houghton Mifflin, 1985.

Leary, William M., ed. *MacArthur and the American Century: A Reader*. Lincoln: University of Nebraska Press, 2001.

———. *We Shall Return: MacArthur's Commanders and the Defeat of Japan, 1942–1945*. Lexington: University Press of Kentucky, 1988.

Luvaas, Jay. *Dear Miss Em: General Eichelberger's War in the Pacific, 1942–1945*. Westport, Conn.: Greenwood Press, 1972.

MacArthur, Douglas. *Reminiscences: Douglas MacArthur, General of the Army*. New York: McGraw-Hill, 1964.

Manchester, William. *American Caesar: Douglas MacArthur, 1880–1964*. New York: Dell, 1978.

Miller, John, Jr., *Cartwheel: The Reduction of Rabaul*. 1959. Reprint, Washington, D.C.: U.S. Army Center for Military History, 2006.

Milner, Samuel. *Victory in Papua*. Washington, D.C.: Department of the Army, 1957.

Morison, Samuel Eliot. *History of the United States Naval Operations in World War II*. Boston: Little, Brown, 1963.

———. *The Oxford History of the American People*. New York: Oxford University Press, 1965.

Morton, Louis. *The Fall of the Philippines*. 1953. Reprint, Washington, D.C.: Office of the Chief of Military History, 2004.

Pearlman, Michael D. *Truman & MacArthur: Policy, Politics, and the Hunger for Honor and Renown*. Bloomington: Indiana University Press, 2008.

Perret, Geoffrey. *Old Soldiers Never Die: The Life of Douglas MacArthur*. New York: Random House, 1996.

Rogers, Paul P. *The Good Years: MacArthur and Sutherland*. New York: Praeger, 1990.

Schifferle, Peter J. *America's School for War: Fort Leavenworth, Officer Education, and Victory in World War II*. Lawrence: University Press of Kansas, 2010.

Sebald, William J. *With MacArthur in Japan: A Personal History of the Occupation*. New York: W. W. Norton, 1965.

Taaffe, Stephen R. *MacArthur's Jungle War: The 1944 New Guinea Campaign*. Lawrence: University Press of Kansas, 1998.

Takemae, Eiji. *Inside GHQ: The Allied Occupation of Japan and Its Legacy*. New York: Continuum, 2002.

Valley, David J. *Gaijin Shogun: General Douglas MacArthur, Stepfather of Postwar Japan.* San Diego: Sektor, 2000.

Weigley, Russell. *The American Way of War: A History of United States Military Strategy and Policy.* Bloomington: Indiana University Press, 1977.

4

Dwight D. Eisenhower

Sean N. Kalic

General and President Dwight D. Eisenhower has come to represent many things to many different people of several generations. For the veterans of World War II, he was the commanding general who planned and oversaw the initial landings in North Africa and Italy. Next, as supreme Allied commander of Europe, he planned, oversaw the preparation of, and made the decision to launch Operation Overlord on the beaches of Normandy. While achieving the Allied victory in Europe, Eisenhower rose to the rank of five-star general. He briefly took a civilian position as president of Columbia University before Harry S. Truman asked him to become supreme Allied commander of the new North Atlantic Treaty Organization (NATO) in the immediate postwar period. After retiring from military service, Eisenhower found another way to continue to serve his country in the midst of the Korean War.

In 1952 Eisenhower ran as the Republican candidate for president of the United States. After winning the presidency, Eisenhower led the United States through a politically turbulent period in the Cold War. Negotiating a truce to the Korean War, supporting covert actions against Communists in Iran and Guatemala, providing funding to the French for their war against Ho Chi Minh and the Viet Minh in Indochina, and firmly entrenching a reliance on nuclear weapons in the United States military are some of the primary actions and decisions made by Eisenhower during his tenure as the president.

Beyond his steadfast efforts to combat the forces of Communism, Eisenhower also supported the development of the National Aeronautics and Space Administration; negotiated treaties for the preservation of the seabed and Antarctica, with an objective of keeping all frontiers free for the sake of scientific research for all; and encouraged the United States to invest heavily in science and math education in the context of the space race with the Soviet Union. While supporting these various military and scientific endeavors, Eisenhower remained persistently committed to ensuring that the United States remained fiscally sound and determined to avoid bankrupting itself, despite its position as the primary bulwark against the expansionistic designs of the Soviet Union and its satellite nations.

From his earliest days in Texas to his final days at his farm in Gettysburg, Pennsylvania, the life of Dwight D. Eisenhower can be characterized as one of "duty, honor, country." He consistently demonstrated a strong work ethic, phenomenal leadership skills, and steadfast belief in the goodness of the United States. This chapter details his strong commitment to service to the United States first in the military and later as president of the United States.[1]

In Denison, Texas, on October 14, 1890, David Jacob and Ida Elizabeth Eisenhower welcomed their third son, Dwight David Eisenhower. David and Ida had met seven years earlier (1883) at Lane University in Lecompton, Kansas.[2] David, who had aspirations of studying to become an engineer, had moved to Hope, Kansas, with his family in the 1870s, as part of a group of River Brethren, a branch of the Mennonite sect that pursued farming. David's father, Jacob Eisenhower, was one of the leaders of the sect and had a 160-acre tract of land in Dickinson County, Kansas.[3] The county seat was Abilene, which was approximately twenty miles northeast of Jacob Eisenhower's farm. In the 1870s the city of Abilene was the railhead for the "northern end of the Chisholm Trail" and served as the embarkation point for cattle as they made their way to the stockyards in Chicago. It was a "rough, wild, and dangerous place" for its 8,000 residents at the time, not yet the quiet, bucolic community where David and Ida would later raise their family.[4]

Ida Stover was from the Shenandoah Valley village of Mount Sidney, Virginia. Upon the death of her mother when Ida was fifteen, Ida's father, who had an additional ten children to care for (seven boys and three girls), sent Ida to live with her maternal grandparents.[5] Starting at age sixteen, Ida worked as a housekeeper and later as a schoolteacher. In 1882 two of Ida's brothers moved to Topeka, Kansas, and Ida joined them there.[6] A year later she enrolled in Lane University with the intention of studying music. There she met David Eisenhower.

David and Ida married on September 23, 1885, without finishing their studies at the university. Using $2,000 his father gave him upon his marriage, David Eisenhower partnered with Milton Good to start a general store in Abilene. In 1888, after only three years, the store failed. By that time David and Ida had one son, Arthur, and were expecting a second child. Needing a livelihood, David left his family in Abilene and went southwest to search for work. He found employment with the railroad in Denison, Texas. In January 1889 David and Ida's second son, Edgar, was born. Shortly thereafter Ida, Arthur, and Edgar moved to Denison to be with David.

Having reliable work and a steady income, David and Ida had a third son, Dwight David, in October 1890, followed by a fourth son, Roy, just a year later. With the expanding demands of his family, David's modest paycheck from the railroad made it increasingly difficult to meet expenses. In 1892 David and Ida decided to move their family back to Abilene, after David's brother-in-law Christian Musser offered him a job at the Belle Creamery there. David accepted the job and would be in charge of maintaining the refrigeration equipment. Abilene would be home for David and Ida and their eventual six sons. More important, Abilene would be the town in which Dwight D. Eisenhower spent the majority of his formative years.

Eisenhower recounts in *At Ease* that, after the family had moved from the house they rented on South Second Street to the three-acre farm on South Fourth Street in Abilene, he and his brothers had a bevy of chores to perform.[7] Eisenhower's father worked at the creamery from 6:00 A.M. until 5:00 P.M. six days a week. This left the majority of the duties of the small farm to be performed by Ida and her sons. After listing the seemingly endless tasks such as cooking, doing dishes, tending to chickens and cows, weeding the vegetable garden, and storing fruits and vegetables for winter, Eisenhower describes the frivolity and competitiveness of brothers in the early years of the twentieth century.[8] By this time Abilene had matured from its boisterous cow-town days into a respectable and quiet community; there Eisenhower and his family lived a very modest and happy life. In fact, he states: "Though our family was far from affluent, I never heard a word even distantly of self-pity. If we were poor—and I'm not sure that we were by the standards of the day—we were unaware of it. We were always well fed, adequately clothed, and housed. Each boy was permitted to earn his own money and spend it according to his taste and best judgment."[9]

The boys worked by selling vegetables and taking other jobs around the town as time permitted while they continued to go to school. Eisenhower recounts that both of his parents stressed education and from the earliest years encouraged each of their sons to go to college.[10] In contrast, the majority of male students in Abilene completed their formal schooling once they finished the eighth grade. In 1904 Dwight started high school in Abilene, which was conducted in the city hall; the fire station was on the same floor and the city jail just below the small classrooms.[11]

Abilene built a dedicated high school in 1905, and Eisenhower's class was composed of twenty-two girls and just eight other males.[12] In most accounts of his life before his departure for West Point, Eisenhower has been noted as being interested in history as well as having a talent for geometry.[13] In addition to his interest in academic pursuits, Eisenhower was athletically inclined. While in high school he played football and baseball and demonstrated a genuine athletic talent, driven by his competitiveness as well as his love of the games. In May 1909 he graduated from Abilene High School, and his classmates noted that he was "Best Historian and Mathematician" in their yearbook, *The Helianthus*.[14] Though he was a talented student-athlete, his future was uncertain, but Eisenhower seemed to want to follow his brother Edgar's lead and go to college.[15] The major problem, however, was that Eisenhower had to pay his own way. According to his biographers, Eisenhower negotiated a deal with his brother Edgar, whereby Eisenhower would work for a year and send what money he could to Edgar as he pursued his studies. Edgar would in turn work a year to help fund Eisenhower's education. The two brothers figured that within eight years they would both be able to complete their respective degrees.[16] To keep his end of the bargain, Eisenhower took a full-time job at the Belle Creamery.

In 1910, however, Eisenhower had a chance encounter with Everett "Swede" Hazlett, a grade school friend who had secured an appointment to the United States Naval Academy. Hazlett proposed that Eisenhower join him at the Academy, and the idea of a free college education appealed to Eisenhower. Though very much interested in taking the entrance exam, Eisenhower quickly found out that by the time of his birthday in 1910, at age twenty he would be too old to gain an appointment to the Naval Academy. The U.S. Military Academy at West Point, New York, however, accepted cadets up to age twenty-two. Thereupon Eisenhower worked to get accepted to West Point.

Having asked prominent members of the Abilene community to write him letters of introduction to Senator Joseph Bristow, Eisenhower on August 20, 1910, wrote a letter to Senator Bristow expressing his desire to secure an appointment to one of the service academies. After waiting two months without a response from Senator Bristow, Eisenhower read in the local paper that the competitive examinations for the service academies were to be administered in Topeka, Kansas, in early October. Not wanting to possibly violate protocol, Eisenhower penned a second letter to Senator Bristow asking if it would be all right if he took the examinations. Senator Bristow responded to Eisenhower's second letter and recommended that Eisenhower indeed take the examinations. On October 4–5, 1910, Eisenhower took the examinations and scored second of the eight men who had taken them. In November Senator Bristow wrote to Eisenhower informing him that he had appointed him to West Point.[17]

Eisenhower began his military career when he arrived at West Point on July 1, 1911. As he traveled from Abilene to New York, he made sure that he planned his cross-country trip to include a week's vacation, during which he visited a friend, Rudy Norman, who lived in Chicago, as well as taking time to see his brother Edgar, who was studying in Ann Arbor at the University of Michigan. Having dispensed with the "vacation" part of his trip, Eisenhower recounts that upon arriving at West Point and making his way up to the administration building, "he got a sense of calculated chaos."[18] After enduring the tumultuous first day, Eisenhower was sworn in as a cadet. He later recounted, "The day had been one of confusion and a heroic brand of readjustment, but when we raised our right hands and repeated the official oath, there was no confusion. A feeling came over me that the expression of 'The United States of America' would now and henceforth mean something different than it ever had before. From here on it would be the nation I would be serving, not myself."[19]

By all accounts, Eisenhower enjoyed his time at West Point. Enduring a curriculum that was heavily focused on math and other engineering-related studies, Eisenhower encountered academic challenges, but he overcame them with hard work and a strong motivation to succeed. In addition to his academic studies, he was steadfastly committed to sports as well, and he made the football

Eisenhower as a West Point cadet. (U.S. Army, 65-173-2)

team at West Point. In November 1912, in a football game against Tufts University, Eisenhower injured his knee and spent five days in the Academy's dispensary.[20] Not wanting to miss the upcoming game against Navy, however, Eisenhower did not get excused from riding class, and he reported to the riding hall to practice "mounted gymnastics" with his fellow cadets. During the class Eisenhower lost control of his horse and was thrown, whereupon he landed on his already injured knee. This ended his ability to play football, although West Point nonetheless awarded him a letter in football for the 1912 season.

For the remainder of his time at West Point, Eisenhower had to decide which branch of the Army he would join after his graduation. Knowing that his ranking was approximately in the middle of his class, he was aware that it was not high enough to secure a commission in the Corps of Engineers, which accepted the top 3 percent of each class. His football injury barred a commission in the Cavalry, and the Artillery branch did not hold the same sense of adventure and prestige as the Infantry. Accordingly, he decided on the Infantry. When Eisenhower graduated from West Point on June 12, 1915, the Army commissioned him as a second lieutenant in the Infantry. After World War II Eisenhower's class would come to be called "the class the stars fell on," since it included so many later prominent officers, such as Omar Bradley, George E. Stratemeyer, and James Van Fleet.[21]

On September 13, 1915, Eisenhower reported to Fort Sam Houston, Texas, to serve with the 19th Infantry. While at Fort Sam Houston, where he remained until 1917, Eisenhower met Mamie Geneva Doud, whom he married in July 1916. Before his wedding, Eisenhower had applied for a transfer to the Aviation section, which was approved. When he shared this news with his future father-in-law, John Doud, however, he received a lecture about how flying was a dangerous and foolish endeavor to contemplate. In *At Ease*, Eisenhower recounted that after a few days of thinking and "looking at the matter seriously," he made the decision to remain with the Infantry.[22]

After the wedding, in response to the escalating troubles on the border between the United States and Mexico, Eisenhower applied to join the punitive expedition under the command of Brigadier General John J. Pershing. At the same time, the Great War continued to rage in Europe, and it increasingly looked as if President Woodrow Wilson would send U.S. troops to assist the war-weary Allies. On April 1, 1917, Eisenhower and several other officers from the 19th Infantry were transferred to Camp Wilson to begin the process of forming the new 57th Regiment.[23]

During this time the Army promoted Eisenhower to captain, and he began to make a name for himself as a strong leader and committed teacher who could be relied on to get the job done. His time at Fort Sam Houston and Camp Wilson brought Eisenhower into association with Robert L. Eichelberger (commander of the Eighth Army in the Philippines campaigns in World War II), as well as Leonard T. Gerow (commander, V Corps, at Omaha Beach on D-Day), who became lifelong friends and future study mates at the Command and General Staff School.

Following his assignment at Fort Sam Houston, Eisenhower went to Fort Oglethorpe, Georgia, to be an instructor at the Officer Training Camp. In essence, Eisenhower was preparing young officers to be effective combat officers. In the midst of this short assignment, however, Eisenhower, who wanted to go to Europe to fight for the United Sates, applied for special duty with a "machine gun battalion, earmarked for overseas combat."[24] The Army disappointed Eisenhower by not fulfilling his request; rather, it provided him with a three-month temporary-duty assignment at Fort Leavenworth. While at Fort Leavenworth, Eisenhower once again proved himself a very capable and effective trainer of troops, as he planned and led the training program for provisional second lieutenants.

In March 1918 Eisenhower was assigned to Camp Meade, Maryland. During this assignment, Eisenhower assisted greatly in organizing and training the 301st Tank Battalion to deploy to Europe.[25] Although he had expected to accompany the 301st to Europe, Eisenhower's desire for combat was once again stymied. Instead, he was ordered to report to Camp Colt in Pennsylvania to organize and train other tank units intended for Europe. Although this assignment came as another disappointment, the Army did promote Eisenhower to the rank of temporary lieutenant colonel.

During his time at Camp Colt, Eisenhower acquired essential skills and experience with managing, coordinating, and maintaining a camp designed to train combat troops. Of his time at Camp Colt Eisenhower would later remark: "I had been singularly fortunate in the scope of my first three and a half years of duty. How to take a cross-section of Americans and convert them into first-rate fighting troops and officers had been learned by experience, not by textbooks. . . . My education had not been neglected."[26] Though he did not get the chance to participate in combat in Europe, Eisenhower's service as a trainer proved invaluable to the Army as well as to Eisenhower himself.

In the years immediately following the war in Europe, Eisenhower first met George S. Patton, who had commanded tanks in combat and had returned to Fort Meade in 1919 as commanding officer of the 304th Tank Brigade. At Meade, Eisenhower served as the deputy commander of the 305th Tank Brigade. He and Patton "shared a passion for tank warfare" and spent time together as Patton prepared to attend the Command and General Staff College.[27] Owing to his close association with Patton, Eisenhower received an introduction to Fox Conner, who had served as the assistant chief of staff for operations of the American Expeditionary Forces. Conner would eventually become a significant mentor and have a profound influence on Eisenhower's career as well as on his chances to attend the Command and General Staff College.

Between February 1918 and January 1922, Eisenhower moved from Camp Meade to Camp Colt, Pennsylvania, and then on to Camp Dix, New Jersey. After a brief stint as a commander of Tank Corps troops at Dix, he went to command Tank Corps troops at Fort Benning, Georgia, before going back to Fort Meade.[28] This period proved to be a critical time in continuing to shape his leadership skills. Furthermore, while at Fort Meade in 1920, Eisenhower wrote an article for *Infantry Journal* in which he declared that tanks, "using terrain properly, could break enemy defenses, create confusion, and exploit the advantage by envelopment."[29] Although his training, experience, and extensive study provided him with a sound argument, Eisenhower received a harsh reprimand from the chief of Infantry, who told Eisenhower that his ideas were "not only wrong, but dangerous, and that he should keep his ideas to himself or face a court martial."[30]

Eisenhower may not have convinced the chief of Infantry, but Brigadier General Fox Conner saw the merits of Eisenhower's ideas and extended an offer for Eisenhower to be his executive officer at Camp Gaillard in the Panama Canal Zone.[31] In addition to reorganizing and modernizing the defenses in the Canal Zone, Conner pushed Eisenhower to begin preparing himself to attend the Command and General Staff School at Fort Leavenworth. In an intense period of mentoring, Conner opened his extensive library to Eisenhower and encouraged his subordinate to read the classic texts of military history. Moreover, Conner questioned his protégé and discussed the books with Eisenhower. This informal yet profound education led Eisenhower to comment that this period served as "a sort of graduate school in military affairs and the humanities, leavened by the comments and discourses of a man who was experienced in his knowledge of men and their conduct."[32] At the end of his assignment in Panama, Conner rated Eisenhower as "superior" and recommended that he was "exceptionally well fitted for general staff training."[33]

In October 1922, at the close of his assignment in Panama, Eisenhower received the Distinguished Service Medal (DSM), which was awarded for his training efforts during World War I. Although Eisenhower is often depicted by historians as an officer who was "plodding" along during this period, his biographer Geoffrey Perret highlights the fact that Eisenhower had "achieved the highest rank of anyone in his class, and was the only one to receive the DSM for service in the Great War."[34] In short, Eisenhower was making a significant impression on the Army and especially on Conner.

In his last efficiency report as Eisenhower's commanding officer, Conner wrote that Eisenhower was "one of the most capable, efficient, and loyal officers I have ever met. . . . Upon completion of his foreign service tour, he should be sent to take the course at the Army Services School at Fort Leavenworth."[35] Although he had an outstanding reputation and had impressed powerful officers such as Fox Conner, Eisenhower's path to the prestigious Command and General Staff School would not be an easy one.[36]

First, Eisenhower had not attended any of the Army's service schools, with the exception of the Infantry Tank School. This did not bode well for him as an Infantry officer. Nevertheless, Conner supported Eisenhower's desire to attend the Command and General Staff School, stating that despite his lack of attendance at other service schools, Eisenhower was "especially fitted to profit by the course," and that he had "marked qualities for the General Staff training."[37] Furthermore, Conner commented that Eisenhower had kept pace with the Benning Infantry course "by special study and contact with recent Benning graduates."[38]

With Conner's endorsement, Eisenhower made a formal request to attend the Command and General Staff School. The Adjutant General's Office processed Eisenhower's request and wrote, "The name of Capt. D. D. Eisenhower has been placed on the tentative list of those officers who will be considered to attend the 1925–26 course at C.&G.S.S. Capt. Eisenhower will be promoted to the grade of Major at the present time."[39] After making its way through the staffing process, Eisenhower's request was tentatively approved

Major Eisenhower. (U.S. Army, 63-340-2)

with the note "usual action," but Eisenhower still had hurdles to overcome before he would attend the Command and General Staff School at Fort Leavenworth. Before his selection for the Staff School, the Army moved Eisenhower from Panama to Fort Meade, as the Army wanted once again to employ Eisenhower's skills as a football coach, a function he had performed earlier in his military career.[40]

While coaching football at Fort Meade, Eisenhower commanded a battalion of tanks as well, a position he had also held earlier. Eisenhower did not think that he was progressing toward the goal of attending the Command and General Staff School. To plead his case, he met with the chief of Infantry, and, as Eisenhower explains in *At Ease*, "he refused to even listen to my arguments, and said that I would have to go to [Fort] Benning to command light tanks."[41] Eisenhower's desire to attend Fort Leavenworth seemed blocked by the chief of Infantry. Eisenhower in the meantime had received a telegram from Fox Conner, however, telling him that "no matter what orders you receive from the War Department, make no protest, accept them without question."[42]

When his new orders arrived, Eisenhower found that he had been assigned to a recruiting command in Denver, Colorado—a very strange and nonstandard assignment for an Infantry officer. Nevertheless, following Conner's advice, Eisenhower did not challenge the orders and made the move to Denver. As Eisenhower began his new duties, a letter from Conner explained the odd assignment. This was a bureaucratic move to circumvent the chief of Infantry. Conner had had Eisenhower "temporarily" assigned to the Adjutant General's Office, which had its own quota of officers allocated to send to the Command and General Staff School. In August 1925 Eisenhower arrived at Fort Leavenworth.

Commenting on his year at Leavenworth, Eisenhower wrote that it "was a watershed in my life."[43] Contemplating attendance at the Staff School, Eisenhower was tentative about his abilities, because he had not attended the preparatory Infantry course at Fort Benning. Fox Conner, however, assured him that he was indeed prepared for the course.[44] Being selected for attendance at the Command and General Staff School was seen as a prestigious career point for officers before they went on to bigger and better positions in the Army. Eisenhower focused on becoming the top student in the class. He pored over tactical problems taught by the faculty members William Bryden, Simon Bolivar Buckner, Horace H. Fuller, James Muir, and James Ord with the assistance of the notes of George S. Patton, who had attended the school earlier.[45] Eisenhower spent countless hours studying with Leonard Gerow, a friend from the 19th Infantry. Although focused and committed, Eisenhower did not do well on his first graded assignment at Fort Leavenworth. Thereupon he committed himself to improving his overall rank in the class. He rose from fourteenth in the class of 250 to graduate first in his class, which included his fellow officers James E. Chaney, Clarence L. Sturdevant, Robert L. Eichelberger, Terry de la Mesa Allen, and Joseph W. Stilwell, all of whom he would encounter again during World War II.[46] These associations would prove very valuable as he rose in rank.

Eisenhower once again proving himself a very capable and outstanding officer, his efficiency report from Brigadier General Edward L. King, the commandant of the Command and General Staff College, referred to him as "alert, resourceful, dependable, and courteous."[47] Moreover, Mark Bender notes that the Command and General Staff School recognized Eisenhower as superior in "attention to duty, initiative, intelligence, energy, resolution, judgment and common sense, and leadership."[48]

When Major Eisenhower reported to Fort Benning, he was told that he would assume a secondary duty beyond his commitments to the 24th Infantry—the Army wanted him to coach the football team at Fort Benning. Eisenhower declined the offer to serve as head coach and instead struck a deal that allowed him to serve as the backfield coach as well as the coach who was in charge of offensive tactics.[49] After a lackluster season, Eisenhower no longer had to endure the tribulations of being a football coach because he received reassignment orders.

In December 1926 Eisenhower was ordered by the War Department to report to Washington, D.C., to serve on the Battle Monuments Commission headed by General Pershing. The objective of the commission was to build and beautify cemeteries that honored those soldiers, sailors, and marines who had sacrificed their lives in the recent war. Additionally, the Battle Monuments Commission had the responsibility of writing guides to the battlefields on which Americans had fought in the conflict. Eisenhower reported for duty in January 1927 and was promptly assigned the duty of writing the battlefield guides. In many ways this was a choice assignment for Eisenhower, who had been a keen student of military history since his boyhood days in Abilene.

Despite his interest and desire to stay with the commission, the Army offered Eisenhower the opportunity to attend the Army War College for the 1927–28 academic year.

In *At Ease*, Eisenhower observes that "for once the Department has given me a choice, and for once I am going to say yes to something that I'm anxious to do."[50] Therefore, despite his continued deep interest in military history, Eisenhower chose to attend the War College. He graduated from that course in June 1928, after which he was again given options by the War Department. This time the options were an assignment to the General Staff or a return to the Battle Monuments Commission. Eisenhower chose to go back to the commission, because it allowed him to finish the battlefield guide that he had worked on previously. This time, however, the assignment entailed travel to France and a tour of the World War I battlefields while based in Paris.

The year in Paris, where Eisenhower "first got acquainted with the European countryside," proved inspiring and beneficial for Eisenhower's future as supreme Allied commander. Eisenhower relished the opportunity to walk the various battlefields of World War I where American units had engaged in combat. When he returned to the United States in the fall of 1929, Eisenhower finished writing the battlefield guides, while also assisting General Pershing in the completion of his memoirs.

After reading Pershing's first draft, Eisenhower determined that the memoir was really just a rewriting of Pershing's wartime diaries, and he suggested to General Pershing: "Everything in that war, as far as the Army is concerned, pointed up to two great battles, Saint-Mihiel and the Argonne. Now I don't believe you should tell the story in those two chapters in the form a diary. It takes the reader's attention away from the development of the battles and just follows your own actions, your own decisions, and your own travels."[51]

This suggestion led Pershing to tell Eisenhower to take the two chapters and rewrite them "how they should be."[52] Eisenhower carefully and meticulously recrafted the two chapters and submitted them to Pershing. Pershing passed the chapters to his trusted friend Colonel George C. Marshall, an officer who had served with Pershing during World War I. After reading Eisenhower's rewrites, Marshall met with Pershing and advised the general to keep his memoirs the way they were, as Eisenhower's chapters, though well written, changed the format and continuity of the text.[53] After briefing Pershing, Marshall stopped by Eisenhower's desk and explained his decision. This was the first time Marshall and Eisenhower met.

After completing his assignment with the Battle Monuments Commission, Eisenhower received an opportunity to work in the assistant secretary of War's office, which was busy drafting and refining studies that dealt with mobilization for future war. Working under General George Moseley, Eisenhower received the assignment of drafting reports that dealt with mobilizing industry. This assignment involved visiting American factories and getting information about their production processes, as well as inquiring how the industries could increase their production when the need arose.

As he widened his knowledge of industrial mobilization, Eisenhower met with Bernard Baruch, a financier who had been chief of the War Industries Board during World War I. Baruch advocated significant government control in times of emergency, and he believed that an agency akin to the War Industries Board needed to have the power to exercise centralized control over vital economic resources. Baruch convinced Eisenhower.[54] In 1930 Congress created the War Policies Commission to perform the duties outlined by Baruch. The new commission wanted mobilization plans as a foundation for its work, and it fell to Eisenhower, Major Gilbert Wilkes, and Moseley to draft the report, the majority of the writing being assigned to Eisenhower. The document was entitled *Industrial Mobilization Plan—1930*. Eisenhower paved the way for this report by publishing an article, "Fundamentals of Industrial Mobilization," in the summer 1930 issue of *Army Ordnance*.[55]

Moseley, Wilkes, and Eisenhower toiled away under Army Chief of Staff Charles P. Summerall, who gave little attention or support to their work. In 1930 General Douglas MacArthur succeeded Summerall. MacArthur encouraged the work on industrial mobilization and saw the need as well as the benefit for the nation. Eisenhower continued his work with mobilization plans and graduated from the Industrial War College in 1931, before he completed his assignment with the assistant secretary of War in February 1933.[56]

Rather than going back to command troops, Eisenhower had the opportunity to serve as MacArthur's military assistant. He accepted the position. Eisenhower commented in *At Ease* that his new position was "on the verge of political, even on the edge of partisan politics," which was an unknown world for most military officers.[57] Despite his initial uneasiness, Eisenhower found MacArthur "a rewarding man to work for."[58] In constant awe of MacArthur's comprehensive knowledge, Eisenhower excelled under MacArthur's style of command. Eisenhower stated that once General MacArthur gave an assignment, he did not needlessly follow up with his subordinates about their progress. MacArthur simply expected the assignment to be completed on time and as ordered.

During his time as MacArthur's military assistant, Eisenhower witnessed the Bonus March incident in Washington, D.C. In 1932 unemployed veterans of World War I gathered in Washington to demand early payment of service bonuses due to them, which were supposed to be paid by the U.S. government in 1945. President Herbert Hoover refused to meet with the veterans, whose numbers had swollen to approximately 5,000 to 7,000. They had erected camps and occupied vacant buildings on the edge of the nation's capital. The Hoover administration wanted the veterans dispersed, and the order went first to the police, who were not trained to deal with "large groups organized under discipline learned in the Armed Forces."[59] The final order went to the Army and General MacArthur. MacArthur, on July 28, 1932, used Cavalry, Infantry, and tanks to disperse the Bonus Marchers and burn their camps. In the context of the Great Depression, MacArthur's actions were viewed by many in the United States as heavy-handed and overly harsh. In his memoirs Eisenhower goes to great length to explain the circumstances that led to the decision to intervene in the marchers' camps, maintaining that it was not MacArthur's boldness or insensitivity that led him to make the final decision, but rather a series of miscommunications. In these passages in *At Ease* there is a real sense of respect and admiration for MacArthur.[60]

Shortly after this time, the U.S. Congress was working on legislation to confer commonwealth status on the Philippines for a period of ten years. The administration of Franklin D. Roosevelt needed to assign a military adviser to oversee the military development of the Philippines. MacArthur would serve this role, and Eisenhower would accompany him.

Although Eisenhower had worked on plans for the Philippine military in the closing months of his assignment with MacArthur, he was not keenly interested in going to the Philippines. MacArthur, however, did not wish to let go of Eisenhower. The general convinced the younger officer that he should accompany him to the Philippines, although MacArthur never gave Eisenhower a straight answer as to the length of the assignment. Respecting MacArthur, Eisenhower agreed to be his special assistant as he served as military adviser to the Philippines.

While in the islands, Eisenhower and Major James Ord, a West

Point classmate, assisted MacArthur in mobilizing and training the Philippine military, as well as developing a defense plan for the major islands. This intensive process required the two staff officers to travel extensively throughout the 7,000 islands that compose the Philippines. To accomplish his duties Eisenhower finally achieved an old dream and received his private pilot's license so he could fly from point to point and accomplish his mission in an efficient and effective manner. Besides minor disagreements with MacArthur, such as MacArthur's recommendation that Eisenhower and Ord take commissions in the Philippine army, Eisenhower and MacArthur worked well together.

As war clouds gathered over Europe, Eisenhower returned from the Philippines in February 1940 to join the 15th Infantry, and within a few months he became chief of staff of the 3rd Division at Fort Lewis, Washington. Despite shortfalls in men, matériel, and experienced officers, Eisenhower worked with his troops to get the division into fighting shape. Of this period back with a line unit, Eisenhower stated that "the experience fortified my conviction that I belonged with troops."[61] As he was training his soldiers, Eisenhower's friend Patton sent him a note stating that he was "about to get a new armor division" that was to be organized soon and that he wanted Eisenhower to be a regimental commander.[62] Eisenhower, who had missed out on combat in World War I to train troops, wanted to be sure that in the event of war he "would not be left at home."[63]

In March 1941 Eisenhower moved to become chief of staff of the IX Army Corps, also at Fort Lewis, and received a promotion to the temporary rank of colonel. Three months later, as he prepared his corps for exercises, he received orders to move to the Third Army in San Antonio, and he became the first deputy chief of staff to Lieutenant General Walter Krueger. Eisenhower was soon promoted to chief of staff for the Third Army.[64] Five days after the Japanese attacked Pearl Harbor, Eisenhower received a telephone message from General Marshall, who summoned him for "emergency duty" and told him to "get on a plane and get up here [Washington, D.C.] right away."[65] World War II had begun for the United States, and Eisenhower would start the war as chief of war plans for the General Staff.

In the opening days of the war, Eisenhower came to respect Marshall, although he was worried that he would not get a combat command.[66] One afternoon, after a promotions board meeting, Marshall stopped by Eisenhower's desk and talked about how field commanders were the ones who needed to be promoted in this war, not staff officers. Marshall said: "Take your case, I know that you were recommended by one general for division command, and by another for corps command. That's all very well, I'm glad they have that opinion of you, but you are going to stay right here and fill your position, and that's that. . . . While this may seem like a sacrifice to you, that's the way it must be."[67]

Not believing what he was hearing, and certainly not wanting to be confined to a desk for the duration of a second war, Eisenhower in a fit of anger responded, "General, I'm interested in what you say, but I want you to know that I don't give a damn about your promotion plans as far as I am concerned. I came into this office from the field and I am trying to do my duty. I expect to do so as long as you want me here. If that locks me to a desk for the rest of the war, so be it!"[68]

Three days later General Marshall wrote an impressive recommendation to President Roosevelt stating that Eisenhower was not a "staff officer" in the traditional sense, but rather a "subordinate commander" who merited promotion. Eisenhower became a major general; he would not be confined to a war plans office in Washington, D.C., but, rather, sent to Europe to command.

After his promotion, General Marshall sent Eisenhower to London to serve as commanding general, European Theater of Operations, in June 1942. By this time the war was not going well for the Allies. The Soviets had suffered significant losses to the Germans, who were about to turn toward the south to seize the vast oil fields of the Caucasus. In Africa, Erwin Rommel had been stopped short of his conquest of Egypt, but Tobruk had once again fallen under the control of the Germans. Eisenhower recounts that despite the situation, President Roosevelt, in consultation with British Prime Minister Winston Churchill, had approved the planning process and buildup for the invasion of Europe, which had been given the code name Roundup. Since the actual invasion, Operation Overlord, could not reach fruition until late 1943 or early 1944, Roosevelt and Churchill wanted to launch some ground operation against the Axis in 1942.[69] To meet this requirement, the decision to invade North Africa was made. This was the first major operation that Eisenhower, promoted to lieutenant general, would command.

In planning for Operation Torch, the invasion of North Africa, Eisenhower came face to face with the lack of training, equipment, and shipping needed for the operation.[70] In preparing for the invasion, Eisenhower selected Major General Mark Clark as his deputy. Clark previously had been training II Corps in England in preparation for Operation Roundup. The first major issue was making sure that the troops were trained and that the proper equipment and logistical supply system were in place.[71] The sheer size of the operation and the vast numbers of men, matériel, and equipment impressed Eisenhower as he flew to his operations center at Gibraltar on the eve of the commencement of Operation Torch.[72] The stakes were high; Eisenhower was aware that the operation might "push two neutral countries—Spain and France—into the Axis, and if it failed, any invasion of Europe might be ruled out for years, until after Japan surrendered."[73]

On November 8, 1942, Operation Torch commenced with landing forces divided into three elements. The Western Assault Force, under the command of Major General George S. Patton, with 35,000 American troops, had the objective of seizing Casablanca, Morocco. The Central Task Force, under the command of Major General Lloyd R. Fredendall, began with 18,500 American troops to seize Oran, Algeria. Finally, the Eastern Task Force, under the command of British Lieutenant General Kenneth Arthur Noel Anderson, with 10,000 American troops and 10,000 British troops, was given the objective of Algiers, Algeria. In addition to the ground forces, Eisenhower had three naval task forces, each assigned to support the landings of the respective ground assault forces, as well as an Eastern Air Command and a Western Air Command. By November 12, 1942, the initial objectives had been secured, and Eisenhower, following through on a political arrangement made earlier, told Mark Clark to place French Admiral Jean-François Darlan in charge of French North Africa.[74] Despite significant public outcry over the "Darlan deal," for which Eisenhower thought he would be fired, both Roosevelt and Churchill stood by Eisenhower, even though Darlan was widely believed to have collaborated with the Nazis. All in all, Operation Torch was a success, providing a vast learning experience for Eisenhower. Between Operation Torch and Operation Overlord, however, Eisenhower oversaw Operation Husky, which was the Allied invasion of Sicily.

On July 10, 1943, an armada of 2,500 ships and 180,000 troops from the United States and the Commonwealth countries approached the shore of Sicily, in the largest amphibious operation before Operation Overlord. Eisenhower was in overall command of Operation Husky; Harold Alexander was his deputy for ground forces and lead planner for the invasion. To oversee the actual invasion forces, Eisenhower had George S. Patton in command of the Seventh Army and Bernard Montgomery in command of the British Eighth Army. The plan called for the Allied forces to land at a stretch of beaches between Licata and Syracuse. Although the Allied invasion force met little initial resistance from the Italians, by July 11 the Germans had mounted a fierce counterattack attempting to push the Allies back into the sea. Under the aggressive leadership of Patton and Montgomery, the Allies held fast and secured their beachheads on July 12. Overall, the invasion proved successful for Eisenhower and his subordinate commanders.[75]

On the basis of his experience in Operations Torch and Husky, in December 1943 Eisenhower was named supreme Allied commander, Allied Expeditionary Forces. With this new position, as well as a new promotion to general in February 1943, Eisenhower was in charge of planning for the invasion of the European mainland, which had been a major Allied objective since 1942. He supervised training, equipping, and planning for the invasion force, which consisted of major land elements from the United States, Great Britain, Canada, and France, supported by a vast flotilla of combat ships and support vessels, to be followed by a massive logistical infrastructure that would be necessary to sustain the drive toward Berlin. The plans also incorporated airborne (parachute and glider) troops as well as massive air support from both the U.S. Army Air Forces and the Royal Air Force.[76]

The process of selecting the appropriate landing sites and coordinating the pre-invasion naval gunfire and aerial bombardment, while also creating necessary deception operations to cover the actual landings, seemed like simple tasks compared to the need to train the approximately 130,000 combat troops that would conduct the initial invasion.[77] The final plan for Operation Overlord included an impressive array of Allied forces. The United States committed ground forces that included the First Army, V Corps, VII Corps, 1st Infantry, 4th Infantry, 29th Infantry, 82nd Airborne, and 101st Airborne divisions. These ground forces were supported by the Eighth and Ninth Air Forces, as well as the Navy's Western

Task Force. The objective was to land at Omaha and Utah beaches in Normandy.

In coordination with the U.S. forces, the British sent the Second British Army, British XXX Corps, and the 3rd British Infantry, 6th British Airborne, 50th British Infantry, and 3rd Canadian Infantry divisions to land at Gold, Juno, and Sword beaches. These ground troops were further supported by the Royal Air Force's Second Tactical Air Force and the Royal Navy's Eastern Task Force.

As the day for the invasion neared, Eisenhower sensed that the tactical situation in France was changing, as the number of German ground forces in the area began to increase. He also had serious concerns about the weather and personally made the decision to invade with the words "Okay, we'll go."[78] The decision made, Eisenhower issued a statement to the Allied troops to explain the significance of the operation, saying:

> You are about to embark upon the Great Crusade, toward which we have striven these many months. The eyes of the world are upon you. The hopes and prayers of liberty-loving people everywhere march with you. In company with our brave Allies and brothers-in-arms on other Fronts, you will bring about the destruction of the German war machine, the elimination of Nazi tyranny over the oppressed peoples of Europe, and security for ourselves in a free world. Your task will not be an easy one. Your enemy is well trained, well equipped and battle hardened. He will fight savagely.
>
> But this is the year 1944! Much has happened since the Nazi triumphs of 1940–41. The United Nations have inflicted upon the Germans great defeats, in open battle, man-to-man. Our air offensive has seriously reduced their strength in the air and their capacity to wage war on the ground. Our Home Fronts have given us an overwhelming superiority in weapons and munitions of war, and placed at our disposal great reserves of trained fighting men. The tide has turned! The free men of the world are marching together to Victory!
>
> I have full confidence in your courage and devotion to duty and skill in battle. We will accept nothing less than full Victory!
>
> Good luck! And let us beseech the blessing of Almighty God upon this great and noble undertaking.[79]

General Eisenhower talks with paratroopers from the 101st Airborne Division at Green Common Airfield, England, on June 5, 1944. (Library of Congress)

While publicly expressing the utmost confidence in the Allied effort, privately Eisenhower wrote a letter in which he accepted full responsibility in the event that the invasion failed. In the aftermath of the landings in France on June 6, 1944, and despite the loss of approximately 10,000 men, however, Eisenhower did not need to submit his letter, as the Allies had gained a foothold on the Continent. Though there was still significant fighting to be done before the collapse of the German and Axis powers, Eisenhower had established himself in the annals of military history as the supreme Allied commander who oversaw the successful invasion of Europe.

Eisenhower's success earned him a fifth star in December 1944. For the next five months Eisenhower continued to command the Supreme Headquarters of the Allied Expeditionary Forces (SHAEF), which had been established in Versailles, France. In April 1945 an advanced headquarters opened in Rheims, France, where on May 8,

1945, Eisenhower oversaw the unconditional surrender of the German military, effectively ending the war in Europe.

In the immediate aftermath of the war in Europe, Eisenhower served briefly as military governor of the United States Occupied Zone until asked by President Harry S. Truman to become the Army chief of staff upon General George C. Marshall's retirement. Though not wanting the position, Eisenhower agreed to Truman's request with the proviso that he would not serve the full four-year term, but, rather, only two years.[80] On November 19, 1945, Eisenhower became the Army chief of staff.

Although the war was over, Eisenhower had to preside over the massive demobilization that took place at the end of the war. The Truman administration had publicly established a goal of 700,000 discharges a month, which proved to be impossible to achieve. Eisenhower explained to Truman that the real issue was the need for transportation to get the soldiers home. After working on a demobilization plan, Eisenhower got the Truman administration to restate its demobilization goal of 300,000 soldiers per month.[81] By the end of 1946, just fourteen months after assuming the position of chief of staff, Eisenhower had supervised the largest demobilization in the history of the United States.

After demobilization, Eisenhower supported President Truman's proposal to unify the three military services. To Eisenhower "victory required a single commander with absolute authority to harness the power of ground, air, and naval forces in a way that brought the strengths of each to maximum effectiveness. No duplication of effort, no untapped resources, no inter-service rivalry."[82] Yet despite his vast experience, there was too much entrenched history to move forward with the concept of a unified military. In the end the United States Air Force became a separate military service and the War Department was reorganized under the National Security Act of 1947, which established a unified organization under a secretary of Defense, created the Central Intelligence Agency, and formed a permanent Joint Chiefs of Staff. This action was not quite unification, but it was an attempt to take the lessons learned during war and apply them to the emerging Cold War.

As Eisenhower's tenure as chief of staff neared its end, he was faced with a series of choices. He had several options. The first was to leave active service and enjoy the quiet life. This did not appeal to Eisenhower. The second was an offer to run as Truman's vice presidential candidate in 1948 in an attempt to reverse Truman's slumping approval rating. Again, this did not appeal to Eisenhower, as he had also been approached by the Republicans to run as a Republican candidate for the presidency. A third offer was to become president of Columbia University. Eisenhower finally accepted this offer in June 1948.[83]

While at Columbia, Eisenhower had to become accustomed to a very different pace and protocol. He recounts in *At Ease* that on one of his first attempts to go to his office on a Saturday, which was his custom in the military, he was confronted with a locked door to the building, as well as by an inquiring policemen who did not believe that he was the president of the university, and had apparently never heard of Eisenhower. The issue was resolved when another police officer vouched for the new university president.[84] After a period of transition, Eisenhower settled into the position at Columbia University and began to enjoy the academic life. As 1950 came to a close, Eisenhower received a call from President Truman that would interrupt his tenure at Columbia.

Truman told Eisenhower that the member nations of the newly created North Atlantic Treaty Organization (NATO) had formally requested that Eisenhower be appointed the first commander of NATO's combined military forces. The position, supreme Allied commander of the North Atlantic Treaty Organization, would allow Eisenhower to go back to Europe and command troops once again.[85] Upon accepting the position, however, he found that it was more a political job than a military one. The real purpose of his command was to build international consensus on the validity of NATO and its mission in the early days of the Cold War. After two years of political wrangling, France, the last country to sign the collective security pact, initialed the treaty in May 1952. Eisenhower believed that this act completed his assigned objective and that he could finally "be released from active duty."[86] He retired from service on May 31, 1952, and resigned his commission in July 1952.

Having left active military duty, Eisenhower was courted by both the Democrat and Republican parties during 1951. Eventually, he succumbed to the Republican "Draft Eisenhower" movement and began his run for the presidency.[87] On November 4, 1952, Eisenhower was elected the thirty-fourth president of the United States. One of the major planks of his platform during the campaign had been a promise to end the Korean War. Accordingly, he helped bro-

President Dwight D. Eisenhower. (Library of Congress)

ker a long-term cease-fire in 1953. Eisenhower's two terms as president entailed confrontation with the Soviet Union, race issues in the United States, concerns about the economic stability of the United States, and the start of the space race.

Having begun his presidency by overseeing a cease-fire in Korea, Eisenhower embraced the tenets of NSC-68, which outlined containment as the basic national security strategy for the United

States during the entirety of the Cold War.[88] Seeing the need to maintain a strong military presence in Europe and Asia, Eisenhower outlined a "New Look" policy that emphasized the use of nuclear weapons from the tactical to the strategic levels of war.[89] As a fiscal conservative, Eisenhower was deeply concerned with the extensive monetary outlays needed to rebuild the conventional elements of the U.S. military to compete with the vast manpower advantages of the Soviet Union and the other members of the Warsaw Pact. To compensate for this shortfall, under the New Look Eisenhower emphasized that the U.S. military could get "more bang for its buck" by relying on nuclear weapons to compensate for the conventional force imbalance.[90]

In addition to reliance on the New Look to reshape the U.S. military, Eisenhower supported the concept of Massive Retaliation, which was formally presented by his secretary of State, John Foster Dulles, in 1954. This policy held that the United States needed to move away from the symmetrical containment policies of the Truman administration and embrace asymmetrical containment, founded on nuclear weapons, in an effort to assert a stronger deterrent against Communist expansion. Although it was an effective policy in the period 1954–57, the Soviet Union's launch of *Sputnik* eroded the validity of Massive Retaliation because the enemy now possessed the ability to strike the United States rapidly with intercontinental ballistic missiles, a capability that the Soviet Union had lacked in 1954 when John Foster Dulles announced the policy of Massive Retaliation.[91] Yet Eisenhower steadfastly supported the tenets of the strategy even under increased pressure from General Maxwell Taylor, who argued that it was dangerous and outdated.

A critical and well-known element of Eisenhower's presidency was his support of the development of military and civilian space programs. In the wake of the Soviet Union's launch of *Sputnik* on October 4, 1957, Eisenhower supported the development of the National Aeronautics and Space Administration (NASA). By establishing a civilian agency, as well as supporting the civilian use of space, Eisenhower believed that the United States could use these examples of its technological and engineering capability as critical tools in the Cold War contest with the Soviet Union. His prime objective was to demonstrate to the world that the United States was the world's leader in advanced technology, science, and engineering.[92] Additionally, Eisenhower's support of NASA emerged as a crucial way to establish that the United States was interested in the civilian and peaceful benefits of space and saw no need to arm the heavens.[93]

Though a champion of the civilian space program, Eisenhower remained conservative about the need to stay focused and constrained in the space race, so as not to bankrupt the nation as it tried to respond to the series of space firsts achieved by the Soviet Union. Eisenhower did not want to charge headlong into "space stunts" just for the sake of publicity. Instead, he believed that the United States needed to maintain steadfastly its intended objective, as it would have additional benefits for the nation and its allies in the long-term context of the Cold War. Eisenhower was correct. By the middle of the 1960s, the United States had finally started to win the space race, largely on the basis of the programs begun in the final days of Eisenhower's administration and certainly because of his calm and steadfast leadership.

As president, Eisenhower also had to deal with domestic social issues. In the landmark legal case *Brown v. Board of Education,* the Supreme Court of the United States reversed the legal ruling of segregation that the Supreme Court had outlined in the 1896 case of *Plessy v. Ferguson.* The Court ruled that the concept of "separate but equal" was no longer valid, and Eisenhower had the difficult task of enforcing the Court's ruling.[94] Although the process of full desegregation would extend beyond his tenure as president, Eisenhower took the early step of sending the 101st Airborne Division into Little Rock, Arkansas, to ensure that school desegregation took place in a peaceful and orderly fashion.

During his two terms as president, Eisenhower firmly established the United States as the free world's leader in the ideological struggle with the Soviet Union. Critical to this position was the U.S. military's embrace of a greater reliance on nuclear weapons, as well as streamlining the process of outlining strategy and plans for strategic nuclear warfare.[95] Eisenhower based his strategic planning on the intelligence gathered from manned overflights of the Soviet Union by the Strategic Air Command and the Central Intelligence Agency (CIA), which he had authorized.

Eisenhower did not just brandish a big stick. He also saw the need to use other elements of U.S. power, such as the pursuit of mutual security. Using NATO as the model, Eisenhower negotiated the

Southeast Asian Treaty Organization (SEATO) and the Australia, New Zealand, and United States Pact (ANZUS) to bolster the defensive posture of U.S. allies in the Pacific. In addition to security pacts, Eisenhower also used the CIA in covert operations in Guatemala and Iran to ensure that leftist governments did not gain footholds in Latin America and the Middle East.[96] Again, his objective was to check the expansion of the Soviet Union and Communism.

Domestically, Eisenhower ushered in a period of social and economic transition as the nation settled down to a period of peace in the aftermath of the Korean War. For Eisenhower this entailed the United States maintaining the right balance between the need for national security and the demands of a peacetime economy that fostered economic prosperity. In addition to the economic demands of the nation, Eisenhower had the duty to enforce school desegregation. Despite his strong leadership, Eisenhower had developed a public reputation as a manager of his administration, rather than a strong, imperial president. Historians writing in the 1980s reexamined his presidency and came to the conclusion that Eisenhower had a much greater role in major policy debates, exercising significant control in the decision-making process.[97] This leadership style has been identified as the "hidden-hand" presidency, and Eisenhower's reputation as a strong chief executive has increased.

As a testament to his abilities and keen intellect, in his farewell address Eisenhower warned the United States about the expansion and growth of the "military-industrial complex" and cautioned the nation about the need to maintain the proper balance between the proverbial "guns and butter." After leaving the presidency, Eisenhower retired to his farm in Gettysburg and lived a relatively quiet life. He wrote three books on his life and experiences in war and peace, played golf, tended to his garden, painted, and focused on establishing his presidential library in Abilene, Kansas, which was to be built on the land of his boyhood home. In March 1969 Eisenhower died. His family buried him in April 1969 in the chapel on the grounds of his presidential library.

"Duty, honor, country" are the three words that characterize the influence Dwight D. Eisenhower had not only on the U.S. military, but also on the nation as a whole. From his first days at West Point he dedicated himself to the nation and strove to make it better, leaving a lasting legacy as a military commander and national leader.

Notes

1. Eisenhower was not held in very high regard as a politician when he left the White House in 1961. Rather, the general public and historians tended to rank him as a mediocre president. In 1982, however, the political scientist Fred I. Greenstein published *The Hidden-Hand Presidency* (New York: Basic Books), which fundamentally challenged the traditional interpretations of Eisenhower's leadership style and argued that Eisenhower was a much stronger president than had been perceived.

2. Geoffrey Perret, *Eisenhower* (New York: Random House, 1999), 6; Piers Brendon, *Ike: His Life and Times* (New York: HarperCollins, 1986), 14.

3. Brendon, *Ike,* 16.

4. Perret, *Eisenhower,* 6.

5. Ibid., 7.

6. Ibid.

7. Dwight D. Eisenhower, *At Ease: Stories I Tell to Friends* (Garden City, N.Y.: Doubleday, 1967), 32.

8. Brendon, *Ike,* 21.

9. Ibid., 36.

10. Ibid.

11. Perret, *Eisenhower,* 29.

12. Ibid.

13. Eisenhower, *At Ease,* 41–43; Perret, *Eisenhower,* 27–29; Stephen E. Ambrose, *Eisenhower: Soldier, General of the Army, President-Elect, 1890–1952* (New York: Simon and Schuster, 1983), 33–36.

14. Perret, *Eisenhower,* 31.

15. Brendon, *Ike,* 25–26; Ambrose, *Eisenhower: Soldier,* 38. Edgar Eisenhower was pursuing a law degree at the University of Michigan.

16. Perret, *Eisenhower,* 37; Brendon, *Ike,* 26; Ambrose, *Eisenhower: Soldier,* 38.

17. Ambrose, *Eisenhower: Soldier,* 40–41.

18. Michael Korda, *Ike: An American Hero* (New York: HarperCollins, 2007), 87; Eisenhower, *At Ease,* 4.

19. Eisenhower, *At Ease,* 4.

20. Perret, *Eisenhower,* 49; Ambrose, *Eisenhower: Soldier,* 49.

21. Eisenhower's West Point class had 164 members, 54 of whom rose to the rank of brigadier general. Some of the other prominent members were Vernon Prichard, Charles Ryder, Stafford Irwin, Joseph McNarney, and Hubert Harmon.

22. Eisenhower, *At Ease,* 118; Korda, *Ike,* 114–15.

23. Ambrose, *Eisenhower: Soldier,* 57; Perret, *Eisenhower,* 66.

24. Mark C. Bender, *Watershed at Leavenworth: Dwight D. Eisenhow-*

er and the Command and General Staff School (Fort Leavenworth, Kans.: Combat Studies Institute, 1990), 18; Ambrose, *Eisenhower: Soldier*, 61–62.

25. Ambrose, *Eisenhower: Soldier*, 62; Bender, *Watershed at Leavenworth*, 18.

26. Eisenhower, *At Ease*, 156; also cited in Bender, *Watershed at Leavenworth*, 20.

27. Brendon, *Ike*, 46; Bender, *Watershed at Leavenworth*, 20.

28. Eisenhower, *At Ease*, 156.

29. Matthew F. Holland, *Eisenhower between the Wars: The Making of a General and Statesman* (Westport, Conn.: Praeger, 2001), 73–74; Bender, *Watershed at Leavenworth*, 20.

30. Perret, *Eisenhower*, 81; Eisenhower, *At Ease*, 173.

31. Korda, *Ike*, 163–70; Holland, *Eisenhower between the Wars*, 17.

32. Eisenhower, *At Ease*, 187.

33. Bender, *Watershed at Leavenworth*, 24; Holland, *Eisenhower between the Wars*, 100–104.

34. Perret, *Eisenhower*, 89.

35. Ambrose, *Eisenhower: Soldier*, 77.

36. Korda, *Ike*, 168–74; Ambrose, *Eisenhower: Soldier*, 78–82.

37. Holland, *Eisenhower between the Wars*, 53; Bender, *Watershed at Leavenworth*, 37.

38. Bender, *Watershed at Leavenworth*, 37; Ambrose, *Eisenhower: Soldier*, 79–82.

39. Ambrose, *Eisenhower: Soldier*, 79–82; Bender, *Watershed at Leavenworth*, 37.

40. Eisenhower, *At Ease*, 197–98; Ambrose, *Eisenhower: Soldier*, 78.

41. Eisenhower, *At Ease*, 198.

42. Ambrose, *Eisenhower: Soldier*, 78–79; Eisenhower, *At Ease*, 199.

43. Eisenhower, *At Ease*, 200.

44. Ibid., 201.

45. Although these officers taught at CGSC the year Eisenhower attended the course, it is difficult to discern if they instructed him specifically.

46. R. Manning Ancell and Christine M. Miller, *The Biographic Dictionary of World War II Generals and Flag Officers, the U.S. Armed Forces* (Westport, Conn.: Greenwood Press, 1996), 375, 311, 96, 5, 307.

47. Bender, *Watershed at Leavenworth*, 54.

48. Ibid.

49. Eisenhower, *At Ease*, 204; Brendon, *Ike*, 55.

50. Eisenhower, *At Ease*, 205–7.

51. Ibid.; Perret, *Eisenhower*, 104.

52. Eisenhower, *At Ease*, 208.

53. Perret, *Eisenhower*, 10; Eisenhower, *At Ease*, 208–9.

54. Eisenhower, *At Ease,* 211; Korda, *Ike,* 188.

55. Eisenhower, *At Ease,* 210–12; Perret, *Eisenhower,* 107.

56. Holland, *Eisenhower between the Wars,* 117.

57. Korda, *Ike,* 207–27; Eisenhower, *At Ease,* 213.

58. Eisenhower, *At Ease,* 214.

59. Ibid., 216.

60. Ibid., 215–18.

61. Ibid., 237.

62. Ibid.

63. Ibid., 249.

64. Holland, *Eisenhower between the Wars,* 111–12; Brendon, *Ike,* 73–74.

65. Brendon, *Ike,* 73–74; Eisenhower, *At Ease,* 245.

66. Korda, *Ike,* 243–67.

67. Eisenhower, *At Ease,* 249.

68. Ibid.

69. Ibid., 251.

70. Korda, *Ike,* 297–307.

71. David Eisenhower, *Eisenhower at War, 1943–1945* (New York: Random House, 1986), 101–12; Korda, *Ike,* 469–74; Ambrose, *Eisenhower: Soldier,* 180–237.

72. The pilot who flew Eisenhower in a B-17 to Gibraltar was Paul Tibbets, who would later be the pilot in command of the *Enola Gay* when it dropped the first atomic bomb on Hiroshima in August 1945.

73. Perret, *Eisenhower,* 177.

74. Brendon, *Ike,* 93–98; Ambrose, *Eisenhower: Soldier,* 204–10; Perret, *Eisenhower,* 181.

75. Perret, *Eisenhower,* 225–26.

76. Ambrose, *Eisenhower: Soldier,* 281–312.

77. Ibid., 201–312; this number does not include the 36,000 U.S. Navy sailors who assisted in the transport operation.

78. Eisenhower, *Eisenhower at War,* 251.

79. "General Eisenhower's Message Sent Just Prior to the Invasion," www.army.mil/d-day/message.html (accessed November 19, 2011).

80. Ambrose, *Eisenhower: Soldier,* 433–57; Perret, *Eisenhower,* 360.

81. Perret, *Eisenhower,* 362; Brendon, *Ike,* 194–96.

82. Perret, *Eisenhower,* 363.

83. Korda, *Ike,* 611–16; Perret, *Eisenhower,* 375–76.

84. Eisenhower, *At Ease,* 338.

85. Ibid., 361.

86. Ibid., 377.

87. Tom Wicker, *Dwight D. Eisenhower* (New York: Times Books, 2002), 10–16; Stephen E. Ambrose, *Eisenhower: The President* (New York: Simon and Schuster, 1984), 13–35.

88. "NSC 68: United States Objectives and Programs for National Security, April 14, 1950," in *American Cold War Strategy: Interpreting NSC 68*, ed. Ernest R. May (Boston: Bedford, 1993), 23–82.

89. Ambrose, *Eisenhower: The President*, 171–72.

90. Ingo Trauschweizer, *The Cold War U.S. Army: Building Deterrence for Limited War* (Lawrence: University Press of Kansas, 2008), 28–47; Ambrose, *Eisenhower: The President*, 224–26.

91. For in-depth histories of the effect of *Sputnik*, see Robert A. Divine, *The Sputnik Challenge: Eisenhower's Response to the Soviet Satellite* (New York: Oxford University Press, 1993); Rip Bulkeley, *The Sputniks Crisis and Early United States Space Policy: A Critique of the Historiography of Space* (Bloomington: Indiana University Press, 1991).

92. Divine, *The Sputnik Challenge*, 113–27.

93. David N. Spires, "From Eisenhower to Kennedy: The National Space Program and the Air Force's Quest for the Military Space Mission," in *Beyond Horizons: A Half Century of Air Force Space Leadership*, ed. Spires et al. (Maxwell Air Force Base, Ala.: Air University Press, 1998), 50–95.

94. Chester J. Pach Jr. and Elmo Richardson, *The Presidency of Dwight D. Eisenhower*, rev. ed. (Lawrence: University Press of Kansas, 1991), 150–55; Wicker, *Eisenhower*, 46–55; Ambrose, *Eisenhower: The President*, 414–26.

95. Scott D. Sagan, *Moving Targets: Nuclear Strategy and National Security* (Princeton: Princeton University Press, 1989), 18–30.

96. John Ranelagh, *The Agency: The Rise and Decline of the CIA* (New York: Simon and Schuster, 1986), 260–68.

97. Greenstein, *The Hidden-Hand Presidency*, 55–154.

References

Ambrose, Stephen E. *Eisenhower: Soldier, General of the Army, President-Elect, 1890–1952*. New York: Simon and Schuster, 1983.

———. *Eisenhower: The President*. New York: Simon and Schuster, 1984.

Ancell, R. Manning, and Christine M. Miller. *The Biographic Dictionary of World War II Generals and Flag Officers, the U.S. Armed Forces*. Westport, Conn.: Greenwood Press, 1996.

Bender, Mark C. *Watershed at Leavenworth: Dwight D. Eisenhower and the Command and General Staff School*. Fort Leavenworth, Kans.: Combat Studies Institute, 1990.

Brendon, Piers. *Ike: His Life and Times*. New York: HarperCollins, 1986.

Bulkeley, Rip. *The Sputniks Crisis and Early United States Space Policy: A Critique of the Historiography of Space*. Bloomington: Indiana University Press, 1991.

Divine, Robert A. *The Sputnik Challenge: Eisenhower's Response to the Soviet Satellite.* New York: Oxford University Press, 1993.

Eisenhower, David. *Eisenhower at War, 1943–1945.* New York: Wings Books, 1991.

Eisenhower, Dwight D. *At Ease: Stories I Tell to Friends.* Garden City, N.Y.: Doubleday, 1967.

Greenstein, Fred I. *The Hidden-Hand Presidency.* New York: Basic Books, 1982.

Holland, Matthew F. *Eisenhower between the Wars: The Making of a General and Statesman.* Westport, Conn.: Praeger, 2001.

Korda, Michael. *Ike: An American Hero.* New York: HarperCollins, 2007.

Pach, Chester J., Jr., and Elmo Richardson. *The Presidency of Dwight D. Eisenhower.* Revised edition. Lawrence: University Press of Kansas, 1991.

Perret, Geoffrey. *Eisenhower.* New York: Random House, 1999.

Sagan, Scott D. *Moving Targets: Nuclear Strategy and National Security.* Princeton: Princeton University Press, 1989.

Trauschweizer, Ingo. *The Cold War U.S. Army: Building Deterrence for Limited War.* Lawrence: University Press of Kansas, 2008.

Wicker, Tom. *Dwight D. Eisenhower.* New York: Times Books, 2002.

5

Henry H. "Hap" Arnold

John M. Curatola

Henry "Hap" Arnold holds a unique place in the pantheon of five-star generals. Not only does Arnold have the distinction of being named the only General of the Air Force, a title bestowed on him after the U.S. Air Force became its own separate service in 1947, but he also held the title General of the Army when he was appointed his fifth star on December 21, 1944, while the Army Air Forces were still part of the U.S. Army. Though he hardly ever wore the blue Air Force uniform, he is largely considered the father of the U.S. Air Force and a chief architect in the development of American airpower. His vision, drive, and perseverance were key elements in creating the largest and most potent air armada the world has ever seen.

Born in Gladwyne, Pennsylvania, on June 25, 1886, Henry Harley "Hap" Arnold was the second son and third of five children born to Dr. Herbert Arnold, a surgeon, and his wife, Louise. The family moved to Ardmore, Pennsylvania, in 1890. Henry's father was a strict Mennonite and a veteran of the Spanish-American War; he was a stern man with a strong work ethic, a low tolerance for horseplay, and a penchant for military service.[1] A longtime member of a Pennsylvania National Guard cavalry unit, Dr. Arnold served with distinction as a reserve officer until retiring in 1922.[2] He wanted his oldest son, Thomas, to pursue a military education and attend the U.S. Military Academy at West Point. The doctor's acquaintance with the local congressman gave him hope that his firstborn would win an appointment to the prestigious institution. Thomas, however, took the unusually courageous stance of refusing to abide by his father's wishes and declined to take the West Point entrance examination. Instead, Thomas chose to study electrical engineering at Pennsylvania State University. With his oldest son steadfast in his decision not to pursue a military career, and having no other recourse, Dr. Arnold looked to Henry.[3]

In his early years Henry was not a great student and was more interested in hunting, athletics, and horses. During his teen years, at his parents' behest, he envisioned a career in the ministry.[4] But after Thomas refused to take the West Point entrance exam, Dr. Arnold looked to young Henry to fulfill his wish for military offspring and take the exam. Despite his lackluster academic performance as a high school student, Henry scored surprisingly well on the exam and placed second within the congressional district. Fortunately for the Arnolds, the applicant who placed first was married, which disqualified him from attending the Military Academy.[5] As a result, in 1903 at the age of seventeen, Henry left Ardmore and started his plebe year at West Point as a member of the class of 1907.

As he had in his earlier academic experience, Arnold proved an unexceptional student. West Point's academic program was one of the toughest in the country, and his highest overall class standing was only 61st of 111 in his junior year; he never rose to the rank of cadet corporal.[6] He did find time, however, to play sports and indulge in his passion for horses. He earned a position as a halfback on the Army's scrimmage football squad and played backup on the varsity squad. He also developed a passion for polo, which coincided with his larger goal of being assigned to the Cavalry branch after graduation. According to Arnold, being assigned to the Cavalry was his only reason for attending West Point, as he described the Cavalry as "the last romantic thing left on the earth."[7]

"Pewt" or "Benny," as he was called by his West Point classmates, was known for his excessive use of profanity. His most notable achievement at the Academy, however, was his leadership of a clandestine student organization known as the "Black Hand." The Black Hand's primary mission was staging and executing pranks and practical jokes on the Academy's grounds. Arnold's most prominent operation came when he lit off a series of fireworks at night that spelled out "1907—Never Again" (1907 was his class's graduating year).[8] Unfortunately for Arnold, he ignited the display just in time to be identified by passersby. For this event he spent many hours "walking the area" as punishment.

When it came time for branch assignment, and despite his overall mediocre performance, Arnold was sure his final class standing, 66th of 111, was good enough for him to be assigned to the Cavalry. Returning home after graduation in June 1907, however, he was dismayed to receive a letter assigning him to the Infantry.[9] Despite his own and his father's attempts to challenge this assignment, they were unable to change it, and Arnold finally accepted his fate. In the process of trying to change his branch assignment, he was afforded the opportunity to pick his first duty station. Eventually Arnold picked the Philippines.

Once in the Philippines, Second Lieutenant Arnold was assigned to the 29th Regiment at Fort McKinley, near Manila, and quickly found the schedule tedious and boring.[10] The routine of an Infantry officer at the fort consisted largely of drill, target practice, administrative duties, and long siestas in the afternoon to avoid the tropical heat, followed by social obligations in the evening.[11] Fortunately for Arnold, an opening became available on a mapping detail designed to survey areas around the islands of Luzon and Corregidor. He quickly jumped at the opportunity and spent months in the Philippine jungle, or *bosque,* as he called it (Spanish for woodland), riding horses and living outdoors.[12] He found the work exciting and frequently came in contact with, as he put it, "monkeys, crocodiles, and the short wolley [sic] haired negritoes galore."[13] Furthermore, the group routinely found what he called "itinerant Japanese peddlers or botanists whose best specimens always happened to be growing just where we had set up our instruments."[14] This assignment not only offered relief from the mundane schedule of garrison duty, but also put him under the charge of Captain Arthur S. Cowan, who was so impressed by the young lieutenant that he remembered Arnold years later and offered him a unique opportunity.

In 1909, after two years in the Philippines, the 29th Infantry Regiment finished its tour and rotated back to the United States. Arnold, having saved some money, decided to take the circuitous way home and sailed to the United States via Hong Kong, Singapore, and Egypt, followed by a tour through Europe. Upon its return, the 29th Regiment was stationed at Fort Jay on Governors Island, New York.[15] Again bored by the daily routine of garrison life, Arnold took the entrance exam for the Ordnance Corps in an effort to switch branches, with the hope of accelerated promotion in that part of the Army.

Other forces were at work, however, and in March 1911 Congress approved $25,000 for military aviation and procured three Wright and two Curtiss airframes.[16] The purchase of the Wright aircraft also included the training of the pilots.[17] Fortunately for Arnold, his mapping expedition commander, Arthur Cowan, now posted to Washington, D.C., had the task of assigning two officers to receive flight training. Remembering Lieutenant Arnold, Cowan sent him a letter offering him the opportunity to attend flight training at the Wright Company's aircraft factory in Dayton, Ohio. Upon receiving the offer, Arnold jumped at the chance and reported to his commanding officer that he was ordered to attend the flight-training program. To this news his superior at Governors Island replied, "Young man, I know of no better way to commit suicide."[18] Undaunted, in April 1911 Arnold reported to the Wright factory.

Arriving at Dayton, he and a fellow student, Lieutenant Thomas Milling, met both Orville and Wilbur Wright. They received no flight instruction from either of the famous brothers, but both officers became welcome guests at the Wright home and were often invited to Sunday dinner. Though the Wrights did provide some ground instruction, Arnold's flight instructor was Art "Owl" Welsh, who took the fledgling aviator on his first flight on May 3, 1911.[19] Arnold soloed ten days later, and after some twenty-eight lessons and a mere three hours and forty-eight minutes of total flight time, his training was considered complete.[20] He did not receive his official military aviator rating, however, until July 22, 1912.[21]

After completion of flight training, he and Milling headed to College Park, Maryland, along with two Wright Model B Flyers, to set up the Signal Corps's flight school. Starting from scratch, the two aviators set about writing manuals and standardizing procedures and nomenclature for both flight and maintenance operations. The newly graduated aviators became flight instructors themselves and trained their new commanding officer, Captain Charles Chandler, and his adjutant, Lieutenant Roy Kirtland. During this tour, in June 1912, Arnold experienced his first brush with death as an aviator. He and Kirtland, flying a heavily loaded Burgess-Wright "tractor" floatplane from Salem, Massachusetts, were forced to land at South Duxbury, Massachusetts, because of the weather. Early aircraft were notoriously underpowered, and every knot of airspeed and ounce of horsepower could make the difference between life and death. They stalled on takeoff and crashed near Plymouth. Taking off without the aid of a headwind for additional lift, the two pilots briefly became airborne, only to be hurtled into the water after stalling. The two hung on to the wreckage of their aircraft until the Coast Guard eventually rescued them. Arnold joked that this crash constituted the "second landing on Plymouth Rock."[22]

Hap Arnold in a Wright Flyer in Dayton, Ohio, 1912. (Courtesy of the National Museum of the U.S. Air Force)

It was during this tour that in October 1912 Arnold won the very first Mackay Trophy, an award given annually for the most meritorious military flight of the year. In this endeavor, both Arnold and Milling were scheduled to fly in the vicinity of Washington, D.C., in an attempt to spot ground troops participating in military exercises.

Experiencing technical difficulties and dealing with a stiff wind, Milling failed to complete his planned flight, leaving only Arnold to do the reconnaissance. Arnold spotted the ground forces and reported his observations to exercise officials. Of greater importance was that this flight provided some definition to the role that aviation might play in the military, that of aerial reconnaissance.[23] Though many saw early aviation as a useless endeavor, airmen at the time struggled to prove airpower's value as a military application. Arnold played a significant role in developing nascent aviation capabilities and missions.

The following month, on November 5, at Fort Riley, Kansas, Arnold experienced another brush with death that shook him to his core. Flying a Wright Model C aircraft, Arnold and a passenger were participating in field maneuver exercises when the aircraft went into a flat spin and plunged some three hundred feet in just ten seconds.[24] The aircraft recovered just above the ground as Arnold was able to gain control of the plane. The experience was so frightening, however, that he landed in a nearby field and proceeded to walk back to the barracks instead of flying the plane to the airfield. Upon seeing Milling after the episode, Arnold quipped, "That's it, a man doesn't face death twice."[25] He requested a leave of absence from flying duties and wrote to his commanding officer, "At the present time my nervous system is in such condition that I will not get in any machine"; he further requested a month's leave.[26] Apparently, Arnold's enthusiasm for aviation was quickly dashed in the wake of this near-death experience. But his avoidance of flying responsibilities would eventually abate, and he would go back to flying.

After the accident, and back in Washington, he worked as the aide to the chief of the Army Signal Corps. His duties allowed him to avoid flying and also provided an opportunity to marry Eleanor "Bee" Pool in September 1913. The two had courted intermittently since their first meeting in 1907, when she had visited West Point. Since then the couple had remained in recurrent contact. Though shy around women, Arnold was taken with Bee and even visited her while she was vacationing in Europe when he took his long journey back from the Philippines in 1909. The marriage also facilitated his avoidance of flying duties, as it was customary at the time for married men to be removed from flight status.[27]

The assignment in Washington was an important step in his professional development. Working for the chief of the Signal Corps helped him not only gain insight into the workings of the federal government, but also meet the major aviation industrialists of the age. He maintained his friendship with the Wright brothers and also came to know Glenn Curtiss and others in the aviation field. His personal relationship with major actors in the U.S. aviation industry would become a key component in the growth of American airpower. Throughout his career he pushed for more advanced aircraft designs, more powerful engines, and increased aircraft performance. Though he was no engineer, he had a workmanlike understanding of aerodynamics. He constantly advocated for faster and more capable airplanes and the development of aviation technology.[28] Arnold's posting in Washington gave him unique insights on how to increase and develop military forces while dealing with the nuances of the federal bureaucracy.

Following his tour in Washington, Arnold was again posted to the Philippines and, with his new bride, arrived in Manila in January 1914. Though he had little to do with the aviation detachment at Fort McKinley, this posting had the Arnolds living next door to young Lieutenant George Marshall. In dealing with Marshall during this period, Arnold gained a quick appreciation for the future chief of staff's skills and abilities. Observing Marshall during exercises in the Philippines, Arnold noted, "[Marshall] holds the job as the main guy for this detachment and tells colonels where to take their regiments and what to do with them . . . everyone agrees that he has the ability to handle the situation so there is no hard feelings."[29] Even more prescient with regard to Marshall and his talents is that Arnold told Bee that Marshall "will be a future Chief of Staff of the Army."[30] He maintained a cordial and respectful relationship with Marshall that would become all the more important during World War II.

Upon completion of their tour in the Philippines, the Arnolds set sail for the United States. While en route, Arnold received a telegram asking him to take a posting at North Island, San Diego, and return to flight status, with the promise of a promotion to captain. Despite his earlier fears of flying following his near-fatal crash at Fort Riley, Arnold accepted the job as the post supply officer at Rockwell Field in May 1916.[31] His initial responsibilities at Rockwell did not require much flying, but by November 1916 he had requalified as an aviator.

It was during this tour that Arnold had the first of a number of conflicts in his career with his immediate superiors. Arnold's boss during this incident was Colonel William A. Glassford. When two fellow aviators went missing, Arnold supposedly conducted an unauthorized search for the two men that violated the wishes of his superior. Arnold had assumed that he had authorization to search for the missing aviators, whereas Glassford argued he had given Arnold no such permission. Though Glassford eventually gave authorization for a rescue flight, he did so only after a long delay. Glassford was later reprimanded for his indecision and delay, but Arnold would feel the repercussions of his own actions, which were perceived as contrary to the wishes of his boss. Arnold's subsequent efficiency report reflected the tension between the two; according to Arnold, that report was "so rotten that it made me stink."[32] This was not the last time Arnold would clash with a superior, but, as it turned out, the adverse efficiency report did not retard Arnold's career.

After a short posting in Panama, Arnold was detailed to the War Department, where he was serving when America entered World War I. Assigned to the Signal Corps Aviation Section, Arnold was promoted to the temporary rank of colonel in August 1917. Despite his requests for a posting to Europe to participate in the war, he remained in the United States to plan and organize the development of America's wartime air fleet. Arnold eventually made it to France, but he arrived at the front literally on the day the war ended. Despite his lack of combat experience and his disappointment over spending the war stateside, Arnold gained a unique appreciation of American production capacity and issues regarding the development of large organizations. He saw firsthand the many requirements for building a large air fleet and realized that an air force required not just planes and pilots, but mechanics, hangars, training programs, maintenance and industrial capacity, all working in harmony through efficient management and organization.[33] He also saw that the United States had not been prepared for the war. Arnold would not forget the lessons of World War I and the lack of American preparation.

He returned from Europe in December 1918, and in the following year he oversaw postwar demobilization efforts in the western United States, during which the Air Service shrank from a wartime high of 190,000 personnel to only 27,000 by June 1919.[34] In January 1920 Arnold reverted to his permanent rank of captain, but by July of the same year he was promoted to major. During this time Arnold had two exceptional officers under his command who would prove key leaders in the rise of the U.S. airpower, Major Carl Spaatz and Lieutenant Ira Eaker. Spaatz would serve as the head of Strategic Air Forces in both Europe and the Pacific during World War II, and Eaker became the commanding general of the U.S. Eighth Air Force at the beginning of the strategic bombing offensive in Europe. Arnold's relationship with Eaker was unique. Though Eaker was Arnold's junior, he was schooled as a journalist and was a skilled writer. The two men collaborated on writing three books addressing airpower's utility and advocating aviation development to the general public.

In 1919 Arnold experienced yet another crash. While he was flying a French LePere biplane, the aircraft suffered a structural failure, but it remained flyable. Arnold carefully flew the plane home and gingerly landed. As he was taxiing, however, the plane's fuselage broke in two, and he was thrown forward, the safety belt digging into his abdomen, which he claimed caused internal injuries. Because of this mishap, he frequently suffered from indigestion.[35] After experiencing gastric ulcers, he was temporarily grounded from July to October 1922. Moreover, physical maladies continued to affect the Arnold household. In July 1923 his son Bill contracted a near-fatal case of scarlet fever, and his two-year-old son, John, fell ill and died after suffering a ruptured appendix. The stress of these events, combined with the lingering effects of her other medical disorders, took their toll on Bee, forcing her to return home to Ardmore for rest and recuperation.[36]

After various postings on the West Coast, Arnold was ordered to attend the Army Industrial College starting in August 1924. This assignment was fortunate, as the school was located in Washington, D.C., and put him closer to Bee and the family residing in Ardmore. Combined with his experiences from World War I, Arnold found the school useful and stated that it "was to stand me in good stead in later years."[37] Following graduation in January 1925, Arnold was assigned as chief of information for the chief of the Air Service, Major General Mason Patrick. This was propitious timing for Arnold, as it put him in the center of the interwar arguments regarding the roles and missions of the various military services, and especially the debate over battleships versus aircraft.[38]

This assignment not only had Arnold working in Washington

again, but also introduced him to the importance of information, the press, and publicity. Arnold became acutely aware that the advancement of aviation required press coverage, which in turn could foster public support and, most important, funding. This funding, he knew, was the seed corn for advances in aviation technology. Additionally, public support was required if there was ever to be a separate, independent air force. For these reasons, he constantly pushed to publicize the accomplishments and capabilities of the Air Corps.

In 1921 Brigadier General Billy Mitchell had sunk the German battleship *Ostfriesland* and demonstrated the vulnerability of ships to air attack. His unrestrained advocacy of airpower, however, forced Army leaders to "exile" him to a somewhat remote posting at Fort Sam Houston, Texas. Still voicing his opinions, in 1925 Mitchell was openly critical of American military leadership with regard to the slow growth of aviation, and in the autumn the general was the subject of a well-publicized court-martial. Before the legal proceedings began, Arnold had been a close friend and associate of Mitchell, and the two agreed on many ideas regarding airpower. This affiliation went so far that Arnold testified at the proceedings in Mitchell's behalf.[39] Arnold hoped Mitchell would temper his words and fall in line with military precedent. But to the dismay of Arnold and others, Mitchell remained steadfast in his zeal and was found guilty of insubordination on December 17, 1925. This verdict would have repercussions on Arnold.

During his time in the Information Office, Arnold provided information to both Congress and the press in an effort to garner support for military aviation.[40] Though this campaign seemed to make good sense to help the cause for airpower, General Patrick took issue with Arnold's actions and those of other officers. Patrick believed that Arnold and others acted "entirely without his [Patrick's] knowledge, and through mistaken zeal," and argued that these officers attempted to influence congressional actions inappropriately.[41] This became an issue for Patrick only after Mitchell's well-publicized court-martial, however. Before Mitchell's trial, Patrick warned Arnold about his close association with Mitchell and the potential effect it might have on his career. In an attempt to distance himself from his pro-Mitchell subordinate following the guilty verdict, Patrick gave Arnold a choice of either resigning from the Army or facing his own court-martial for passing information to Congress and the media without express permission.[42] Patrick gave Arnold only twenty-four hours to make his decision.

Much as he had in San Diego, Arnold again found himself at odds with his superior. Given a Hobson's choice, Arnold decided to call the general's bluff and request a court-martial. Possibly not willing to endure another public legal proceeding surrounding the Air Service and not wanting to risk potential personal and professional embarrassment, Patrick decided not to court-martial Arnold. Patrick "exiled" his subordinate to a distant post, as Mitchell had been, rather than force him from the service.[43] By February 1926 the Arnold family was at Fort Riley, Kansas, which by chance was commanded by Brigadier General Ewing E. Booth, a judge in the Mitchell court-martial.[44]

Although Arnold did not know what kind of reception he would receive at Fort Riley, and despite the manner in which he had left Washington, the tour at the Cavalry post proved to be one of the most enjoyable in his career. Arnold assumed command of the 16th Observation Squadron and was warmly welcomed by Booth and the other officers at the post. The squadron initially had only a few tired DH-4s and JN-4 Jenny aircraft, but Arnold made the most of his assets and provided reconnaissance services to units throughout the Midwest.[45] Despite his exiled status, he still served as an advocate for aviation by instructing promising officers who were attending the Cavalry School at Fort Riley on the use of the airplane in support of ground maneuvers. He incorporated aviation into the school curriculum and influenced students who might one day become general officers.[46]

During this tour Arnold was given the task of providing airmail service to President Calvin Coolidge while the chief executive vacationed in the Black Hills of South Dakota, a job that brought out his creative management skills. Arnold was instructed to provide mail delivery to the president every Tuesday and Thursday morning.[47] Knowing the unpredictable nature of midwestern weather patterns and flying conditions, Arnold adroitly had half of the daily mail held back by the ground crews so that there would always be something to deliver to the president on Tuesdays and Thursdays.[48] The mail may have been late, but there was at least an uninterrupted flow.[49] Accomplishing the mission, Arnold earned a letter of commendation from the secretary of War.

By the time he arrived at Fort Riley, Arnold was reaching his twentieth year of military service, thereby making him eligible for retirement. During this tour, Pan American Airways offered Arnold an employment opportunity. As aviation became more popular, the idea of air travel began to grow and airlines began to appear. One of the largest carriers was Pan American, and its president, Juan Trippe, personally called the Arnold residence seeking his services. Arnold would have done well financially if he had decided to retire and accept the job. Despite the promising offer, and concerned about the future of American military aviation, he declined, stating, "I couldn't very well quit the service under fire."[50]

Arnold did so well in his exile tour that General Booth recommended him for a seat at the Army's prestigious Command and General Staff College (CGSC) at Fort Leavenworth, Kansas. In his recommendation Booth wrote, "I consider that the progress in training between the Air Corps and the other combat units of this post has been of exceptional value and is improving all the time. His [Arnold's] method of instruction and training of observers, 90 of whom are taking the course here, is exceptionally good. . . . I shall be very sorry to see Major Arnold leave this post but feel that his excellent services here entitle him to as favorable recommendation as I can give him."[51]

Unfortunately, the commandant of the school at Leavenworth, Brigadier General Edward L. King, who was also a member of the Mitchell court-martial panel, thought that Arnold's presence might be a distraction to the other students attending the ground-centric school, and discouraged Arnold's attendance. Despite King's reservations, Arnold attended the course but found the overall curriculum prosaic and thought that the aviation curriculum was both lacking and outdated; Army doctrine at the time did not give aviation a significant support role in ground operations. One evening after class he told Bee, "Well we fought the battle of Gettysburg again today, and guess who won. Right, Meade did it again, but think what Lee could have done with just one Wright airplane."[52] The experience Arnold had gained at Fort Riley, however, allowed him to surprise his Cavalry classmates by his understanding of their tactics and his ability to withstand long rides in the saddle.[53]

While Arnold attended the course, a fellow airman crashed an aircraft into the Missouri River. General King called the aviators in the class into his office and began to admonish them about their flying skills and ability.[54] Being lectured about flying by a man who

Major Arnold, 1927. (Courtesy of the National Museum of the U.S. Air Force)

was not an aviator himself did not sit well with Arnold. After the lecture, and while within earshot of the general, Arnold said, "That guy doesn't know a damned thing about flying."[55] According to one account, the general grabbed Arnold by the belt and told him to take the comment back, to which Arnold replied, "No, Sir, you don't know anything about flying and you can't tell these men how to fly."[56]

Despite this incident with the general, Arnold performed well at the college. Perhaps to further prod the general, Arnold wrote a paper addressing how topics such as air operations should be included in the curriculum of the college.[57] Ironically, years afterward, in 1931, Arnold met General King again, and the senior officer informed the junior that he "appreciated very much the paper [he] had submitted . . . outlining . . . ideas of the proper instruction in air operations at the Command and General Staff School."[58] Arnold's experience at CGSC had been a disappointment, and when it came time for graduation, he could not leave the post fast enough. On graduation day in 1929, Arnold attended the formal ceremonies alone. Bee and the kids waited in the car outside the building, with the engine running, so that after the graduation ceremony "he could get out of the goddamned place just as fast as possible."[59] Nevertheless, he had made the acquaintance of a number of fellow students with whom he would work again in later assignments.

After graduation the Arnolds headed for the Fairfield Air Depot at Dayton, Ohio, where he assumed responsibility for managing the distribution of aviation-related supplies and scheduled maintenance of aircraft. During this assignment, he, like the rest of America, felt the effect of the stock market crash and the beginning of the Great Depression. He lost much of his own personal savings, but by remaining in the service and not having jumped at Pan American Airways' offer, he at least remained employed. The same could not be said for both his parents and his in-laws, however, who lost much of their holdings and were financially ruined. It was also during this period that Arnold's mother passed away, in January 1931.[60] Though his mother, as well as Bee, had always referred to him as "Sunny," after his mother's death he began to sign his correspondence with the nickname "Hap."[61] Many speculate that the nickname was short for "Happy," but the origin of this nickname remains a mystery.[62] So does the reason for his choosing to assume the new nickname after his mother's death. Regardless of its origins or the rationale for its use, Hap became the nickname most closely associated with him.

In 1931 Arnold, promoted to lieutenant colonel, was once again sent to the West Coast and this time assumed command of an operational flight detachment at March Field, near Riverside, California. In this assignment Arnold made the most of his proximity to Hollywood and used his command to publicize airpower as much as possible. Holding air shows and courting celebrities at March Field put the Air Corps in public view while garnering much favorable press.[63] As he had learned in his time in Washington, publicity was a key component in the development of American aviation. In addition to the public relations efforts, this command also reunited Arnold with both Spaatz and Eaker and offered him the opportunity to work with other talented officers destined for the flag-grade ranks.

This assignment again found Arnold at odds with his superior. On March 10, 1933, nearby Long Beach experienced a 6.4-magnitude earthquake that killed some 115 people and caused $40 million in property damage. In an effort to assist, Arnold authorized the use of Army trucks and supplies and dispatched them to the stricken area. By the organizational command structure of the time, however, use of Army materials for such an effort fell under the authorization of the 9th Corps Area, of which General Malin Craig, located in San Francisco, was in charge. Arnold had inadvertently violated command protocols, and Craig summoned Arnold to his office to explain his actions. Arnold flew up to San Francisco to meet with Craig. As a result of this meeting, Craig came away with a favorable impression of Arnold, forgave him for overstepping his authority, and established a friendly professional relationship with him. Nothing further came of Arnold's unauthorized use of equipment. What Arnold did not know at the time was that he was establishing a rapport with a future Army chief of staff.

During this assignment, Arnold again made a name for himself as an aviator by leading a flight of newly designed Martin B-10 bombers from Washington, D.C., to Fairbanks, Alaska. This public relations event came on the heels of the airmail debacle that occurred when the Army Air Corps was found woefully deficient in providing scheduled postal services in early 1934. The B-10 mission was designed to counter the Air Corps's bad publicity resulting from the airmail incident and to publicize its new advanced, all-metal monoplane bomber. Furthermore, the flight was made to display

Arnold in front of a B-10 from his 1934 Alaskan expedition. (Courtesy of the
National Museum of the U.S. Air Force)

the capability of the service to conduct long-range missions. Though Arnold was named the mission commander well after planning had begun, he understood the logistics required for such an event and ensured the availability of spare parts and other supplies during the operation. On July 19, 1934, ten bombers left Washington, D.C., covering some 800 miles a day; all aircraft arrived at their destination.[64] While in Alaska, the flight photographed more than 20,000 miles of wilderness, including Mount McKinley.[65] During the deployment, one pilot mishandled the fuel switches on takeoff, causing the bomber's engines to cut off owing to fuel starvation.[66] The powerless plane flew into a lake, where most of the damage came from its partial submersion.[67] Because of Arnold's logistical planning and some very capable mechanics, however, the plane was recovered and quickly made airworthy. All ten B-10s flew back to Washington, D.C., on August 20, to much fanfare. For this mission Arnold received a second Mackay Trophy and the Distinguished Flying Cross.

Despite the acclaim Arnold received for the 1934 Alaska flight, he was chagrined to find that he had not been selected for promotion to brigadier general. Less than a year later, however, in March 1935, he was promoted to flag rank. Coincidentally, in late 1935 there were a number of changes in Army leadership. General Craig, Arnold's superior at the time of the Long Beach earthquake, was appointed Army chief of staff, and General Oscar Westover replaced General Benjamin Foulois as chief of the Air Corps. Both incoming generals knew of Arnold's professional abilities, and he was ordered to Washington to serve as Westover's deputy. In January 1936 Arnold left March Field for what became his final permanent military posting and one in which he would remain for the next ten years—Washington, D.C.

His tenure as Westover's assistant lasted only until September 1938, when the Air Corps chief died in a crash of his A-17 aircraft at Burbank, California. The logical replacement for the deceased Air chief was his assistant, Arnold. But Arnold's appointment as chief was not a fait accompli. Unfounded rumors arose about Arnold's being a drunkard when stationed in Hawaii. The origins of this rumor are unknown, especially since Arnold was never stationed in Hawaii and drank only sparingly. Despite the rumor, Arnold filled in temporarily as chief of the Air Corps, until he was formally appointed and on October 28 was promoted to major general, a rank commensurate with his new duties.

Days after Westover's death, President Roosevelt, alarmed by the results of the Munich Conference in September 1938, where Neville Chamberlain appeased Hitler over control of the Czech Sudetenland, called a meeting at the White House with both his military and civilian advisers. As Arnold filled in for the recently deceased Air chief, the president expressed his concern about America's lack of military preparedness and addressed the issue of an expansion of the military, especially the Air Corps.[68] Roosevelt asked for an assessment of foreign air forces, and Arnold responded with numbers that illustrated the weakness of the U.S. air fleet in comparison with other nations. Alarmed by these numbers and the relative size of foreign air forces, Roosevelt proposed that the Air Corps grow to 10,000 aircraft, a far cry from the 1940 budget's allocation.[69] Possessing a greater understanding of the requirements for fielding a large air fleet than the president, Arnold warned Roosevelt, "The strength of an air force cannot be measured in terms of airplanes only . . . other things are essential—production capacity of planes, of pilots, of mechanics, and bases from which to operate. A sound training program is essential to provide replacements."[70]

With war looming on the horizon, Arnold agreed that the Air Corps needed to expand. The small American Air Corps was no match for the air forces of some European nations, and the only modern airframes the United States possessed were a few precious early-model B-17 bombers.[71] Though the B-17 was an impressive aircraft for its day and showed promise as a long-range weapon, most Air Corps purchases during this time focused on shorter-range, ground support aircraft. Furthermore, the budget for 1940 provided the Air Corps with only 178 new airplanes.[72] In 1940 the Air Corps had a total of 5,054 airplanes, of which only 2,500 were combat designs.[73] The monumental task of expanding and modernizing the fledgling Air Corps into an armada capable of fighting a global war fell directly on Arnold's shoulders.

Focused on the expansion of the Air Corps, Arnold understood that the growth of the service also required extensive cooperation with various elements of the civilian sector. To modernize the air fleet, the Air Corps needed to leverage civilian scientists, engineers, and designers. Aircraft manufacturers would need to improve, and substantially increase, the number and size of factories and facilities, as well as the rates of production. Furthermore, the Air Corps would have to use civilian facilities, airports, and instructors to in-

General Arnold as chief of staff, Army Air Forces. (Courtesy of the National Museum of the U.S. Air Force)

crease military training capacities. Before America's entry into the war, the Air Corps produced approximately 750 pilots a year, but to support the entire war effort it needed as many as 100,000 trained aviators.[74] These tasks needed to be done at a time when the country was not yet at war and the funding floodgates had yet to be opened. Before American participation in the war, Arnold worked at a feverish pace, setting up training programs, working with congressional leaders on legislation, and reorganizing the Air Corps for the upcoming hostilities.[75]

Aside from the difficulties of getting American industry on board with the development of a larger, more advanced Air Corps, Arnold was faced with an equally daunting political obstacle. Despite America's isolationist leaning during the early years of World War II, President Roosevelt was interested in supporting those countries that stood against Nazi Germany, specifically France and Great Britain. Toward this end, Roosevelt concerned himself with selling aircraft and engines to foreign countries that were standing against the German threat and therefore needed the weapons more urgently than the United States. This larger political objective, however, contradicted the directive to build up and modernize the Air Corps. How could Arnold build up the U.S. air fleet while America was sending its newest designs and engines overseas?

This issue came to a head in March 1940, when Arnold testified before the House Military Affairs Committee, stating that the production of aircraft for foreign air forces was adversely affecting the Air Corps's modernization and growth program.[76] This issue of foreign support was also complicated by the inquiry into the death of a French national who in January had crashed in an early experimental version of the Douglas A-20 attack bomber in California. The deceased French aviator's presence in a U.S. aircraft was an apparent violation of the Neutrality Acts of the 1930s. After Arnold's congressional testimony regarding these incidents, the Air chief was chastised by Roosevelt during a March 12 meeting at the White House. As Arnold put it, "He [Roosevelt] expressed dissatisfaction with the manner in which questions had been answered in the past, particularly by the War Department witnesses. And then looking directly at me, he said there were places to which officers who did not 'play ball' might be sent—such as Guam."[77] When he got home that night, Arnold told Bee to be ready to pack their belongings.[78]

Arnold avoided exile to Guam, but his apparent break with the president over his intent to provide matériel and support to Allied nations made him persona non grata within the Roosevelt administration, and he was not invited back to the White House for months. Resolute in his concerns, Arnold told newly appointed Secretary of War Henry Stimson that giving priority to aircraft and engine production for Great Britain meant that the Air Corps could not meet its expansion schedules.[79] Eventually, Roosevelt began to appreciate the burden his policy had placed on the Air Force, and in December Arnold was once again invited to the White House. Roosevelt requested that Arnold arrive early, before the start of a small dinner party, so that the two men could meet privately. Once they met, the president asked Arnold if he could fix Hap an "old-fashioned" cocktail. To this offer Arnold replied, "Thanks, Mr. President, I haven't had one for about 20 years, but I assure you I'll enjoy this one with you tremendously."[80] Thereafter, whatever reservations Roosevelt had about Arnold were forgotten, and by the time of the Pearl Harbor attack, Arnold had become a trusted confidant within Roosevelt's war council.[81] Indicative of the president's trust was Arnold's promotion to lieutenant general a year later, on December 15, 1941.

Another important relationship during the war years was his association with his friend from his days in the Philippines, General George C. Marshall, who had become Army chief of staff. Marshall placed great faith and trust in Arnold, and he too became an advocate for an independent air force after the war was over. Marshall fully empowered Arnold and stated, "I tried to give Arnold all the power I could, I tried to make him as nearly as I could Chief of Staff of the Air without any restraint."[82] In return, Arnold held Marshall in the highest esteem; as he told Eaker, "If George Marshall ever took a position contrary to mine, I would know I was wrong."[83] By February 1942 Arnold was a member of the Joint Chiefs of Staff. His presence as a full-fledged member of the Joint Chiefs was not welcomed by everyone, however, especially within the Navy. Chief of Naval Operations (CNO) Admiral Ernest J. King and his staff never fully accepted Arnold as a member of the Joint Chiefs. This snub came about largely because the CNO's head of Naval Aviation, Admiral John Tower, was not himself a full member.[84]

Throughout much of the prewar period and then during the war itself, Arnold set himself a hurried pace for a fifty-four-year-old man. He worked seven days a week, and for the duration of the war he expected much of the same from his staff, installing phones in their homes so he could reach them at any time.[85] According to his personal pilot, Gene Bebee, "His [Arnold's] idea of a good time was to work all day in the office, and he'd probably come in from the last conference with the Secretary . . . then we'd rush out to Bolling Field, jump in a plane and fly all night to LA . . . arrive in the morning, visit five aircraft factories and then go to someone's house for dinner that night."[86] Bee, too, had a busy schedule, as Arnold appointed her head of the Air Force Relief Society, a charitable organization assisting the families of Air Force personnel.[87] Their collective frantic pace was to exact a toll on Arnold's health and on their marriage.

In addition to his role in building a large, modern air force once America was engaged in the war, Arnold had a hand in the conduct of the global air war. Though he was not necessarily overseeing day-to-day operation of combat units, his influence was felt in air campaigns conducted on all American fronts. In this role Arnold held great sway in the manner in which airpower was employed, as many of the men conducting the air war were his friends and colleagues. More important, he held their professional destinies in his hands. If an air commander was not producing the results expected, Arnold had no compunction about addressing the subordinate's failings or even relieving him of command. He was often impatient with subordinates because he was focused on making the most out of the Army Air Force's efforts. Thus, even friends and close associates were not exempt from his wrath.

Indicative of this characteristic is a quotation from his longtime associate Carl Spaatz, who, when finally assigned overseas during World War II, told his wife not to worry: "I'll be home in six months, by that time Hap will fire me."[88] In fact, in late 1942, when Arnold was disappointed in the number of B-17s Spaatz had dispatched in bombing raids over Europe, he wrote to his friend a rather pointed inquiry: "It is believed that some powerful reason must obtain which limits your heavy-bomber operations to an apparent average of less than one per week. Weather conditions alone are not believed the cause, nor the preparation of some of the two hundred heavy bombers under your control . . . request full information on the subject."[89]

When Arnold's longtime subordinate and coauthor, Ira Eaker, failed to produce the expected results with the Eighth Air Force in 1943, the Air chief sent a number of messages venting his frustration. To these messages Eaker finally retorted, "I shall always accept gladly and in the proper spirit, any advice, council, or criticism from you. I do not feel, however, that my past service which has come under your observation indicates that I am a horse which needs to be ridden with spurs."[90] Several air commanders from various theaters of war would suffer the wrath of Arnold's displeasure over the course of the conflict.

After attending the Casablanca Conference in January 1943, where the Army Air Force and Great Britain's Royal Air Force established the foundation for the Combined Bomber Offensive in Europe, Arnold continued his travels and flew to China to consult with Chiang Kai-shek on Sino-American efforts against the Japanese. On his trip over the Himalayas, however, he came close to becoming a casualty of war himself. He and several other general officers flew over the mountain range, referred to as "the hump," at night to the Chinese airfield at Kunming. The crew of the plane assured Arnold that they were familiar with the 525-mile flight path, which was to take about three hours.[91] Flying in the rarefied air for the first time, however, the navigator suffered from hypoxia (lack of oxygen in the bloodstream) and became disoriented.[92] The radio operator could not locate the navigation beacon from Kunming and found only other Chinese and, ironically, Japanese radio aids.[93] The aircraft had consumed enough fuel to have already passed the point of no return, and they were forced to carry on, the risk of crashing in the mountainous terrain growing each minute. Eventually the pilot located the beacon and realized they had overflown Kunming, and they landed six hours after takeoff with only a few gallons of fuel left.[94] The next day Arnold dryly remarked to the pilot, "I think we ought to plan our trips better."[95]

Following his arrival back in the United States on February 28, Arnold attended a White House meeting and returned to his Fort Myer home to relax. Once at home, however, he complained of chest pains and the post's duty doctor was called to his residence. After arguing with the doctor, a young captain who ignored Arnold's protestations that he required no further medical attention, Arnold eventually acquiesced and went by ambulance to Walter Reed Army Hospital.[96] Diagnosed with coronary thrombosis, he grudgingly took a few weeks' leave in Florida to recover. Army regulations at the time required a medical retirement for those suffering from a coronary condition. The issue regarding Arnold's health and his remaining on active duty went all the way up to Marshall and eventually to the president. Since doctors had given Arnold a good prognosis for recovery, Roosevelt overrode the Army regulation and kept the Air chief on the active list.[97] After this episode, however, Marshall kept abreast of Arnold's medical condition on a regular basis. Despite his heart ailment, in March 1943 Arnold was promoted to full general.

Nevertheless, this was not Arnold's only coronary incident but, rather, only the first of many. Two months later, in May, when preparing for the Trident Conference, Arnold suffered yet another attack. This time his heart rate rose to 160 beats per minute, and he was again taken to Walter Reed and forced to take a vacation.[98] In a letter to Marshall regarding his absence from the upcoming conference, Arnold wrote, "This is one hell of a time for this to happen. My engine started turning over at 160 when it should have been doing 74 to 76. For this I am sorry."[99] After a few weeks of rest, he returned to work and resumed his normal duties. Despite this serious medical condition, Arnold did his best to hide this ailment from members of his staff.[100]

If 1943 was a hard year for Arnold medically, it was also a dark year for the strategic bombing campaign in Europe. Disastrous raids against the ball-bearing factories in Schweinfurt in both August and October were less than effective, and the Air Force's high loss rates, about 20 percent for just these two raids, were a sobering reality.[101] For October 1943 alone the Eighth Air Force in England experienced an overall loss rate of 9 percent.[102] Statistically speaking, U.S. aircrews could not expect to complete their assigned tour of twenty-five missions successfully. Though Arnold was sending airplanes and aircrews to Europe as fast as he could, the losses the Eighth Air Force experienced shook Arnold and his belief in daylight strategic bombing. According to Secretary Stimson, "Hap was having a hell of a time hanging on [to the concept of daylight bombing]. . . . I can't document it, but I think he was beginning to worry about it because the attrition rate was too high."[103]

Exercising his prerogative as Air chief and looking for better effects with the Combined Bomber Offensive, in December 1943 Arnold changed his senior air commanders in the European theater. Unhappy with the results of the Eighth Air Force, he approved General Eisenhower's request to transfer Spaatz from the Mediterranean theater to England to help the supreme Allied commander plan Op-

Arnold inspecting the *Memphis Belle* during a war bond tour. (Courtesy of the National Museum of the U.S. Air Force)

eration Overlord. Furthermore, Arnold placed Spaatz as the head of a larger air organization, the U.S. Strategic Air Forces in Europe, responsible for coordinating the entire U.S. air effort. In conjunction with Spaatz's reassignment, Arnold placed the famous aviator Jimmy Doolittle in command of the Eighth Air Force, much to the consternation of its incumbent commander, Ira Eaker.[104] Despite Eaker's arguments for retaining his command, Arnold reassigned his longtime acquaintance to command of the Mediterranean Allied Air Forces. Though the transfer of Spaatz at Eisenhower's request made for a somewhat convenient justification, Arnold left no doubt among those around him about his displeasure with Eaker's performance, despite their longtime relationship.[105]

Arnold wanted to prove the efficacy of strategic bombing doctrine, while also promoting the idea of the need to establish an independent air force separate from the Army and Navy. Toward this end, and with a keen understanding of the importance of publicity, he was adamant about having significant press coverage of the air war and the Army Air Force's efforts. In addition to relating bombing rates, sorties, and tonnage numbers, Arnold wanted to make a statement to the American people about the importance of airpower. He frequently leveraged the mass communications means available to him to publicize the efficacy of American airpower.[106] Arnold was chagrined by Eaker's low sortie rates in comparison to the RAF's Bomber Command's. In January 1944 he wrote to Spaatz and argued that the American press was giving the impression that the damage inflicted by the RAF exceeded that of the USAAF. Arnold requested that Spaatz someday "not too far distant, send out a big number—*and I mean a big number*—of bombers to hit something in the nature of an aircraft factory and *lay it flat?*"[107] The emphasis he added to "and I mean a big number" and the intent to "lay it flat" speaks to the idea that one of Arnold's main goals during the war was to have the Air Force contribute to winning the war to the greatest extent possible, while ensuring that the service receive its due credit in the public eye.[108]

Arnold shouldered large responsibilities in Washington, but he also continued to travel and meet with commanders in the field. In December 1943 he toured the Mediterranean area of operations, not only visiting Eisenhower and Spaatz but also seeing his son Hank, who was an artillery officer participating in the Monte Cassino campaign. While in Italy, General Mark Clark, Fifth Army commander, invited the Air chief to visit the front. Arnold accepted the offer, and Clark took Arnold to areas exposed to enemy fire. At one point a German 88-mm artillery shell exploded near their jeep, forcing some in the entourage to seek cover. Seeing the carnage of battle, Arnold was moved by the wounded men he observed, noting that he saw "a man with only half his innards, dying, but still smiling and saying, I am all right."[109] Ironically, despite his rank as one of the most senior officers in the U.S. military, this incident was the first and only time Arnold actually experienced battle firsthand.[110]

On May 10, 1944, Arnold suffered his third heart attack and flew to Coral Gables, Florida, for recovery and rest. Bee accompanied Arnold to Florida, but her presence was less than comforting.[111] She too was stressed by her own responsibilities with the Air Force Aid Society, and the two had grown apart over the years. Given their large responsibilities during the war, their relationship suffered. By June he had recovered from this latest incident and was well enough to travel to Europe and see the results of the D-Day invasion in person. Arnold, along with other senior leaders, landed on the Normandy coast on June 12, just six days after the invasion. When he returned home, he resumed his normal schedule.[112]

In April 1944 the first Boeing B-29 Superfortress bombers began leaving the United States for service overseas. Arnold had been a strong advocate for the bomber since its inception and authorized the contract to build the first wooden mock-ups in 1940. He concerned himself personally with the development, deployment, and use of the bomber. The Superfortress had greater range and payload than the B-17s and B-24s the Army Air Force was then using, and Arnold thought that the airframe held great promise for the American war effort. He served as the biggest proponent of the immensely expensive B-29 program and put both his personal and professional reputation at risk in this effort. Regarding Arnold's role in the development of the Superfortress, General Curtis LeMay wrote, "Arnold more than anyone else in the Air Corps, took the chances, cut the corners, and ordered this unique aircraft."[113] Called the "3 Billion Dollar Gamble," the B-29 was a very complex airframe requiring the involvement of a significant portion of the American aircraft industry. Its four R-3350 engines were fire prone and problematic, however. Because of this problem, during early B-29 operations the crews talked more about the ability to take off safely at their home field than they did about flying over enemy territory. Wartime exigencies required that the plane be rushed into production without the normal test-and-development period. Arnold knew that both he and the Air Force would be held accountable if the program proved to be a white elephant.

While Arnold kept himself abreast of the B-29's progress, his special interest in the bomber also forced him to assume his first combat command, albeit from Washington, D.C. Because there was no unity of command in the Pacific war, Arnold feared that the B-29s sent to the Pacific would be siphoned off for missions other than strategic bombing. None of the theater commanders in the Pacific were advocates of strategic bombing. Douglas MacArthur in the south Pacific, Joseph Stilwell in Southeast Asia, and Chester Nimitz in the central Pacific saw little promise in the strategic air effort. As a result, Arnold was loath to put the bomber under the charge of a single theater commander, who might then use the asset for tactical missions. Concerned about the lack of unity of command in the Pacific, and believing the unique capabilities of the new bomber demanded its own campaign, on April 4, 1944, Arnold created the Twentieth Air Force and assumed command two days later. Though he retained control of the organization from his office, he delegated authority to his subordinate commanders at forward bases in both China and the Mariana Islands.

On December 21, 1944, Arnold was finally awarded his fifth star as General of the Army. The leadership he displayed in running the global air war, his management of the world's largest air fleet, and his willingness to make tough decisions proved his worthiness for the rank. The difficult replacement of underperforming friends and subordinates that Arnold made in Europe also occurred in the Pacific theater. During the early phases of the B-29 employment, the aircraft failed to meet its expectations, as operations in China were severely curtailed owing to logistical constraints. Additionally, the B-29 strikes flying out of the Marianas proved to be largely ineffectual. As he had done earlier in Europe, Arnold relieved the commander of the XX Bomber Command in China, General Kenneth Wolfe, and replaced him with General Curtis LeMay. Months later, as the China bombing effort proved logistically unfeasible, Arnold withdrew all the B-29s from China and consolidated them under the XXI Bomber Command on the Marianas. Here, too, Arnold found the commander of the XXI Bomber Command falling short of expectations. General Haywood Hansell, a framer of the Army Air Force's precision strategic bombing concept, was relieved on January 19, 1945, and also replaced with LeMay. LeMay understood the B-29's need for validation as a program and Arnold's special interest in the aircraft. Toward this end LeMay stated, "General Arnold was absolutely determined to get results out of this weapon system [the B-29]. The turkey is around my neck. I've got to deliver."[114]

In March 1945 LeMay developed an application that indeed validated the development of the B-29. On the night of March 9 the Twentieth Air Force conducted its first low-level incendiary raid on Tokyo. This raid became the harbinger of the American firebombing efforts over Japan that eventually razed over 180 square miles of Japanese urban area in the spring and summer of 1945. Upon learning of the results of the March 9 raid, Arnold congratulated LeMay and wrote, "This mission proves your crews have the guts for anything."[115]

On January 17, two days before he relieved Hansell, Arnold experienced his fourth and most serious heart attack.[116] While eating dinner at home he suffered a coronary occlusion and was again taken to Coral Gables for rest and treatment. At the time of the attack, Bee was in California on Air Force Aid Society business and flew to Florida to be at his bedside, but her presence was again less than comforting. She chastised her husband for his busy work schedule and for how he had driven himself to this poor medical state. The conversation between the two became heated and caused Hap's blood pressure to rise. As a result, the attending physician, fearing for Arnold's health, had Bee removed from the room.[117] Frustrated with both Arnold and the doctor, Bee departed Florida for Washington. By February Arnold was recovering and joked about his health in a letter to his daughter, Lois, stating, "One of my cylinders blew a gasket and I had to get down here and have an overhaul job done."[118] Hap and Bee separated for a short time, but they eventually reconciled, and the general finally understood that he needed to make a lifestyle change.

After this latest medical episode, he relinquished some of his responsibilities to his subordinate Lieutenant General Barney Giles and went so far as to send his chief of the Air War Plans Division, Lieutenant General Larry Kuter, in his stead to attend the Yalta Conference in February 1945.

By March, however, he had returned to Washington and subsequently traveled to Europe as VE Day approached. While in Europe, he once again visited his son Hank, who penned a letter to Bee saying, "He [Arnold] is really enjoying himself and acting more like a tourist than anything. I personally think this trip has done him a world of good."[119] On VE Day, Arnold was again in a Florida hospital, but this time only to have some follow-up tests.[120] While in Florida, he received a letter from President Harry Truman stating that the new commander in chief wished to have Arnold stay on as the Air chief. According to Arnold, Truman expressed "complete confidence in me and would like to keep me on the job."[121] After receiving a clean bill of health, Arnold traveled to the Pacific in June to visit with LeMay, other Army Air Force leaders, and Douglas MacArthur.

Arnold's hard work, leadership skills, and managerial abilities were reflected in the growth of the Army Air Forces during the conduct of the war. He was a linchpin in the wartime marriage between American aircraft manufacturers and the U.S. military. American aircraft production for all types of aircraft increased from a paltry 6,028 in 1940 to a high of 95,272 during 1944.[122] In addition, the Air Force grew from just over 20,000 men in June 1938 to 2,372,293 in June 1944.[123] Overall, the Army Air Force grew from just 11 percent of the Army's total strength to more than 30 percent.[124] During his tenure Arnold built the world's largest, most advanced, and most potent air armada, while managing an air fleet that conducted operations in every corner of the world.

Arnold did not play a significant role regarding the decision to drop the atomic bomb, although the Army Air Force was the method by which the device was delivered. Target selection was determined by a group of both military and civilian experts who reported their selections to Stimson, Marshall, and the head of the Manhattan Project, Major General Leslie Groves, and execution was left to the discretion of the Pacific air commander, Spaatz. While cognizant of the Manhattan Project and its potential, Arnold was not necessarily in favor of using the weapon. He submitted to the Joint Chiefs an assessment of the Twentieth Air Force's ongoing bombing effort and argued, "Acceleration and augmentation of the strategic air program culminating in a land campaign, will bring about the defeat of Japan with a minimum loss of American lives."[125] He agreed with Marshall that airpower alone could not win the war and believed that at least one of the two planned amphibious invasions of Japan was required. Regardless of his opinions, he was informed of the atomic bombings via private communication line to his house; when the Japanese announced their surrender, Arnold had no real celebration at his home until fellow officers began to drop by and offer their congratulations.[126]

Victory over the Axis powers claimed many casualties, including Arnold. By VJ Day he was an exhausted man. Having suffered four heart attacks, a frantic work pace for the preceding few years, and marital strife, he was ready to retire.[127] Early in 1945 he had already made the decision to leave active duty service, and with peace at hand, the timing was propitious.[128] Demobilization became the new challenge facing the services, but Arnold left much of that planning and effort to his subordinates and successor.[129] On November 8, 1945, he forwarded a memo requesting retirement on February 6, and he left Washington on March 1, 1946.[130]

A few years earlier, in 1943, he and Bee had purchased a ranch, El Rancho Feliz, quietly tucked away in the hills near Sonoma, California. After some forty years of military service and living on a military pension, he could not claim to be a rich man. Though he had led the largest air force in the world and was an international figure of some renown, Arnold's lifestyle changed appreciably, as he had a sizable mortgage and only a few thousand dollars to his name.[131] He lived tranquilly at his ranch with Bee and spent much of his time making furniture and tending to his animals. He served for a short time as the California Game and Fish commissioner and in 1946 began working on his memoirs. Thinking that his autobiography might be a way to help improve his financial situation, he worked with William Laidlaw on writing the manuscript. The two men at times had an acrimonious relationship, but they finished the book in 1949. By the time he submitted his manuscript to the publishers, however, they had lost much of their initial interest. Despite good reviews, the book experienced only modest sales.

In January 1948 Arnold suffered his fifth heart attack and was bedridden for three months. Despite this medical setback, his spirits were buoyed when in May 1949 he received yet another military accolade. President Truman wrote to Arnold stating that he had approved his promotion as the first General of the Air Force. He flew to Washington to receive the promotion from Truman personally; the official rank was designated on May 7, 1949.

Eight months later, in the early morning of January 15, 1950, Arnold passed away quietly in his home at the age of sixty-three. He was buried at Arlington National Cemetery with full military honors on January 19. Funeral plans called for a huge military flyover in respect for the father of the Air Force, but weather conditions precluded the event. Bee died years later, at the age of ninety-one, and was buried alongside him.

The Air Force owes much of its very existence to Arnold and his belief in airpower. Despite his lack of real combat command and experience, he fought other kinds of battles in Washington, D.C., in the halls of Congress, in aviation factories, and in corporate boardrooms to create an independent Air Force. Though his battles were less glamorous, and certainly less exciting, they were no less important than those fought in overseas theaters. His victories and the legacies he established last to this day.

Notes

1. H. H. Arnold, *Global Mission* (New York: Harper and Row, 1949), 5. Thomas Coffey, *Hap: The Story of the U.S. Air Force and the Man Who Built It, General Henry H. "Hap" Arnold* (New York: Viking Press, 1982), 12.

2. Coffey, *Hap*, 15.

3. Arnold, *Global Mission*, 6; Coffey, *Hap*, 15.

4. Ibid.

5. Coffey, *Hap*, 16.

6. Dik Daso, *Hap Arnold and the Evolution of American Airpower* (Washington, D.C.: Smithsonian Institution Press, 2000), 235; Arnold, *Global Mission*, 7.

7. Daso, *Hap Arnold*, 26–27.

8. Coffey, *Hap*, 22.

9. Ibid., 32–33.

10. Ibid., 31; Daso, *Hap Arnold*, 34.

11. Daso, *Hap Arnold*, 35.

12. Arnold, *Global Mission*, 11.

13. Ibid., 12; Daso, *Hap Arnold*, 37.

14. Arnold, *Global Mission*, 12; Daso, *Hap Arnold*, 37.

15. Dik Daso, "The Origins of Airpower: Hap Arnold's Early Career in Aviation Technology, 1903–1935," *Airpower Journal* (Winter 1996): 71.

16. Daso, *Hap Arnold*, 43.

17. Ibid.

18. Arnold, *Global Mission*, 15; Coffey, *Hap*, 40; Daso, *Hap Arnold*, 43.

19. Arnold, *Global Mission*, 19.

20. Ibid.

21. Daso, "Origins of Airpower," 72.

22. Arnold, *Global Mission*, 39–40.

23. Daso, *Hap Arnold*, 57.

24. Daso, *Hap Arnold*, 58; Coffey, *Hap*, 62.

25. Coffey, *Hap*, 63.

26. Ibid.

27. Arnold, *Global Mission*, 43; Daso, *Hap Arnold*, 59.

28. Daso, *Hap Arnold*, 73.

29. Ibid., 77; Coffey, *Hap*, 80.

30. Coffey, *Hap*, 80.

31. Arnold, *Global Mission*, 45.

32. Ibid., 46; Daso, *Hap Arnold*, 84; Coffey, *Hap*, 90.

33. Daso, "Origins of Airpower," 75.

34. Daso, *Hap Arnold*, 101.

35. Arnold, *Global Mission*, 107; Coffey, *Hap*, 101; Daso, *Hap Arnold*, 105.

36. Daso, *Hap Arnold*, 107.

37. Ibid., 111.

38. Coffey, *Hap*, 119.

39. Daso, *Hap Arnold*, 112.

40. Ibid., 113.

41. Coffey, *Hap*, 126.

42. Daso, *Hap Arnold*, 113; Coffey, *Hap*, 126.

43. Daso, *Hap Arnold*, 114.

44. Arnold, *Global Mission*, 122–23.

45. Coffey, *Hap*, 128.

46. Arnold, *Global Mission*, 123; Coffey, *Hap*, 128.

47. Arnold, *Global Mission*, 125.

48. Coffey, *Hap*, 133.

49. Ibid.

50. Daso, *Hap Arnold*, 118.

51. Ibid., 116.

52. Coffey, *Hap*, 136.

53. Ibid.

54. Ibid.

55. Ibid.

56. Ibid., 137.

57. Ibid.

58. Arnold, *Global Mission*, 131.

59. Coffey, *Hap*, 137.

60. Ibid., 140.

61. Daso, *Hap Arnold*, 126.

62. Ibid., 129, 271–72.

63. Coffey, *Hap*, 148–49; Daso, *Hap Arnold*, 129.

64. Arnold, *Global Mission*, 146; Coffey, *Hap*, 159.

65. Coffey, *Hap*, 159.

66. Daso, *Hap Arnold*, 138.

67. Ibid.

68. Coffey, *Hap*, 184–85.

69. Arnold, *Global Mission*, 179.

70. Wesley Frank Craven and James Lea Cate, *The Army Air Forces in World War II*, vol. 6, *Men and Planes* (1955; repr., Washington, D.C.: Office of Air Force History, 1983), xi; Coffey, *Hap*, 184.

71. Craven and Cate, *Army Air Forces in World War II*, 6:xii.

72. Arnold, *Global Mission*, 179.

73. Office of Statistical Control, *Army Air Forces Statistical Digest: World War II* (Washington, D.C.: Office of Statistical Control, 1945), corrections page.

74. Coffey, *Hap*, 196.

75. Daso, *Hap Arnold*, 161.

76. Coffey, *Hap*, 211.

77. Arnold, *Global Mission*, 186; Coffey *Hap*, 211.

78. Coffey, *Hap*, 212.

79. Ibid., 218.

80. Ibid., 220.

81. Daso, *Hap Arnold*, 171.

82. Coffey, *Hap*, 232.

83. Ibid., 346.

84. Ibid., 258.

85. Ibid., 247.

86. Coffey, *Hap*, 223; Daso, *Hap Arnold*, 170.

87. Coffey, *Hap*, 283.

88. Ibid., 279.

89. Richard G. Davis, *Carl A. Spaatz and the Air War in Europe* (Washington, D.C.: Center for Air Force History, 1993), 103.

90. Coffey, *Hap*, 316; Michael Sherry, *The Rise of American Air Power: The Creation of Armageddon* (New Haven: Yale University Press, 1987), 150–51.

91. Arnold, *Global Mission*, 411; Daso, *Hap Arnold*, 299.

92. Arnold, *Global Mission*, 411; Daso, *Hap Arnold*, 299–300.

93. Arnold, *Global Mission*, 412; Coffey, *Hap*, 299.

94. Coffey, *Hap*, 300.

95. Ibid.

96. Ibid., 305.

97. Ibid., 309.

98. Daso, *Hap Arnold*, 183.

99. Coffey, *Hap*, 312.

100. Daso, *Hap Arnold*, 183.

101. Richard G. Davis, *Bombing the European Axis Powers: A Historical*

Digest of the Combined Bomber Offensive, 1939–1945 (Maxwell AFB, Ala.: Air University Press, 2006), 158–59, 182–83.

102. Wesley Frank Craven and James Lea Cate, *The Army Air Forces in World War II*, vol. 2, *Europe—Torch to Pointblank, August 1942 to December 1943* (Chicago: University of Chicago Press, 1949), 708.

103. Coffey, *Hap*, 321.

104. Ibid., 328–29; Davis, *Bombing the European Axis Powers*, 209–11.

105. Davis, *Bombing the European Axis Powers*, 209.

106. Daso, *Hap Arnold*, 230.

107. H. Arnold to C. Spaatz, January 24, 1944, box 14, General Carl Spaatz Papers, Manuscript Division, Library of Congress, Washington, D.C.; emphasis in original.

108. Conrad Crane, *Bombs, Cities, and Civilians: American Airpower Strategy in World War II* (Lawrence: University Press of Kansas, 1993), 33.

109. Coffey, *Hap*, 331.

110. Ibid.

111. Daso, *Hap Arnold*, 199; Coffey, *Hap*, 343–44.

112. Coffey, *Hap*, 348–49.

113. Curtis LeMay and Bill Yenne, *Superfortress* (New York: Berkley Books, 1988), 23.

114. Curtis LeMay with MacKinlay Kantor, *Mission with LeMay: My Story* (Garden City, N.Y.: Doubleday, 1965), 338.

115. Alvin Coox, "Strategic Bombing in the Pacific 1942–1945," in *Case Studies in Strategic Bombardment*, ed. R. Cargill Hall (Washington, D.C.: U.S. Air Force History and Museums Program, 1998), 321.

116. Daso, *Hap Arnold*, 199.

117. Coffey, *Hap*, 359; Daso, *Hap Arnold*, 199.

118. Coffey, *Hap*, 361.

119. Daso, *Hap Arnold*, 204.

120. Ibid., 206.

121. Arnold, *Global Mission*, 560.

122. Office of Statistical Control, *Army Air Forces Statistical Digest: World War II*, 112.

123. Craven and Cate, *The Army Air Forces in World War II*, 6:xix, xvii.

124. Ibid., xxv.

125. Arnold, *Global Mission*, 596.

126. Ibid., 597.

127. Coffey, *Hap*, 376.

128. Arnold, *Global Mission*, 608.

129. Daso, *Hap Arnold*, 214.

130. Arnold, *Global Mission*, 608–9.

131. Coffey, *Hap*, 379.

References

Arnold, H. H. *Global Mission*. New York: Harper and Row, 1949.

Coffey, Thomas. *Hap: The Story of the U.S. Air Force and the Man Who Built It, General Henry H. "Hap" Arnold*. New York: Viking Press, 1982.

Coox, Alvin D. "Strategic Bombing in the Pacific 1942–1945." In *Case Studies in Strategic Bombardment*. Edited by R. Cargill Hall. Washington, D.C.: U.S. Air Force History and Museums Program, 1998.

Crane, Conrad. *Bombs, Cities, and Civilians: American Airpower Strategy in World War II*. Lawrence: University Press of Kansas, 1993.

Craven, Wesley Frank, and James Lea Cate. *The Army Air Forces in World War II*, vol. 2, *Europe—Torch to Pointblank, August 1942 to December 1943*. Chicago: University of Chicago Press, 1949.

———. *The Army Air Forces in World War II*, vol. 6, *Men and Planes*. 1955. Reprint, Washington, D.C.: Office of Air Force History, 1983.

Daso, Dik. *Hap Arnold and the Evolution of American Airpower*. Washington, D.C.: Smithsonian Institution Press, 2000.

———. "The Origins of Airpower: Hap Arnold's Early Career in Aviation Technology, 1903–1935." *Airpower Journal* (Winter 1996): 70–92.

Davis, Richard G. *Bombing the European Axis Powers: A Historical Digest of the Combined Bomber Offensive, 1939–1945*. Maxwell AFB, Ala.: Air University Press, 2006.

———. *Carl A. Spaatz and the Air War in Europe*. Washington, D.C.: Center for Air Force History, 1993.

General Carl Spaatz Papers. Manuscript Division, Library of Congress, Washington, D.C.

LeMay, Curtis, and Bill Yenne. *Superfortress*. New York: Berkley Books, 1988.

LeMay, Curtis, with MacKinlay Kantor. *Mission with LeMay: My Story*. Garden City, N.Y.: Doubleday, 1965.

Office of Statistical Control, *Army Air Forces Statistical Digest: World War II*. Washington, D.C.: Office of Statistical Control, 1945.

Sherry, Michael. *The Rise of American Air Power: The Creation of Armageddon*. New Haven: Yale University Press, 1987.

6

Omar Nelson Bradley

Joseph R. Fischer

Omar Nelson Bradley became the last general to reach five-star rank, doing so well after the completion of World War II and a year after the creation of the position of chairman of the Joint Chiefs of Staff. In many ways he was also the most unusual of those to attain this exalted rank. There was nothing of the showmanship that Mac-Arthur brought to the rank. Nor was there the charm that Dwight D. Eisenhower used to weave and hold together a coalition of war-time partners. The war correspondent Ernie Pyle described Bradley to the American public as looking like a schoolteacher whose face, even in the worst of times, wore a sense of composure that reassured those around him.

During the war years there was little flashy in his dress to mark him. He often preferred to wear none of the various decorations he had earned in his career, or, if he did wear a decoration, a lone Bronze Star marked his solidarity with his soldiers. And he was painfully aware of the burden his soldiers bore. In his autobiography he noted, "Those who are left to fight, fight on, evading death but knowing with each day of evasion they have exhausted one more chance for survival. Sooner or later, unless victory comes, the chase must end in the litter or in the grave."[1] Pyle noted that Bradley's simple style and sparing of lives brought him the nearly universal love and respect of his men.

When World War II came to an end, Bradley had commanded from division through Army group level, the latter, Twelfth Army Group, being the largest grouping of U.S. soldiers ever fielded. He had worked to bring the Army from its prewar doldrums to the proficiency it possessed at war's end, shaping its leadership as well as its approach to war along the way. It would be a road that would take him from stateside posts to the debacle of the Kasserine Pass, to Sicily, then to France, and finally to the heart of the Nazi Reich and victory.

Little in the early years of Bradley's life suggested his future achievements. He had been born in a log cabin to John Smith Bradley and Sara Elizabeth Hubbard Bradley in Clark, Missouri, on February 12, 1893. His father farmed and taught school. Omar spent his youth hunting and, when he had a chance, playing baseball. There having been little in the way of finances to see him through college, he had taken a job with the Wabash Railroad. When his Sunday school superintendent suggested he apply for admission to West Point as an inexpensive route to an education, he did so. The entrance examinations would prove a challenge. Bradley's problem was that he had been away from school for a year. His skills in geography, geometry, algebra, and English, the subjects assessed in the examination, had diminished in that time. He hit the books in preparation, and when he took the test, his scores were sufficient to earn him selection as an alternate. When the primary candidate found himself unable to attend, second place became good enough.

Bradley's years at West Point were uneventful. He played on the school's baseball and football teams, attended to his studies, and graduated 44th of 165 in the class of 1915. He was commissioned a second lieutenant of Infantry, and his first assignment was to the 14th Infantry Regiment at Fort George Wright, outside Spokane, Washington. Perhaps the high point of this assignment was his marriage in June 1916 to Mary Quayle, a woman from his hometown of Moberly, Missouri, whom he had met and courted during his two months of "graduation leave" the previous year. His early postings to various Army posts both stateside and overseas (Hawaii) were not particularly noteworthy, except that they included various teaching assignments at West Point and at Fort Benning, Georgia, something Bradley credited with shaping his approach to leadership.

Through no fault of his own, he missed combat in World War I and feared that the whims of the personnel system might well have limited his career. In 1920 the Army assigned him back to West Point as a mathematics instructor. In 1924 he attended the Infantry Officer Advanced Course at Fort Benning, receiving permanent promotion to the rank of major at the end of the course. From Benning he received assignment to the 27th Infantry Regiment in Hawaii, where he first encountered George S. Patton Jr. His performance caught the attention of his superior officers, which led to his receiving selection to Fort Leavenworth's revamped Command and General Staff College, the Army's premier school for officers it believed capable of senior-level commands. The course had been based on the Prussian Kriegsakademie, focusing heavily on history as well as operational planning built around 124 map problems and numerous terrain walks. Most of the exercises were at division, corps, and army level. The point of the exercises was to have the student make a decision and then defend it.[2] Bradley found the Leavenworth experience somewhat disappointing, however, noting that the lectures were "trite, predictable, and often unrealistic." Nonetheless, he conceded that it created a corps of officers with a common operational language, something that would prove invaluable when war came again.[3]

Bradley's next assignment, this time as an instructor at the Infantry School, brought him to the attention of George C. Marshall, the school's assistant commandant.[4] Marshall had directed the rewriting of the school's curriculum. He had been a proponent of John Pershing's view that warfare needed to be mobile, rather than something akin to the slugfest of the Western Front's trenches. Building largely on this vision, Marshall fashioned the training around the management of the chaos combat created. The curriculum aimed at preparing officers for command two levels above their current grade, a goal that reflected the reality of officer combat mortality. Bradley found himself assigned as an instructor in the Tactics Department, teaching battalion-level operations. A year later Marshall made Bradley chief of the Weapons Section, a key position he held until reassignment across post in support of a new program.

In the spring of 1933 the United States was suffering through the depths of the Great Depression. With nearly 25 percent of the workforce unemployed and much of the rest underemployed, Franklin D. Roosevelt, the nation's newly elected president, instituted a work program known as the Civilian Conservation Corps (CCC). The CCC was designed to employ out-of-work young men in various conservation programs, such as planting trees, building dams, and cutting firebreaks in national forests, and the Army received the job of organizing and directing the project. The Army reassigned Bradley to the CCC base camp at Benning, where he assumed command of six companies of men, nearly all African American, from Georgia and Alabama.[5] The Army's performance in support of the CCC program proved one of the high points of the interwar years and helped immeasurably in the War Department budget battles of the early 1930s.

By the fall of 1933 Bradley found himself a student again, this time at the Army War College at what was then Fort Humphreys (following World War II it was renamed Fort McNair), Washington, D.C. From there Bradley went on to another instructor assignment, in the Tactics Department at West Point, an assignment very much to Bradley's liking. From West Point it was back to Washington, D.C.

With war clouds threatening Europe, Bradley found himself assigned first to the Army G-1, where he worked on mobilization issues. Then, in 1939, Marshall, now Army chief of staff, pulled Bradley to his own office.[6] These two assignments exposed Bradley to a wider variety of problems, not the least of which was that of mobilizing the National Guard. He strongly questioned the National Guard system as it existed, arguing that state-level politics ensured that most Guard units were officered by well-connected but militarily incompetent officers. He noted that frequently company-grade officers were too old for their duties and often physically unfit to perform them.[7]

The coming year found him reassigned, obedient to Marshall's wishes, to the Infantry School at Benning, but this time as its commandant. Here Bradley put his own stamp on the nation's Army. Marshall had given Bradley the task of creating an officer-commissioning program in anticipation of national mobilization. The Army's enlisted ranks would provide most of the pool from which officer candidates would come. Bradley's creation became known as the Officer Candidate School (OCS) and served as the model for other branches. It was built loosely on the cadet experience at West Point; candidates were up at 0600, in classes from 0730 to 1745, permitted two hours of study time in the evening, and in bed by lights-out at 2200. "The Benning method," as Bradley's teaching pedagogy came to be called, was simple: demonstrate the skill desired, explain it, then have the cadet do it. By the end of World War II, fully 75 percent (more than 45,000) of the Army's company-level officers were OCS graduates.[8]

Bradley's contributions to training the prewar Army at Benning did not stop with the OCS. He understood, particularly in light of the German Army's swift victories over Poland in 1939 and France in 1940, the growing importance of armor on the modern battlefield. Marshall had established two armored units, 1st Armored Division based at Fort Knox, Kentucky, and 2nd Armored Division at Benning. Bradley did everything in his power to support the development of the division and of the doctrinal development of armored warfare. He became an early proponent of airborne operations, noting Germany's successful use of paratroopers in the Netherlands and later in Crete. Though Bradley did not initiate airborne training at Benning, he did oversee its growth.[9]

With the early successes of Axis armies in Europe and Asia, the necessity for a larger military became apparent. Marshall, realizing this fact, next assigned Bradley to command of the 82nd Infantry Division, one of three Organized Reserve divisions (the others being the 77th and 85th) activated after the Japanese attack on Pearl Harbor. Upon taking the assignment, Bradley quickly came to realize that his initial assessment of the preparedness of the Guard was equally true of the Army Reserves.

Bradley began by instituting a rigorous training program. The most pressing weakness of the 82nd was the terrible physical condition of many of its members. Nearly a third of his enlisted personnel failed to pass minimum fitness standards. To address this, Bradley instituted an obstacle course, insisting that everyone, including himself, run it. On one of his runs through the course, Bradley's hands slipped from a rope swing, and he plunged into a pit of sewage. Colonel Matthew B. Ridgway, one of the regimental commanders and the division's future commanding general, noted that seeing their commanding general splashing his way out of the foul muck brought both respect and smiles from the enlisted men present.

Another of Bradley's training innovations included changing the way the 82nd did marksmanship training. Sergeant Alvin York, the division's most famous World War I veteran, accepted an invitation from Bradley to visit. York remarked that most of his wartime shooting had been at distances of not more than fifty yards. As a result, Bradley added a marksmanship range in which soldiers engaged small targets, often nothing larger than cans, from various positions at no greater distance than fifty yards.[10]

The 82nd showed marked improvement under Bradley's leadership, to the extent that Marshall thought his subordinate's talents better used commanding a National Guard division undergoing mobilization.[11] Marshall assigned Bradley to command Pennsylvania's 28th Infantry Division. The 28th had been used as a replacement unit, its regiments stripped of men to fill other, more nearly ready units. Bradley became the division's third division commander in six months. He stopped the hemorrhaging of personnel, replaced

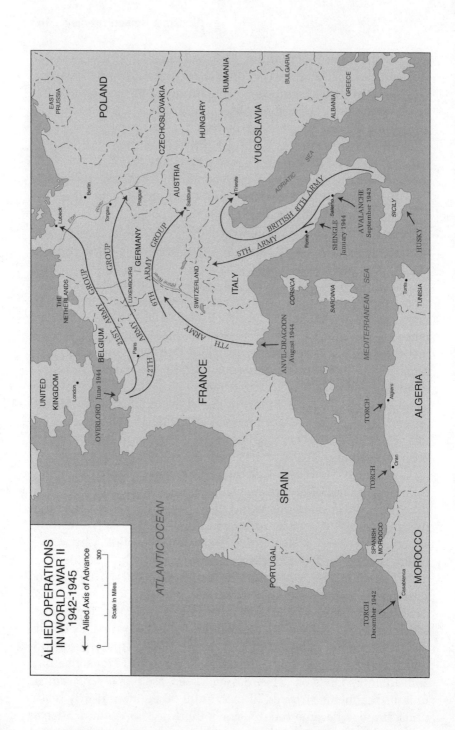

ALLIED OPERATIONS
IN WORLD WAR II
1942-1945

→ — Allied Axis of Advance

0   300

Scale in Miles

the leadership as necessary, and then started the division along the path already followed by the 82nd. Both the 82nd and the 28th established superb reputations in the European theater.

Bradley would never have the opportunity to lead a division in combat. Marshall had other plans for his protégé. Shortly after the 1942 Operation Torch landings in North Africa, Marshall assigned Bradley to Eisenhower to serve as a deputy and as an additional set of eyes for an inexperienced American Army.[12] The initial performance of many of the units in that Army did not bode well. The American II Corps had suffered a devastating defeat at Kasserine Pass, in Tunisia, in February 1943. American forces had fought poorly. German units reported that captured British and French officers referred to the Americans as "our Italians," an expression of disdain for their newly arrived allies.[13] Bradley's job was to find out what had happened and recommend ways to fix the situation.

Although a number of issues came to light, undoubtedly the most important proved to be the performance of Major General Lloyd Fredendall, the II Corps commanding general. Increasingly, as Bradley interviewed subordinate officers, a lack of faith in Fredendall's leadership abilities became evident—to the point that Bradley recommended Fredendall's relief.[14] Eisenhower, after reading the report, agreed, removing Fredendall and placing Patton in command of II Corps. Rather than allow access to his command by another general officer not answerable to himself, Patton arranged to have Bradley assigned as his deputy corps commander.[15]

As the North African campaign progressed, Eisenhower saw fit to relieve Patton of II Corps to permit him time to create Seventh Army headquarters in anticipation of Operation Husky, the invasion of Sicily. Bradley was Patton's natural successor to command II Corps. The difference between the two leadership styles was clearly marked. Gone was the pomp of Patton and in its place the no-nonsense midwestern manner of Bradley, but Bradley understood that one of the chief tasks facing him was resurrecting the corps's reputation in the aftermath of the defeat at Kasserine Pass.[16]

The final push toward Tunis was initially intended to have British First and Eighth armies converge on Tunis with the U.S. II Corps in support. British First Army was to attack west to east in the north toward the city while British Eighth Army attacked south to north along Tunisia's east coast. The proposal effectively pinched U.S. II Corps out of the final defeat of the Africa Corps. Bradley argued

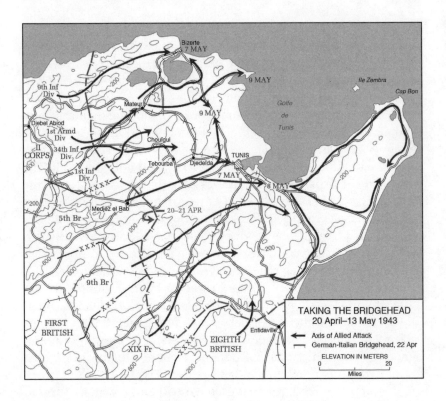

TAKING THE BRIDGEHEAD
20 April–13 May 1943

◄— Axis of Allied Attack
⊢— German-Italian Bridgehead, 22 Apr

ELEVATION IN METERS

0   20

Miles

that for morale purposes, if nothing else, his soldiers needed to be in on the kill; he proposed that, instead of British First Army, his corps assume responsibility for the northernmost sector. British commanders, particularly General Sir Harold Alexander, believed it difficult if not impossible for the Americans to move an entire corps 160 miles through the rear area of British First Army. Bradley insisted it could be done and, when he was given approval, accomplished the mission, moving 110,000 Americans and their equipment northward to their new positions in a matter of days.

The attack of II Corps toward Tunis provides a good look at Bradley's tendencies in command, many of which, for better or for worse, remained with him throughout the remainder of the war. He understood the need for brevity. The corps's operations plan for the drive toward Bizerte, Tunisia, included a single page of instructions, along with a map.[17] Bradley, as much as Patton, was the master of the unforgiving minute. Once the corps's attack began, it moved forward relentlessly, slowed at times, but never stopped. Furthermore, he was willing to accept risk. The frontages he assigned to some divisions were well beyond their ability to control by fire, let alone occupy. At one point in the attack, Manton Eddy's 9th Infantry Division frontage totaled twenty-eight miles. Bradley even permitted a nine-mile gap to exist between the 9th and Terry Allen's 1st Infantry Division, relying on patrols to maintain contact along the division boundary.[18] By the time the North African campaign had drawn to a close, II Corps was functioning on a par with its British Allies. The next hurdle facing the Allies would be the invasion of Sicily, their first venture onto the soil of Axis-controlled Europe.

The Allies had long debated where to go after completing their conquest of North Africa. During a series of meetings held in Casablanca, French Morocco, in January 1943, British and American planners worked out their differences. The Americans favored a direct approach to Europe, landing on the French northwest coast as soon as resources, particularly landing craft and men, would permit. They argued that this made the best use of limited resources, particularly shipping; promised to take the pressure off a badly pressed Red Army in the east; and most directly targeted the German center of gravity. The British favored a more indirect approach. The vulnerability of their supply lines through the Mediterranean, threatened as they were by Axis air and naval power operating from bases in Italy, suggested the next offensive should be against Sicily.[19] They argued that the loss of Sicily might well result in the toppling of the Mussolini government. Once Italy was out of the war, German military units would have to be repositioned from France and the Low Countries to compensate for the loss of Italian forces, thereby creating a more favorable operational picture for the cross-Channel invasion. Furthermore, taking Sicily would make good use of Allied combat power operating in North Africa once the campaign there came to a conclusion. The invasion of Sicily (code-named Husky) became a compromise decision.

The Combined Chiefs of Staff selected Eisenhower to be in overall command, and three British flag officers served as land, sea, and air component commanders, the most important of whom was Harold Alexander, Eisenhower's land force commander in North Africa. Alexander would command Fifteenth Army Group, which would include two Allied armies. Patton's Seventh Army included Major General Ernest J. Dawley's VI Corps, which was to provide most of Patton's ground forces. British Eighth Army under Bernard

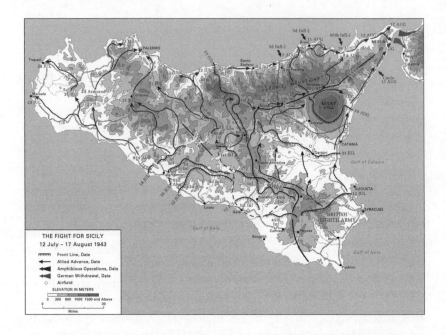

THE FIGHT FOR SICILY
12 July – 17 August 1943

Montgomery would provide the British contingent. Patton, uneasy with the inexperience of Dawley's corps headquarters, requested that Bradley's II Corps headquarters be substituted for VI Corps to permit the latter additional time to train. Eisenhower yielded to Patton's wishes, and Bradley's corps assumed command of the primary U.S. ground force for the operation.

Operation Husky went through a number of iterations. Initial plans called for Eighth Army to land along the southeast coast of the island below Syracuse while Seventh Army landed along the northern coast near Palermo. The two armies would then drive on to Messina. This plan would allow an efficient use of Sicily's ports for logistics and permit the immediate suppression of the island's key airfields. Montgomery objected to this, arguing that the two armies needed to move together to support one another. Alexander came to agree and modified the plan. Seventh Army would land along the southern coast from Licata to the boundary of Eighth Army, and both armies would advance northward toward Messina. Airborne units from the 82nd would support the attack by cutting the east-west interior roads, thereby isolating Italian and German positions. Bradley rightly criticized the plan as providing little thought to follow-on operations after the landings.[20] In its execution the operation would not be marked by excellence. Nor was it notable for the degree of harmony demonstrated between British and American commanders.

The landings themselves went well despite inclement weather. The Axis problem was too much shoreline to defend with too few troops. Allied deception plans added to the friction. Some 200,000–300,000 Axis troops occupied the island. Most were Italian; there were only slightly over 30,000 German combat troops as well as another 30,000 Luftwaffe airmen present to steel the defenses. Primary responsibility for Sicily's coastal areas fell to six Italian coastal divisions, the least well trained, least motivated of the Italian army on the island. The limited numbers of antitank guns available to them, essentially amounting to one gun for every five miles of beach, made an effective defense problematic.[21] Low morale and equipment shortages were compounded by Italian-German coalition problems. Although Axis forces were technically commanded by General Alfredo Guzzoni and under Italian Sixth Army, the two primary German units, the 15th Panzer Grenadier and the Hermann Göring Panzer divisions, operated to varying degrees independent of the Italian command.

The Axis plan to defend Sicily was to contest the landings as much as possible with coastal defense forces and reinforce them with tanks and armored infantry before the Allies could amass sufficient power to break out from the beaches. Guzzoni believed that his only hope was to station his most mobile units (largely German) close to the most likely landing beaches. Believing these to be on the southeast side of the island, he proposed concentrating both German divisions there. Fortunately for the Allies, Field Marshal Albert Kesselring refused, sending 15th Panzer Grenadier Division to the west, where, as the landing progressed, it would be ineffective until it moved back to the east, where Guzzoni had initially wanted to place it. As a result, when the landings came, Guzzoni lacked both the firepower and the mobility to push the Allies back into the sea, although he certainly tried.

Eighth Army landed against only minimal opposition and was quickly on the road to Augusta. Only in the Seventh Army sector did the Italians and Germans put up a fight. Bradley's II Corps had come ashore with Troy Middleton's 45th Infantry Division on the right near Scoglitti. It was to move inland to Ragusa and link up with Eighth Army's left flank. In the center, Terry Allen's experienced 1st Infantry Division, reinforced with two Ranger battalions, was to seize Gela and then move north toward Niscemi. Lucian Truscott's 3rd Infantry Division formed II Corp's left flank but remained under Patton's direct control. Patton retained most of 2nd Armored Division as well as the remainder of the 82nd Airborne Division and part of the 9th Infantry Division in reserve.

Axis forces responded with more courage than coordination to the landings of Bradley's corps. At Gela, 1st Infantry Division defeated two determined Italian counterattacks. Farther inland, paratroopers from the 82nd Airborne Division, with the help of naval gunfire support, turned back columns of Italian and German armor. Only in the 45th Infantry Division's area, where the Hermann Göring Division attacked with Tiger I tanks, did Axis forces have any success, and this was soon reversed. At the end of the first day's fighting, II Corps held fifty miles of beach to a depth of two to four miles.

The second day, Guzzoni again hit the Americans, attempting to cut their beachhead in two. He committed the better part of the Hermann Göring Division and the Italian Livorno Division, backed by close air support, against II Corps. Bradley found that the congestion on the landing beaches made it difficult to move armor forward to blunt the attack. As a result, anyone who could fire a weapon found himself pressed into service as infantry. Naval gunfire support and artillery weighed in, effectively stopping the enemy a mere 2,000 yards from the landing beaches near Gela.

Over the next few days Bradley's divisions shifted to the offensive, driving inland. All seemed to be going well until German reinforcements in the form of 1st Parachute Division entered the line opposite Eighth Army. Montgomery's advance ground to a halt. Rather than press on, he elected to ask Alexander for a boundary change that would place Route 124, Patton's primary axis of advance toward the island's northern coast, under Eighth Army control, effectively cutting the Americans off from any approach to Messina. Alexander assumed Messina would be a prize left for Montgomery and granted the request.[22] Patton and Bradley took the change of boundary as a slap in the face, believing that British generals, most notably Montgomery, were committed to allowing American forces to do the bleeding while British armies took the laurels. Bradley had to stop and disengage 45th Infantry, pull it back nearly to the landing beaches, and then move it to the left of 1st Infantry.

Patton's response was to create a provisional corps out of his reserve and dispatch it, under the guise of a reconnaissance, toward Palermo, Sicily's capital. Bradley's corps would continue to press northward toward the coast. Patton saw the opportunity to swing Bradley's corps eastward toward Messina after it reached the northern coast, particularly if German resistance in front of Eighth Army stiffened. For Patton, taking Messina ahead of Montgomery became a fixation. Relations between Patton and Bradley had been professional to this point but not particularly friendly. Though Bradley respected his superior's drive and skill, Patton's showboating style bothered the midwesterner. In Patton's rush to get II Corps to Messina, he admonished Bradley, "I want you to get to Messina just as fast as you can. I do not want you to waste time on these maneuvers, even if you've got to spend men to do it. I want to beat Monty to Messina!"[23] Bradley found the haste would gain little and cost much, particularly in blood.[24]

Thanks largely to the tenacity of the American soldier, Patton got his wish. The 45th Division reached the northern coastal road, turned east, and pressed on toward Messina. German and Italian units had created a series of defensive lines designed to delay the Seventh and Eighth armies long enough to make an evacuation of Sicily possible. The terrain in Sicily's northeast corner favored the defense. To bypass Axis positions, Bradley, at Patton's direction, staged a series of amphibious landings that helped speed II Corps soldiers to Messina ahead of the lead elements of British Eighth Army. Sicily rested in Allied hands; Italian dissidents deposed Benito Mussolini, and Allied lines of supply through the Mediterranean were secure. The victory was not all it could have been, however.

American reluctance to go any farther in the Mediterranean than Sicily, as well as concerns over the intentions of the Italian navy, meant that no plans had been made to blockade the Strait of Messina, which separates Sicily from the Italian mainland. The Allies did try to interdict the evacuation using airpower, but Axis antiaircraft fire rendered the effort ineffectual.[25] As a result, 40,000 German soldiers and airmen, along with 10,000 vehicles, escaped the island. So too did 70,000 Italian soldiers before Allied forces could close the strait. Bradley saw it as one of the largest Allied failures of the war; indeed, he was right, as the three and a half German divisions that escaped would be reconstituted to fight another day.[26]

Nonetheless, the campaign provided an unexpected opening

for Bradley. His rise to army commander may have been helped by Patton's maltreatment of a number of his soldiers, most notably Private Charles H. Kuhl. Reports of Patton's slapping of Kuhl made their way into the American press, where the publicity temporarily overshadowed Patton's accomplishments on the battlefield.[27] Bradley, on the other hand, continued to have friends in high places, most notably Marshall and Eisenhower.[28] Ike directed him to pack his bags, take those of his II Corps staff whom he wished, and find his way to England. There he would command the First Army, the American ground contingent for Operation Overlord, the Normandy landings. In addition, Bradley was to form an Army group headquarters in anticipation of an Allied buildup, breakout, and pursuit from the Normandy beachhead.[29]

First Army headquarters became operational in October 1943. The slapping incident aside, Marshall believed that, although Patton had demonstrated a flair for rapid movement in open terrain, it was Bradley whose prowess in handling units in constricted terrain over a contested battlefield was more appropriate to the anticipated problems of a landing in France.[30] Eisenhower seconded Marshall's view.[31] Allied planners foresaw the road to the Rhine as just such a battlefield. British shortages in manpower, particularly infantry, implied that operations in France would increasingly rely on American soldiers to carry the attack.[32]

British planners had laid the groundwork for a cross-Channel assault as early as 1941, but the earliest plans (Operation Roundup) envisioned a much smaller action that would be accompanied by a series of peripheral operations focused on wearing the Germans down. The assumption inherent in the original plan was that the German military would be engaged in a retrograde operation to the borders of Germany and would therefore probably offer only token resistance to the landings. Marshall not only questioned that assumption, but also saw this indirect approach as a waste of time and resources, perhaps considering the degree to which the American public would accept a long war.[33] The Soviets backed Marshall's view, hoping that a serious Anglo-American threat in France would provide the Red Army some respite.

Allied planning for a cross-Channel attack considered a number of different possibilities before electing to land in Normandy. At the heart of the planning rested a new assumption, namely that the Germans would be able to provide significant resistance to the

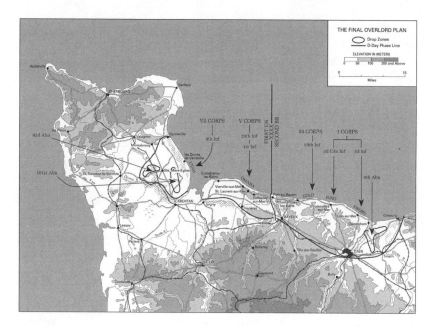

landings. The final plan envisioned Bradley's First Army, consisting of VII and V Corps, landing on the westernmost beaches, closest to Cherbourg, whose early capture was essential if additional manpower and supplies were to be brought quickly to the lodgment. XIX Corps would be in reserve. British Second Army, consisting of British XXX and I Corps, would land to the east, along the approaches to Caen. The interarmy boundary would be near Bayeux. The beaches assigned to each army reflected the staging areas the Allies would use in Great Britain. American units had generally arrived in Britain in its southwestern ports and were bivouacked close to what would be their embarkation ports for the invasion. British and Canadian divisions were located farther north and east.[34]

Bradley played a leading role in putting together the overall plan for the American landings. The operational questions inherent in such an ambitious undertaking yielded no easy answers. One of the most important questions dealt with how much Allied air cover could be expected over the beaches and whether it would be sufficient to hold the Germans at bay during the critical early hours of the landings. Allied armies ashore could expect as many as fifty-eight German divisions to be concentrated against them if airmen failed to provide adequate air cover or if airborne divisions failed to cut the beach approaches.[35] How many divisions could go ashore on D-Day? With the disastrous landings at Dieppe in 1942 in mind, Montgomery, who would be overall land force commander, had pressed for more extensive landings than earlier plans had entailed, but that would require landing craft in numbers not yet available in the theater. Near-herculean efforts and the postponement of Operation Anvil (later renamed Operation Dragoon, the invasion of southern France) produced the landing craft.[36] All or part of six divisions of American, British, and Canadian infantry would storm ashore in the first wave while three airborne divisions landed inland to secure the approaches to the landings. How many German divisions were available for defense of the beaches themselves, and how much capacity, particularly in the form of armored units, could the Germans employ to attack the beachheads? An Allied air campaign would cut the railroad bridges and staging areas from which the Germans could move reinforcements. How many tons of supplies would units need, given beach and port capabilities?[37] The invasion would be a race in which the Allies had to secure the beachhead and then build up significant forces to prevent being thrown into the sea by a German counterattack. The construction of two artificial harbors (code-named Mulberry) would give the logisticians some ability to push supplies to the beaches, and the taking of Cherbourg would, if it could be taken relatively intact, open a major port to Allied shipping.

These were the challenges that Bradley faced before the landings, but to make it all work would require more than exceptional staff effort. An opposed amphibious landing is one of the most difficult missions for any unit. The disastrous landings at Gallipoli during World War I had shown how not to do it. More recently, the U.S. Marine Corps's landing on Tarawa, in the Pacific, though successful, had been a bloody affair. Bradley made a point of being present to observe training, to reassure soldiers that he understood how much he was asking of them.

The invasion windows for Normandy were tight thanks to a requirement to land near low tide, preferably with a full moon and as close as possible to dawn. German strength was building, and the lunar calendar made clear that only three days in each lunar cycle were ideal for landing. Although planners hoped to go in May 1944, weather forced delay. In the following month, only June 4–6 worked well. The Germans had built extensive obstacles designed to rip the bottom out of landing craft under the assumption that allied landings would come at or near high tide. Landing in low tide would permit engineers to cut paths through the obstacle belt preparatory to the main landings. A low-tide option had the drawback of creating a deadly killing zone between the place where the landing craft would beach and the relative safety of the seawall, but this, planners believed, was the lesser of two evils.[38] Naval and aviation planners had made clear that their support could neutralize but not destroy many of the German defensive positions along the beach. To stop or hinder German reinforcement, Bradley insisted on the use of paratroopers landing behind the beaches to cut the roads and causeways leading to the beaches.[39] The paratroopers needed moonlight between midnight and dawn to make consolidation on the drop zones possible.

The Allies had done all in their power to confuse the Germans about the exact location and date of the landings. Until March 1944 Hitler had been convinced that the landings would come at Pas-de-Calais. A deception plan built around a fictitious American First Army Group commanded by Patton had helped sell the idea. At the end of March Hitler changed his mind, believing that the Allies would come ashore in Normandy, in the process accepting the belief of Field Marshal Erwin Rommel that the landings had to be defeated as early and as close to the beach as possible. The overall field commander in the West, Field Marshal Gerd von Rundstedt, disagreed with the assessment and argued against moving panzer units close to the beaches.[40] In May Hitler changed his mind again, deciding that landings would come at Normandy, but that they would be a diversion designed to bring about the shifting of German panzer units south, away from Calais, where the main Allied attack would fall. As a result, Hitler placed three of six panzer divisions under Rommel, but kept two SS panzer divisions under his own control some fifty miles from the beaches. Another panzer division would be in Belgium when the Allied naval flotilla set sail for Normandy on June 5, 1944.[41] The dispersal of German armored divisions, as well as problems in the German chain of command, hindered the German response and bought the Allies time once the invasion began.

Bradley watched the landings on June 6, 1944, from the heavy cruiser USS *Augusta*. After some early tense moments on Utah Beach, VII Corps's 4th Infantry Division gained a foothold and began to push inland. On Omaha Beach it was another matter.

Throughout the morning of June 6, Bradley waited, by his own admission largely powerless, while the V Corps's 1st Infantry Division and 29th Infantry Division struggled to move forward from the seawall. To avoid German coastal artillery, the Navy had launched many of the landing craft over ten miles offshore. German guns had ample opportunity to take them under fire well before they reached the beach.[42] Most of the amphibious tanks assigned to support the landings foundered in the surf. Men arrived seasick, cold, and wet if they arrived at all. In addition, the Germans had recently positioned the 352nd Infantry Division in the area behind Omaha Beach. The Germans defended their positions well, and little that Allied air or naval gunfire could do proved sufficient to dislodge them. Bradley considered pulling his forces from Omaha, but his soldiers saved him the choice. Increasingly, as company-grade officers and sergeants led frightened men forward, German soldiers began to give ground.[43] By the end of the morning, Omaha Beach belonged to the First Army. On Gold, Juno, and Sword beaches, British and Canadian troops had also landed successfully. Allied forces had a lodgment on what Hitler had boasted would be Fortress Europe.

Over the following weeks, Eisenhower saw to it that his Army commanders built up their forces. The limited port facilities hindered the buildup, and after seven weeks at no place was the beachhead more than thirty miles deep.[44] The reality was that the Allies were behind schedule. The original plans called for all of Normandy to be in Allied hands by the end of June, but they held only a fifth of the province by month's end.[45] In the American zone, Bradley had three corps (V, VII, and XIX) ashore. He would add VIII Corps as well. With the arrival of the additional strength, Bradley pushed his forces inland against stiff German defenses. As V Corps pressed south toward Caumont, VII Corps, with 9th Infantry Division in the lead, raced to cut the Cotentin Peninsula before turning north toward Cherbourg, and 4th Infantry Division moved north along the opposite coast. Cherbourg fell to Bradley's soldiers on June 27. The Allies now had their port, but German demolition crews had ensured it would be of little use for months. Over most of July Bradley expanded his beachhead southward.

The problem with the area beyond the American beaches was that it was hedgerow country, usually referred to as the *bocage*. This series of small fields surrounded by dirt and stone walls five feet tall usually covered in underbrush created difficulties for any attacking force. The Germans had understood this. Fields of fire were constricted, visibility difficult, and camouflage for the defender ample. The hedgerows made it difficult for tanks and infantry to support one another. The terrain limited advances to yards rather than miles; many believed that the situation was quickly re-creating something akin to the battlefields of World War I. The casualty figures certainly suggested as much. Increasingly, Allied leaders, including Bradley, were coming in for criticism. Patton, still in England but slated to command what would be Third Army in France, claimed that if he were commander of First Army, he would break through to open country in three days.[46] As casualties mounted, particularly in the infantry, Bradley's next challenge was to find a way to break through the hedgerows and turn his soldiers toward the Rhine. Operation Cobra, the breakout from the Normandy beachhead, would be Bradley's signature victory of World War II. Meant as only a limited-objective penetration, it created the conditions that took Allied armies nearly all the way to the German border.

Bradley envisioned the use of heavy, medium, and light bombers to blast an opening in German Seventh Army positions before unleashing first VII Corps and then the rest of First Army into a penetration that he hoped would become an exploitation of a shattered foe. Infantry divisions would punch the initial holes in German defenses, and then two armored divisions and one motorized infantry division would conduct the exploitation. The employment of heavy bombers in support of ground troops was not something that strategic bombing advocates saw as a wise employment of a limited asset. Lieutenant General Carl A. Spaatz, who commanded the United States Strategic Air Forces, adamantly opposed the idea, but Bradley, with support from Marshall and Eisenhower, was able to get Spaatz to dedicate 1,500 of his heavy bombers to the attack.[47] Cobra called for saturation bombing of an area one mile by five miles just south of the Saint-Lô–Périers road. The bombing was to take an hour to complete; to maximize the blast effect while minimizing cratering, which might slow the attack, light bombs (one hundred pounds) rather than heavier ordnance were used. Furthermore, Bradley proposed that to negate the possibility of fratricide, the bombers were to approach on a path parallel to the forward line of troops (FLOT).

Bradley personally briefed his plan to Eighth and Ninth Army Air Force planners and met immediate opposition to parts of the plan. Flying parallel to the FLOT would expose planes flying at low altitudes to excessive antiaircraft fire. Instead, the air avenue of approach needed to be perpendicular to the FLOT. In addition, air planners argued that they would need ground forces to withdraw 3,000 feet from forward positions.[48] Bradley countered that ground forces needed to hit German positions as rapidly as possible after the bombing to take full advantage of the confusion the bombardment would create and argued for an 800-yard withdrawal. The two sides compromised, agreeing to 1,250 yards. An additional 250-yard strip for fighter bombers meant that 1,500 yards of ground should exist between the impact area and Bradley's soldiers. Bradley believed he had won the argument on the parallel versus perpendicular approach to the target area. He had not, and this proved a costly mistake.[49]

Army Air Force planners believed that the only workable approach to the bombing was to come in perpendicular to the target largely because of the difficulties weather and terrain might present in computing bomb release points. The Saint-Lô road, it was feared, would not be easily discernible to the heavy bombers at 15,000 feet. The Normandy coast could serve as an initial checkpoint and the Saint-Lô road as the final for confirmation of range to the target. In addition, funneling 1,500 bombers through a one-mile-wide target box in an hour was not possible.[50] The Air Force's concerns were real and prompted changes to the plan; unfortunately and inexplicably, none of these changes was provided to Bradley or his subordinates.

Ninth and Eighth Air Forces were to open Operation Cobra on July 24. Planes departed their airfields in England, but weather over the target forced an inflight cancellation. Unfortunately, not all the planes got the word in time, and 317 planes dropped their loads over what they presumed to be the target. Some of the bombs landed in the 30th Infantry Division area, killing 25 soldiers and wounding 131 others. Bradley demanded to know what had happened, and only then did he discover the changes. Rescheduling the attack was possible, but only if he would accept the fact that a subsequent attempt would also be perpendicular to the FLOT. Bradley reluctantly assented, passing the changes to corps and division commanders.

On July 25 the planes again set out for Normandy. Again, not all went according to plan. Ninth Air Force fighter bombers tore up the ground in front of VII Corps, creating clouds of smoke and dust that drifted southward over the bombing area designated for heavy

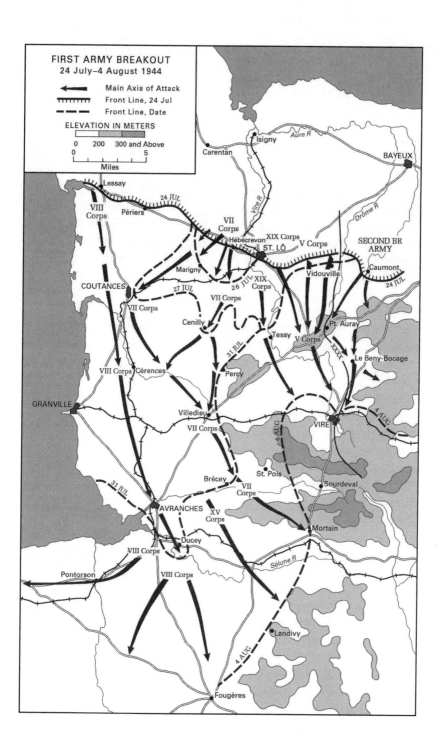

FIRST ARMY BREAKOUT
24 July–4 August 1944

⟵ Main Axis of Attack
⊤⊤⊤⊤⊤⊤ Front Line, 24 Jul
▬ ▬ ▬ Front Line, Date

ELEVATION IN METERS

0   200   300 and Above

0   5
Miles

Aure R

Isigny

Carentan

BAYEUX

Lessay

24 JUL

VIII
Corps

Périers

Vire R

Drôme R

VII
Corps

Hébécrevon

XIX Corps

V Corps

SECOND BR
ARMY

ST. LÔ

Marigny

Vidouville

Caumont

24 JUL

COUTANCES

27 JUL

26 JUL

XIX
Corps

Pt. Auray

VII Corps

VII Corps

Cenilly

31 JUL

Tessy

V Corps

Le Beny-Bocage

XXX

VIII Corps Cérences

Percy

GRANVILLE

Villedieu

VIRE

4 AUG

VII Corps

4 AUG

Brécey

St. Pois

Sourdeval

VII
Corps

AVRANCHES

XV
Corps

Mortain

31 JUL

Ducey

VIII Corps

Pontorson

Sélune R

VIII Corps

Landivy

4 AUG

Fougères

bombers. Nearly all of the 1,500 heavy bombers assigned to the mission dropped their bombs. Most hit within the target box, but some bombs again fell on the unlucky 30th Division, killing another 61 soldiers and wounding 374 others. Among the dead was Lieutenant General Lesley J. McNair, commanding general of Army Ground Forces.[51] Nonetheless, VII Corps divisions pressed forward, initially experiencing considerable opposition before German units began to give ground. The VII Corps commander, Lawton Collins, sensed that German defenses, under pressure from his infantry, were losing their coherence. With Bradley's approval, Collins unleashed his armored divisions on the morning of July 26 with devastating effect. By the afternoon, his forces had penetrated German forward defenses to a distance of several miles. The following day, as the extent of German collapse became apparent, Bradley turned his corps due south toward Avranches, in preparation for an attack into the Brittany peninsula in hopes of seizing additional ports.

To keep German reinforcements from Bradley's front, Montgomery had British Second Army open an offensive in the vicinity of Caen. The attack worked, keeping the bulk of German armor focused on Caen even as German defenses collapsed to the west. By the middle of July Patton had most of his Third Army in Normandy, whereupon Bradley relinquished command of First Army to Courtney H. Hodges and assumed command of newly activated Twelfth Army Group. The roles were now reversed: Patton now worked for Bradley. Third Army would assume the task of seizing Brittany's ports. The lack of cohesion German Seventh Army was showing allowed Patton to do this with only one corps, and the remainder of his army became available in support of Bradley's next move, a turning movement designed to destroy German Seventh Army west of the Seine River. The plan was daring and made exceptional use of the American Army's advantage in mobility. Eisenhower had early on made it clear that his approach to defeating Germany was to destroy its army before it could retreat behind the Rhine. Bradley was intent on doing exactly this. Unbeknown to Eisenhower, Montgomery, and Bradley, Hitler was soon to help the Allied armies in their task.

Hitler's initial response to the Allied landings in Normandy had been to assume that they were but a diversion. By the end of July it was clear, even to him, that this was not the case. Rather than order Army Group B's commander, Field Marshal Günther von Kluge, to withdraw to better positions along the Seine, Hitler directed a coun-terattack near Mortain. Twelfth Army Group was vulnerable there: the Mortain-Avranches corridor was all that linked First Army with Third Army. Hitler ordered the commitment of a complete panzer army, but by this stage there was neither time nor resources to cob-ble one together. Kluge did what he could, and the panzer divisions available pushed the Americans back six miles but could go no far-ther. The Americans counterattacked and, with overwhelming air support, stabilized the line. The combination of the German pene-tration and Allied counterattacks had made German Seventh Army vulnerable to an attack on its open southern flank. Montgomery's armies, along with part of the American First Army, held the north-ern side of the pocket. Bradley saw an opportunity to send Patton's Third Army east and then north toward Falaise, into the vulnerable flank.[52] Canadian First Army would attack southward to close the pocket. Montgomery established an Army group boundary south of Falaise to permit fire support coordination and to prevent fratricide.

The plan came close to working perfectly. Though Third Army performed superbly, Canadian First, facing heavy resistance, was unable to close to the boundary. Patton begged for permission to cross the boundary, but Bradley, perhaps with memories of the frat-ricide that had occurred at the beginning of Cobra, refused, halt-ing Third Army at Argentan. He could have requested a boundary change to allow Patton to move forward, but he chose not to do so. As a result, thousands of German soldiers escaped to fight an-other day. This left little in the way of a coherent defense in front of American forces, however. Both First and Third armies began a monthlong press toward the Rhine against little German resistance.

Bradley assumed responsibility for stopping Patton, but he ar-gued that had Montgomery's First Canadian Army been more vig-orous in its attack toward Falaise, the Allies would have closed the pocket as planned. Nonetheless, Operation Cobra and the pursuit that followed were decidedly the result of Bradley's vision. The lost opportunity of Falaise aside, the weeks ahead would be heady in-deed for Allied forces as they raced toward the Rhine and what they hoped would be an early end to the war. Their optimism would run out in the face of the hard reality of logistics.

Cobra had worked beyond anyone's wildest imagination, but the resulting exploitation began to stretch the Allies' supply lines. Logistics, particularly in the area of fuel and ammunition, presented a problem for Allied operations as British and American armies pressed deeper into France. Allied strategy largely followed Eisenhower's vision. He had early on favored a broad front, and although he wavered in that during the fall of 1944, in August the impending collapse of German armies pulled Twenty-first Army Group (Montgomery) and Twelfth Army Group (Bradley) ever forward in a front that was growing not only in depth but also in width. Logisticians had planned on a measured advance and ample time to bring up supplies. They had assumed that a system of depots would provide the stores necessary to propel the Allied attack and had anticipated a lengthy halt at the Seine to build them. The rapid pursuit by Allied armies, particularly Third Army and First Army, undermined those plans, as did the delay in capturing the ports. In addition to the challenge of getting ammunition and fuel to the European mainland, there was the problem of transporting it to attacking armies. Logisticians calculated they would need 240 truck companies, but only 160 landed in France.[53] Allied air attacks had destroyed French railroads, which Allied logisticians had hoped to use. While the railroads were being repaired, a continual express of trucks from ports to armies and then back again attempted to pick up the slack. Traffic jams and problems with maintenance hindered the effort, but truck supply made possible some degree of movement until September, when the well ran dry.[54] No degree of leadership could coax forward a tank lacking fuel, and in the operational pause that ensued, the German Army was able to reconstitute itself.

Eisenhower had directed Bradley and Montgomery to press their attacks forward with due haste. Montgomery's key mission in the late summer and early fall had been to seize and open the port of Antwerp and press ahead to the Ruhr Valley, Germany's industrial heartland.[55] Antwerp was Europe's largest port and promised to solve Allied supply problems if it and its approaches could be taken. Montgomery's focus, however, became that of gaining the Ruhr and if possible striking out across the north German plain to Berlin. He had hoped that Eisenhower would assign First Army to guard his flank while Patton's Third was effectively halted along the Meuse River. Antwerp became an afterthought until Eisenhower made it clear that the port had to be opened. Antwerp fell to Montgomery in September, but he failed to clear the approaches until November 28, 1944, effectively crippling Bradley's ability to move forward.[56]

Bradley adamantly opposed Montgomery's narrow front, arguing that it permitted the Germans to concentrate their limited resources against one army group. Conceding that the terrain favored Montgomery's army group over his own, Bradley saw the need for a secondary attack that, if Montgomery's efforts failed, would offer an alternative approach to the German heartland. This two-front approach (the addition of Alexander Patch's Sixth Army Group driving up the Rhône River offering a third front) compounded the German Army's inability to defend the German heartland.

German defenses had stiffened, and the heady days of August were a thing of the past. Montgomery managed to convince Eisenhower that if given command of the three airborne divisions that Supreme Headquarters Allied Expeditionary Force (SHAEF) held in reserve, a series of parachute landings in conjunction with a determined armored attack up the Highway 69 corridor the paratroopers controlled would propel the British across the Rhine and into the Ruhr. Beyond the Ruhr lay the north German plains and the seduction of an open road to Berlin. Montgomery hoped to have control over First Army to guard his flank. The operation was code-named Market Garden, and Montgomery got his airborne drop with First Army assigned to support him. The remainder of Bradley's Army group marked time. When the Germans stopped Montgomery's assault short of the Rhine, Eisenhower returned to a broad-front approach. Eisenhower freed Bradley to resume his offensives, making Twelfth Army Group, with First Army back under his control, the Allied main effort in November. First Army would move toward Aachen and the Ruhr while Third Army would move into Lorraine, cross the Moselle in the vicinity of Metz, and seek crossing points over the Rhine that would lead to Frankfurt. Encircling the Ruhr from the south became a possibility for future operations. The problem with the approach was that as Allied armies pressed forward, the amount of frontage grew. Bradley found himself stretched thin; there was little in the way of an Army group reserve available either to leverage a breakthrough or to block an attack.

Eisenhower saw fit to strengthen Bradley's hand by assigning William Hood Simpson's Ninth Army to Twelfth Army Group. Bradley initially placed Ninth Army between First and Third armies, but then in November, fearing that Montgomery might again gain control over one of his armies in his push northward, he shifted Ninth to form his flank with Montgomery's Twenty-first Army Group. Bradley had no intention of letting First Army fall under Montgomery's control, but he was willing to sacrifice the less experienced Ninth if need be.

The war on the Western Front from September through November was largely an infantryman's fight.[57] What had been a war of maneuver became one of attrition. The taxing battles of November pressured U.S. Army resources. Freezing rains, flooded streams, and the accompanying cases of trench foot, as well as determined German defenders, drained the optimism of summer.[58] Patton's thrust through Lorraine slowed to a crawl in front of Metz. Hodges had requested permission from Bradley to take control of the Hürtgen Forest to secure his flanks before a larger offensive into the Ruhr. Bradley agreed. The Hürtgen proved a bloodbath for the units Hodges committed. Two badly battered but well-dug-in German infantry divisions chewed up four U.S. Infantry divisions during November.[59] Costing over 33,000 casualties, control of the forest may have been worth the toll had it materially contributed to access to the Ruhr. It did not, and the limited mobility of the German units in the woods made suspect the assumption that they could do much to threaten Hodges's flanks.[60] By the time November was over, Bradley conceded that his hopes to "smash through to the Rhine" had failed.[61]

With the coming of December, Bradley's armies were stretched thin, particularly in the Ardennes. Eisenhower had directed Bradley to attack toward the Ruhr, First Army swinging to the north of the Ardennes and Third to its south. In the Ardennes itself, Bradley elected to accept the risk of assigning the area to First Army's VIII Corps under Troy Middleton. The VIII consisted of four divisions, including the badly damaged 28th Infantry Division and the 106th Infantry Division, a division new to combat.

Bradley was repeating what he had done in North Africa, namely holding an extensive front with minimum forces. Middleton's four divisions were covering a front of seventy-five miles in heavily wooded, compartmentalized terrain, roughly eighteen miles per division. Neither the corps nor the Army group had any real reserves, nor was it expected that any would be needed. Allied intelligence had come to rely on Ultra intercepts (intelligence gained by breaking encrypted German communications), none of which indicated a major offensive was in the offing.[62] The Ardennes seemed a quiet, safe sector, but it would soon prove to be exactly the place Hitler elected to wager one last throw of the dice.

The Germans had used the Ardennes in the Franco-Prussian

War, as well as in their 1940 attack on France, to good effect. Bradley was well aware of the area's history; however, in the two earlier campaigns, the Germans had managed to overcome the limited road network through superior mobility in relation to their foes. Hitler's plan for Army Group B (now under the command of Field Marshal Walter Model), consisting of three armies (Sixth SS Panzer, Fifth Panzer, and Seventh Army) that he would send into the Ardennes, was that they penetrate First Army positions, cross the Meuse near Namur, and then wheel right and drive north toward Antwerp. Sixth SS Panzer Army in the original plan would provide the main attack while also expanding and holding the northern flank of the penetration. Seventh Army, with only four infantry divisions, would secure the southern flank. Fifth Panzer would secure Sixth Panzer's left flank and press toward Brussels.[63] Fifteenth Army would provide a supporting attack to the northeast toward Maastricht from Aachen. When Antwerp fell, Allied armies would be split and the way open for a negotiated settlement—or so Hitler hoped.

It was a gamble German field commanders, most notably Rundstedt and Model, believed beyond their capabilities, for though men and machines were available, fuel was not.[64] Allied fuel depots would have to be captured intact, a highly questionable proposition. The plan also rested on inclement weather minimizing Allied air superiority. It assumed the complete collapse of American frontline divisions. Underlying it all was a strict schedule. Hitler assumed his panzers would reach the Meuse in two days. Rundstedt thought it would take four. Plans are only as good as the validity of the facts and assumptions that underlie them, and in this case the assumptions proved false.

When the German attack came on December 16, it came with eight panzer divisions, twenty-eight infantry divisions, and two mechanized brigades, a total of 200,000 men. Over 500 tanks supported the assault.[65] Facing Fifth Panzer Army, the U.S. 106th and 28th divisions could not hold, the former essentially disintegrating on the second day and the latter being encircled and forced back, one of its regiments shattered.[66] The American front collapsed as planned; resistance did not. American soldiers caught in the maelstrom fought back against the German advance. The tight schedule for German units to reach the key crossroad towns of Bastogne and St. Vith unraveled, first by minutes, then by hours, finally by days.

The Allies had been caught off guard by the German attack and

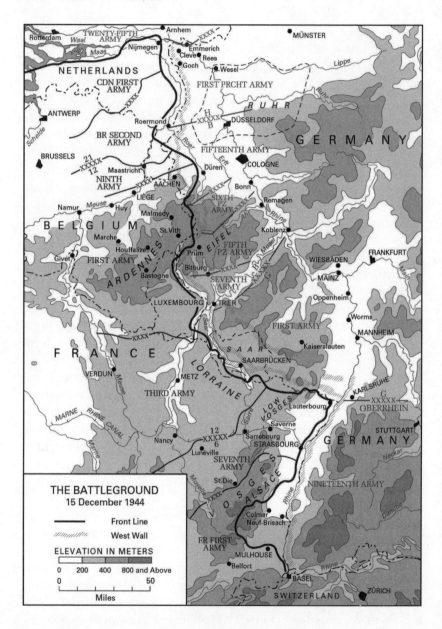

THE BATTLEGROUND
15 December 1944

——— Front Line

////// West Wall

ELEVATION IN METERS

0   200   400   800 and Above

0   50

Miles

were arguably slow to react.[67] Bradley mistakenly believed it a spoiling attack and dispatched, with Eisenhower's approval, two armored divisions (7th Armored from Ninth Army and 10th Armored from Third Army) to the support of Middleton's VIII Corps.[68] As

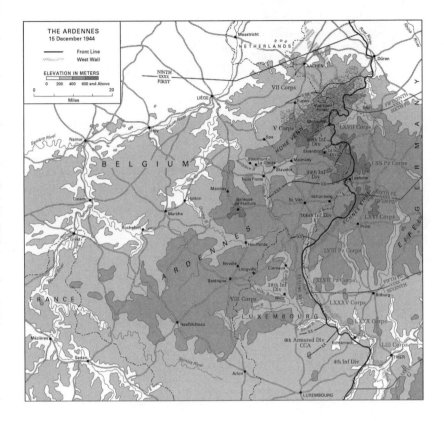

the enemy picture worsened, Bradley maintained his composure. When subordinates pointed out that Twelfth Army Group headquarters in Luxembourg City, then located near the path of the German onslaught, was threatened, Bradley responded: "I will never move backwards with a headquarters. There is too much prestige at stake."[69]

Eisenhower's view of the situation was that he had to prevent the German Army from crossing the Meuse. To do this, he assigned Montgomery the task of securing the Meuse River crossings behind the American VIII Corps. By December 19 Montgomery held the river's west bank and its bridges with the tanks of his XXX Corps. The emerging enemy order of battle suggested that this might well be the last large-scale operational reserve remaining on the Western Front, and with that realization Bradley saw an opportunity to create a second Falaise pocket—one he intended to close.

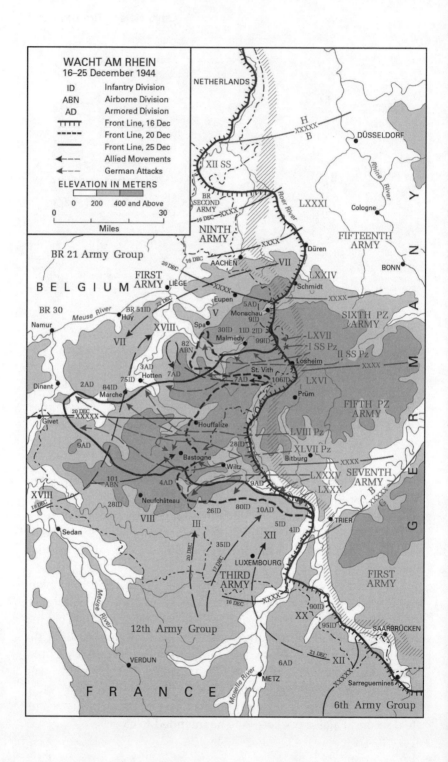

WACHT AM RHEIN
16–25 December 1944

ID   Infantry Division
ABN   Airborne Division
AD   Armored Division
⊤⊤⊤⊤⊤   Front Line, 16 Dec
- - - -   Front Line, 20 Dec
———   Front Line, 25 Dec
←- - -   Allied Movements
←———   German Attacks

ELEVATION IN METERS

0   200   400 and Above

0   30
            Miles

NETHERLANDS

H
XXXXX
B

DÜSSELDORF

XII SS

BR SECOND ARMY
16 DEC   XXXX

LXXXI

Rhine River

Cologne

NINTH ARMY

FIFTEENTH ARMY

BR 21 Army Group

20 DEC   16 DEC

AACHEN

XXXX

Düren

VII

BONN

B E L G I U M

FIRST ARMY   LIÈGE

Roer River

Schmidt

LXXIV

SIXTH PZ ARMY

BR 30

Meuse River   BR 51   Huy
22 DEC

XVIII

VII

Eupen

5AD

Monschau
9ID

Spa

V

XXXX

Namur

Dinant

82 ABN

3AD

75ID   Hotten

7AD

30ID   1ID 2ID
Malmédy   99ID

LXVII
I SS Pz

II SS Pz

Losheim

St. Vith

7AD   106ID

LXVI

Prüm

XXXX

FIFTH PZ ARMY

2AD

84ID
Marche

20 DEC
XXXXX

Givet

9AD

Houffalize

Bastogne

Wiltz

28ID

Bitburg

LVIII Pz

XLVII Pz

XXXX

101 ABN

4AD

Neufchâteau

9AD

LXXXV   SEVENTH ARMY

LXXX

B

XVIII

28ID

VIII

19 DEC

Sedan

26ID   80ID
III

35ID

20 DEC

17 DEC

10AD

5ID   4ID

XII

LUXEMBOURG

TRIER

FIRST ARMY

12th Army Group

THIRD ARMY

16 DEC   XXXX

90ID

XX

95ID

SAARBRÜCKEN

G E R M A N Y

VERDUN

Moselle River

METZ

6AD

21 DEC

XII

XXXXX

Sarreguemines

F R A N C E

6th Army Group

Bradley directed that St. Vith and Bastogne, two key crossroads towns, be reinforced and held as long as possible. He requested that Eisenhower give him the SHAEF reserve consisting of XVIII Airborne Corps (101st and 82nd Airborne divisions) to assist in contesting the two towns. Middleton assigned St. Vith to 7th Armored Division, and there they stayed for several critical days before overwhelming enemy pressure forced the town's evacuation.[70] Combat Command Reserve (CCR) of the 10th Armored Division and 101st Airborne Division reached Bastogne just in time to prevent its fall, winning the race in no small measure owing to remnants of American units that contested the German advance. Though the 101st and CCR were soon surrounded, they held the key crossroads town, effectively slowing the German advance to the Meuse bridges. On the edges of the penetration, Bradley ordered that the shoulders be held, limiting the roads available to pass German units forward and constricting their logistics flow. Hodges assigned four U.S. divisions (1st, 2nd, 9th, and 99th Infantry divisions) the task.[71] They too held. In the south, at Bradley's direction, Patton effectively changed Third Army's direction of advance by ninety degrees, slamming his divisions into the flank of the German Seventh Army.[72] Bradley further directed that 4th Armored Division relieve Bastogne.[73] The German timetable had fallen seriously behind in the face of unexpected American resistance. To make matters worse for the Germans, the skies cleared, bringing American bombers.

Had Bradley retained command of an intact Twelfth Army Group, the German penetration might well have been cut off and destroyed as he had envisioned. It was not. The blame fell, perhaps unjustly, on Montgomery, who, during the darkest hours of the German attack, had lobbied Eisenhower for and received command of Ninth Army and those elements of First Army north of the penetration, effectively leaving Bradley command of only Third Army and XVIII Airborne Corps. Accepting the argument that the German penetration threatened Twelfth Army Group's two armies north of the penetration, Eisenhower, with Bradley's grudging acceptance, agreed to the transfer, but he noted that it was only a temporary change.

Had Montgomery seen the operational picture in the same light, the result should have been the same; he did not. Following Eisenhower's orders, he (as mentioned previously) secured the Meuse River bridges but failed to do anything of substance in attacking

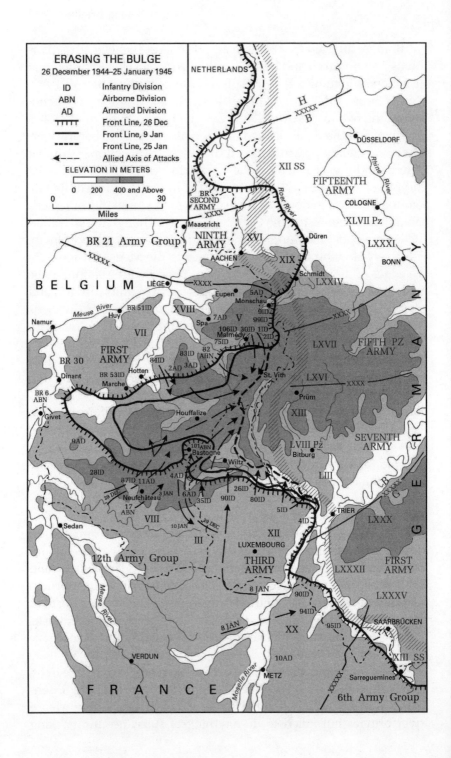

ERASING THE BULGE
26 December 1944–25 January 1945

ID   Infantry Division
ABN   Airborne Division
AD   Armored Division
⊤⊤⊤⊤⊤   Front Line, 26 Dec
━━━━   Front Line, 9 Jan
- - - -   Front Line, 25 Jan
◄–·–·   Allied Axis of Attacks

ELEVATION IN METERS

0   200   400 and Above

0   30
        Miles

NETHERLANDS

H
B

XXXXX

DÜSSELDORF

XII SS

FIFTEENTH
ARMY

Roer River

Rhine River

BR
SECOND
ARMY

XVI

Maastricht

NINTH
ARMY

XIX

COLOGNE

XLVII Pz

LXXXI

BR 21 Army Group

AACHEN

Düren

BONN

BELGIUM

LIÈGE

Schmidt

LXXIV

Eupen   5AD
Monschau

Meuse River

BR 51D

XVIII

7AD   V   9ID
99ID

Namur

Huy

VII

Spa   106ID 30ID 1ID
Malmédy   2ID
75ID

LXVII

FIFTH PZ
ARMY

FIRST
ARMY

84ID   83ID

82
ABN

2AD 3AD

St. Vith

LXVI

XXXX

BR 30

Dinant

BR 53ID
Marche

Hotten

Houffalize

Prüm

XIII

BR 6
ABN

Givet

9AD

101ABN
Bastogne

LVIII Pz
Bitburg

SEVENTH
ARMY

28ID

87ID 11AD

4AD

Wiltz

LIII

29 DEC

Neufchâteau

17
ABN

3 JAN

6AD

35ID

26ID

80ID

90ID

5ID

4ID

TRIER

LXXX

VIII

10 JAN

29 DEC

III

LUXEMBOURG

XII

THIRD
ARMY

FIRST
ARMY

Sedan

12th Army Group

Meuse River

8 JAN

90ID

LXXXII

94ID

LXXXV

8 JAN

XX

95ID

SAARBRÜCKEN

VERDUN

10AD

METZ

Moselle River

Sarreguemines

XIII SS

FRANCE

6th Army Group

GERMANY

the penetration from the north until early January, arguing that the Americans had taken such a beating that he would need time to "tidy up" the situation before a sustained offensive could be attempted; the opportunity slipped away. Over the first several weeks of January 1945, the Allies closed the salient. The Germans conducted an orderly delay as they evacuated those units and equipment that could possibly get out of the Ardennes. Backward they fell toward the Rhine and the hoped-for safety of the Siegfried Line. Out of fuel or destroyed, little of the armor that had spearheaded the offensive came back through the Ardennes.

At this time Eisenhower received notice that he had been promoted to a fifth star. Understanding that splitting Twelfth Army Group and putting Ninth and most of First Army under Montgomery's control might be seen as an expression of a lack of confidence in Bradley, Ike asked that Bradley receive a fourth star. Marshall agreed, as did President Roosevelt. The promotion may have lessened some of the sting, but the effect did not last long.

The German Army had lost heavily in the Ardennes, but the Allies had suffered as well. Estimates vary from a low of 67,000 to a high of 100,000 German soldiers killed, captured, or wounded, compared to 80,000 Allied soldiers lost, most of them American.[74] In addition to the killed and wounded, however, Montgomery managed to make a casualty of the Allied coalition, for in a press conference after the Battle of the Bulge, he suggested that First Army had been badly served by its leadership and that he had saved the cause. In truth, Montgomery and Twenty-first Army contributed to the outcome. Montgomery did assemble a coherent defense along the northern half of the German penetration. He had rushed XXX Corps to the Meuse River bridges, and a few British units had seen combat, such as the 6th Airborne Division and the 52nd Lowland Division.[75] Nonetheless, the fight had been largely an American fight, involving the whole or partial engagement of thirty-two U.S. divisions. It had been the Americans who had upset the timetable and the Americans who had ensured that much-needed fuel did not fall into the hands of the Germans. Only a handful of German soldiers ever got within sight of the Meuse, thanks to the efforts of Bradley's soldiers.[76] American units had been surprised in the Ardennes, to be sure, but as Bradley had believed, mobility compensated for numbers. There would be no repeat of the German attack of 1940 against second-echelon French divisions. Had Montgomery been willing to gamble his reputation on the ability of his First and Ninth Army units to close the pocket from the north, as Patton had done in the south, the way ahead might well have been open. It was a wager he only belatedly made.

The reduction of the Ardennes salient was complete by January 28, 1945. Bradley's Army group, again containing First and Third armies, pushed on toward the Rhine as part of Eisenhower's plan to close the three Allied army groups on the river before crossing and driving into the heart of Germany. One major German pocket existed in Lieutenant General Jacob Devers's area. Eisenhower ordered it reduced. Bradley's orders were to continue to push forward until stopped and then go on the defensive. The one exception to this directive was that Ike freed Bradley to take advantage of any opportunity that offered a way to seize control of the Roer River dams. In February Eisenhower brought Twelfth Army Group to a stop. The task at hand became that of crossing the Rhine.

Eisenhower's plan for the Rhine campaign called for Twenty-first Army Group to provide the main thrust with a drive to the north of the Ruhr while Twelfth Army Group delivered a secondary attack aimed at Frankfurt. Neither Bradley nor his subordinates, Hodges and Patton, intended to see their mission as a supporting attack for Montgomery. Eisenhower had given them enough leeway to presume that, if they were successful, Eisenhower would make Twelfth Army Group the main effort. The plan called for First Army to drive toward the junction of the Ahr and Rhine rivers, then swing south to meet Patton's Third Army. Once in motion, the two armies picked up momentum as German resistance began to collapse. First Army units began to reach the Rhine, only to find that German engineers had blown up the bridges, in some cases as the Americans looked on. All the usable bridges fell, except one—the bridge at Remagen. First Army had its bridge across the Rhine. Rather than wait for orders, Bradley ordered Hodges to get as many men as possible across the bridge. Eisenhower seconded the decision, telling Bradley to get five divisions across and expand the bridgehead. It was an unnecessary order, as Bradley was already reinforcing the bridgehead.

Patton, in the meantime, was to attack German defenses along the Moselle east from Trier toward the Rhine. Bradley feared Eisenhower would tell him to give some of his divisions to Devers; rather than allow this to happen, he meant to get Patton engaged so that such a diversion of his forces would be impractical. Patton ensured that Bradley got his wish. When Patton pushed the German forces, they soon gave ground, their defense becoming more disjointed the deeper the Americans advanced. In the ten days between March 11 and 21, Third Army moved from the Moselle to the Rhine. Allied armies soon controlled the Rhine's west bank from Switzerland to the North Sea. By the end of March all three Allied army groups had bridgeheads across the Rhine. Ninth Army would soon rejoin Twelfth Army Group for the final push. Hitler's Germany was in its death throes.

The last offensive for Bradley's armies would be ensuring that the remnants of the Nazi leadership did not find haven in the German Alps. In hindsight, it now seems this mission was unnecessary. Surrounded by the Red Army in his bunker, Hitler committed suicide. With the German military now shattered and the morale of the German people broken, there would be no last Nazi stand in the Alps. The war in Europe drew to a close on May 7, 1945. For Bradley this spelled the end of his combat experience, for although he quickly asked for reassignment to the Pacific, General Douglas MacArthur made it clear that he had no need for another Army group commander. Marshall elected not to push the issue in Bradley's behalf, having another mission in mind for his friend.

Marshall understood that the scope of the war would create a tremendous demand for services to take care of returning veterans. The Veterans Administration (VA) held this charge. It was here that Marshall believed Bradley's skills would best serve the country, for the agency had become ossified over the years.

The VA faced a daunting task. Estimates were that 10 percent of World War II veterans would seek services from the administration. By the end of 1946 it was clear that number would top 25 percent.[77] Expanding and improving medical services became Bradley's first challenge. Opening educational benefits for 15 million returning veterans proved his second. He convinced Congress to drop the age ceiling, then twenty-five, for receiving educational benefits, and college enrollments increased from 1.3 million at war's end to 2.3 million by 1947.[78] During his tenure as director of the VA, Bradley extended services to more than 17 million veterans in programs ranging from health care to job training. The effort did not escape the attention of President Truman when General Eisenhower, then chief of staff of the Army, elected to retire.

Bradley was the natural successor to Eisenhower as the Army's chief of staff. Ike had been given the painful task of taking apart the Army he had helped create. Demobilization happened quickly following the end of the war, and the downsizing left an army consisting of what seemed more like police and clerks than soldiers. Truman had made it clear that he intended to bring federal deficits down, and the U.S. military would pay for the reductions. Events in Europe and Asia brought a reevaluation of this decision. The Soviet Union's Joseph Stalin increasingly seemed to see the Red Army as an occupation force in areas it had conquered during the war, while it systematically created puppet governments to solidify its gains. The question facing American military leadership was how to ensure that the Soviets were contained within the areas they already held. Bradley faced this issue as well as others when he became the Army's chief of staff in February 1948.

The War Department's answer to the Soviet threat rested on airpower in the form of Operation Halfmoon, the first unified war plan of the postwar era. In the event of war with the Soviet Union, the U.S. military would hit seventy Soviet cities with 133 atomic bombs. U.S. Army units would secure the airbases from which the air attacks would be launched and then, following full mobilization, occupy western Europe and the Soviet Union. The plan required eighteen combat-ready divisions at the onset, and would cost $30 billion, two and a half times what the Truman administration was willing to spend. Operation Off Tackle was the successor to Halfmoon. Depending on airpower to decide the conflict, the plan called for the dropping of 292 atomic bombs as well as 17,000 tons of conventional munitions. Its requirements for ground forces were less clear. In the disparity between war plans and budgets, the Truman administration came increasingly to rely on airpower and atomic weapons to fight war on the cheap. Dubbing the effort "cheap-easy-victory through air power alone," Bradley increasingly found himself on the defensive, believing the reliance on atomic weapons to be shortsighted and too rigid. He would prove to be right on both accounts.[79]

During the last two years of his tenure as Army chief of staff, Bradley adamantly defended his service—with mixed results. He successfully won the argument to increase pay and allowances for the military, arguing that little had been done to address the buying power of military salaries in the face of postwar inflation. Under-

Omar Bradley as chief of staff, in a portrait by C. L. MacNelly. (National Archives)

standing the need to have a mobilization plan available that could quickly generate capable units, he unsuccessfully lobbied Congress for universal military training.[80] A war-weary nation had no interest in a universal draft. He proclaimed the National Guard "virtually useless in a national crisis" and proposed that the Guard be federalized.[81] The suggestion was dead on arrival in Congress. When Truman announced he wanted the U.S. military desegregated, Bradley warned that however good the idea, the devil was in the details, and that if done in haste, integration had the potential to cripple combat readiness.[82] Throughout his tenure as Army chief of staff, he remained steadfast in stating his beliefs, regardless of their popularity. When Truman proposed a reorganization of the War Department into what would become the Department of Defense, Bradley was among a select few considered for the chairmanship of the Joint Chiefs of Staff.

Not surprisingly, Truman's first pick for the new position was Eisenhower. For various reasons, Eisenhower declined the offer, and Truman offered the position to Bradley, who became the nation's first chairman of the Joint Chiefs of Staff in August 1949. The following month Truman asked Congress for authorization to promote Bradley to his fifth star. The decision proved a wise one, for Bradley would need the prestige the rank provided him when the last challenge of his army career presented itself in Korea.

In the fall of 1950 Communist forces in North Korea crossed the 38th parallel driving south, overwhelming poorly trained and equipped South Korean and U.S. forces sent to slow them down. U.S. airpower immediately came into play, impeding but not halting the invasion. The North Koreans pinned South Korean and U.S. forces to the southeast corner of the peninsula around the port city of Pusan. With the approval of both Truman and the Joint Chiefs of Staff, Douglas MacArthur conducted a daring amphibious landing at Inchon, north of Seoul, effectively cutting the lines of supply and communication to North Korean forces to the south. What followed was an American–South Korean advance to the north similar in some respects to the American pursuit following the Normandy breakout. North Korean forces appeared in disarray. Rather than stop at the 38th parallel, MacArthur pushed northward toward the Yalu River and the border with Communist China.[83] MacArthur, citing his own intelligence sources, said that the possibility of Chinese intervention was minimal and that the war would be over by Thanksgiving.[84]

It was Bradley's position as chairman that combatant commanders such as MacArthur be given as much freedom of action as possible to allow them to do their jobs. He was not about to micromanage MacArthur, had that even been possible. He, as well as the

General Bradley as chairman of the Joint Chiefs of Staff. (Department of Defense, courtesy of the Harry S. Truman Library)

Joint Chiefs of Staff, accepted MacArthur's view of the situation; this proved shortsighted. When Chinese units began to infiltrate in large numbers across the Yalu, U.S. intelligence noted their presence but discounted their numbers, intentions, and capabilities. When the Chinese attack came, it caught MacArthur by surprise, driving his forces back down the peninsula, a situation not stabilized until

January 1951. MacArthur's planning had failed to anticipate the offensive, let alone determine what to do if it came.

Truman realized that U.S. policy might well have to change and accept the idea of a truce at the 38th parallel. Seemingly in direct violation of the president's intentions, as well as guidance that the White House approve all policy pronouncements, MacArthur stated that the successful conclusion of the conflict required reunification of Korea. MacArthur followed this by asking the Joint Chiefs not to impose any further military restrictions, particularly regarding the use of airpower. He warned that bombing restrictions against the Chinese "made it completely impractical to clear North Korea."[85] He went on to comment openly that the Chinese had proven themselves militarily incompetent. Truman believed this remark would jeopardize chances of reaching any settlement in Korea that would be acceptable to Communist China. What MacArthur wanted was a wider war. Ridgway noted in his account of the Korean War that MacArthur intended to strike Communism "a blow from which it would never recover." As part of this vision, MacArthur not only wanted to drive American forces to the Yalu, but also wanted an air campaign to destroy air bases and industrial capacity in Manchuria and a blockade of the Chinese coast. All this he saw as preparatory to a U.S.–supported invasion of the Chinese homeland by Chiang Kai-shek's Nationalist Army.[86] Implicit in MacArthur's vision was the possible employment of atomic weapons.[87] With earlier issues such as the landing of the Chinese Nationalist Army on the Chinese mainland and the possible use of atomic weapons weighing on his mind, Truman wanted MacArthur relieved. Bradley, as well as Secretary of State Marshall, argued for a go-slow approach. Bradley was unsure whether MacArthur had actually disobeyed Truman's orders, as the president contended. Nonetheless, in what would become one of his last acts as chairman, Bradley recommended the relief of MacArthur. Though the relief was without prejudice, the ticker-tape parades that greeted MacArthur upon his return to the United States failed to mask the break between Truman and MacArthur.

MacArthur's relief proved hard for Bradley, for despite his reservations about MacArthur's behavior, he understood that the general's return marked the passing of an age. By the end of the summer, it would be Bradley's turn to fade from public view. He had served two tours as the nation's first chairman of the Joint

Chiefs. Those years had been contentious, as the services argued over missions and budgets. He had served largely as a mediator. He had helped give birth to the North Atlantic Treaty Organization (NATO) and had served as a faithful counsel to President Truman. In August 1953, thirty-eight years after his commissioning at West Point, he yielded his position as chairman of the Joint Chiefs and retired. Bradley would live another twenty-eight years before his death on April 8, 1981. He filled the years between 1953 and 1981 well, directing Bulova Watch Company as well as being a popular speaker in the military's service colleges. In the 1960s President Lyndon B. Johnson called on him for advice regarding the war in Vietnam. He saw the passing of many of his wartime peers, marking more than one funeral at the graveside of a departed friend. No friend stood dearer than his wife, Mary, who passed away in 1964. He took the death hard but would marry again, wedding Kitty Buhler, who remained his constant companion until his own death. The Army laid him to rest at Arlington National Cemetery, in the company of his soldiers.

In the years since his death, historians have debated his position among the nation's military greats. Some have called into question his handling of the race to the Rhine. Others have argued that the decision to accept risk in the Ardennes without an adequate reserve constituted recklessness. Some or all of the criticisms may have their validity, yet, in truth, no American field commander ever faced his challenges or possessed his knack for commanding the respect of soldiers. He could handle the likes of a Patton, bringing out the best while compensating for the flaws. To superiors, he was a loyal subordinate while at the same time a vocal advocate on behalf of his men. Ernie Pyle summarized the men who waded ashore at Normandy as simply "Brave Men," and so they were, made so by their soft-spoken commanding general. He always carried an awareness of the responsibilities of command, the gut-wrenching realization that his decisions determined the lives of men. For a Missouri boy born of humble parents, the journey across a life to five stars and chairmanship of the Joint Chiefs of Staff was the stuff of Horatio Alger stories. Though never intending to be one, he became an icon to the Willies, Joes, and Rosies of an era.

Notes

1. Omar N. Bradley, *A Soldier's Story* (New York: Henry Holt, 1951), 485.

2. Geoffrey Perret, *There's a War to Be Won: The United States Army in World War II* (New York: Random House, 1991), 117.

3. Omar N. Bradley, *A General's Life: An Autobiography* (New York: Simon and Schuster, 1983), 60.

4. Following World War I, the U.S. Army created an Infantry Board, whose purpose was to capture the lessons of the war as well as to create new schooling to teach those lessons. Ibid., 10

5. Ibid., 71–72.

6. Jim DeFelice, *Omar Bradley: General at War* (Washington, D.C.: Regnery, 2011), 46.

7. Bradley, *A General's Life*, 108.

8. Ibid., 115.

9. Ibid., 97, 99–101.

10. Ibid., 107.

11. The 82nd Division would go on to be the first U.S. division selected for duty as paratroopers.

12. Bradley clearly saw the job of being Eisenhower's eyes as meaning just that. He intended to go as far forward as necessary, if need be down to platoon and even squad level. He backed his intentions with actions. Rather than the standard .45-caliber Colt pistol carried by most general officers, Bradley picked out a 1903 Springfield as an additional personal firearm. Bradley, *A General's Life*, 133.

13. Russell Weigley, *Eisenhower's Lieutenants: The Campaigns of France and Germany, 1944–1945*, 2 vols. (Bloomington: Indiana University Press, 1981), 1:119.

14. Ibid., and Rick Atkinson, *An Army at Dawn: The War in North Africa, 1942–1943* (New York: Henry Holt, 2002), 500.

15. Weigley, *Eisenhower's Lieutenants*, 1:120.

16. Perret, *There's a War to Be Won*, 165, and Bradley, *A Soldier's Story*, 67, 87.

17. Bradley, *A Soldier's Story*, 78.

18. Ibid., 80–81.

19. Allied planners had considered an invasion of Sardinia (Operation Brimstone), but the island's location seemed to offer no real advantages for subsequent operations on the continent of Europe. Furthermore, Marshall believed that an invasion of Sardinia carried the risk of greater shipping losses, something that would jeopardize the cross-Channel attack into northwestern France he strongly favored. Sicily was somewhat of an ad hoc compromise. Though a major move-

ment of German Army units into Italy might require operations on the Italian mainland, both the Americans and the British hoped to avoid getting embroiled there. A successful invasion of Sicily would, it was hoped, secure the Mediterranean's sea lines of communication, meet Stalin's plea for an Anglo-American second front, and cause Italy to exit the conflict. See Albert N. Garland and Howard McGraw Smyth, *Sicily and the Surrender of Italy*, U.S. Army in World War II (Washington, D.C.: Center of Military History, 2002), 7–11.

20. Bradley, *A General's Life*, 186.

21. Michael Veranov, ed., *The Mammoth Book of the Third Reich at War* (London: Constable and Robinson, 1997), 306.

22. Though the preliminary plans for the invasion of Sicily calling for the Americans to land on the northern coast and the British on the east left the capture of Messina more or less open to whichever army pressed faster, the actual landing plan in which Patton's Seventh Army provided flank security to Montgomery's Eighth assumed Messina's fall to the latter. See Garland and Smyth, *Sicily and the Surrender of Italy*, 89.

23. Bradley, *A General's Life*, 199.

24. Bradley's style of leadership clashed with that of Patton. While complimentary of Patton as Third Army commanding general in France, in Sicily Bradley bit his tongue and wrote in his diary: "To his troops an army commander is little more than a distant figure who occasionally shows himself at the front. As a consequence the impressions of those men come directly from what they see. George irritated them by flaunting the pageantry of his command. He traveled in an entourage of command cars followed by a string of nattily uniformed staff officers. His own vehicle was gaily decked with oversize stars and the insignia of his command. These exhibitions did not awe troops as perhaps Patton believed. Instead, they offended the men as they trudged through the clouds of dust left in the wake of that procession. In Sicily Patton, the man, bore little resemblance to Patton the legend." See Bradley, *A Soldier's Story*, 159–60.

25. Garland and Smyth, *Sicily and the Surrender of Italy*, 412.

26. Ibid., 198, and Veranov, *Mammoth Book of the Third Reich at War*, 319.

27. Bradley had received a report from his medical staff about Patton's slapping of Kuhl. Kuhl had been diagnosed by the physicians as suffering from "psychoneurosis, anxiety state moderately severe." At the time of the slapping, Kuhl had been evacuated three times, was suffering from severe chronic diarrhea, and had malaria and a temperature of 102.2 degrees. Bradley made no attempt to forward the report to Eisenhower out of deference to the reality that Patton was his immediate superior at the time. See Bradley, *A General's Life*, 195.

28. Weigley, *Eisenhower's Lieutenants*, 1:120.

29. Bradley, *A General's Life*, 211.

30. Weigley, *Eisenhower's Lieutenants*, 1:120.

31. Dwight D. Eisenhower, *Crusade in Europe* (Garden City, N.Y.: Doubleday, 1948), 215.

32. Ibid., 211.

33. Gordon A. Harrison, *Cross-Channel Attack*, U.S. Army in World War II: The European Theater of Operations (Washington, D.C.: Center of Military History, 2007), 15.

34. The arrangement of Allied forces based on ports of debarkation created its own set of problems once the landings occurred. The British manpower pool was nearly expended by 1944, whereas American numbers were still on the rise. The Americans were going to carry most of the combat burden in the drive across France. Furthermore, U.S. industries were producing a wide variety of good-quality armored vehicles in astonishing numbers, so that it was clear that once Allied forces were established on the European mainland, the Americans were going to generate the greater number of armored units. Because the British landed to the east of the Americans, their forces were closest to the best mechanized avenues of approach into Germany while lacking the mobility American armies possessed.

35. Gerhard L. Weinberg, "Some Myths of World War II," *Journal of Military History* 75.3 (July 2011): 714.

36. Operation Anvil was initially to coincide with Overlord (originally code-named Sledgehammer). Anvil would send at least one and preferably three divisions against German defenders in the south of France for an offensive northward along the Rhône River. Planners hoped that opening up a line of communications (LOC) north along the Rhône would help alleviate the logistics problems that threatened a wider Allied advance into France. The air war against French railroads had been too successful, which made it difficult for logisticians to use them to resupply Allied armies without significant and lengthy repairs. Anvil's initial cancellation came as an answer to Overlord's growing need for amphibious lift as well as the Allied losses suffered in support of the Anzio landings. Allied planners did reschedule and execute Anvil in August 1944. See Bradley, *A Soldier's Story*, 219, and Jeffrey J. Clarke and Robert Ross Smith, *Riviera to the Rhine*, U.S. Army in World War II (Washington, D.C.: Center of Military History, 1993), 13–21.

37. Bradley, *A Soldier's Story*, 215.

38. Allied planners sought to give combat engineers thirty minutes in advance of the main landing force to clear lanes through the obstacles. The assault craft would ride the rising tide onto the beach and as close to the seawall as possible. Ibid., 261.

39. There had been considerable debate over the use of airborne units in support of the Normandy landings. James M. Gavin, later commanding general of the 82nd Airborne Division, wrote that Bradley had threatened to cancel the assault on Utah Beach unless the airborne drop went according to plan. None other than Chief Marshal Sir Trafford Leigh-Mallory had warned that to drop the 82nd and 101st Airborne divisions behind Omaha and Utah beaches would result in the "futile slaughter of two fine divisions." In the face of very real opposition, Bradley got his way. See James M. Gavin, *On to Berlin: Battles of an Airborne Commander, 1943–1946* (New York: Viking Press, 1978), 94.

40. In overall command Rundstedt neither commanded the panzer divisions assigned to western France and Belgium nor controlled either German sea or land assets assigned to defend the English Channel ports. Rundstedt only nominally controlled SS units, as their commanding officers could appeal directly to Reichsführer Heinrich Himmler if they did not approve of Rundstedt's orders. See Veranov, *Mammoth Book of the Third Reich at War*, 492.

41. Ibid., 493–94.

42. Bradley, *A General's Life*, 247.

43. Weigley, *Eisenhower's Lieutenants*, 1:131.

44. Forrest Pogue, *The Supreme Command*, U.S. Army in World War II (Washington, D.C.: Center of Military History, 1954), 192.

45. Martin Blumenson, *Breakout and Pursuit* (Washington, D.C.: Center of Military History, 1961), 4.

46. John J. Sullivan, "The Botched Air Support of Operation Cobra," *Parameters* 18 (March 1988): 98.

47. Ibid., 99.

48. Ibid., 100.

49. Bradley states in his autobiography that he had made it clear that nothing but a parallel approach was acceptable. See Bradley, *A General's Life*, 276.

50. Sullivan, "The Botched Air Support of Operation Cobra," 101.

51. Blumenson, *Breakout and Pursuit*, 236.

52. Bradley, *A Soldier's Story*, 372.

53. Weigley, *Eisenhower's Lieutenants*, 1:395.

54. There were other factors as well. First, too few ports supported the supply effort. German demolitions had significantly damaged nearly every port in Allied hands. Second, the Allies had planned to bypass Paris to avoid the additional demand the population of the city would place on supplies. Factors beyond the battlefield brought Paris under Allied control and along with it the supply drain logisticians feared. Third, not only were there too few truck companies, but there was also not an ideal mix of heavy and light trucks. There were too few of the

former and too many of the latter. Ibid.

55. Eisenhower's orders to Montgomery dated August 24, 1944, were clear: "Take Antwerp; advance eastward on the Ruhr." See John A. Adams, *The Battle for Western Europe, Fall 1944: An Operational Assessment* (Bloomington: Indiana University Press, 2010), 191; Weigley, *Eisenhower's Lieutenants,* 2:91; and Pogue, *The Supreme Command,* 310.

56. Pogue, *The Supreme Command,* 301.

57. Bradley concedes that planners had failed to man the force adequately, particularly in the numbers of infantry available. Infantry divisions at full strength numbered roughly 14,000 soldiers, but only one soldier in seven actually served as infantry. See Bradley, *A Soldier's Story,* 445, and Pogue, *The Supreme Command,* 305.

58. Bradley admits that part of the problem came from the supply crisis. As transportation was limited, he had elected to favor the movement of fuel and ammunition over that of winter clothing. Bradley, *A Soldier's Story,* 445.

59. The 9th, 28th, 45th, 8th, and elements of the 1st Infantry divisions all took casualties in the Hürtgen Forest. The 28th alone suffered 6,184 casualties there. By contrast, 1st and 29th Infantry divisions suffered just over 4,000 casualties on Omaha Beach. See Adams, *The Battle for Western Europe,* 246.

60. U.S. Army doctrine as written in the 1940 edition of *FM-100.5* advised that woods be bypassed if possible. Believing their flank threatened by the German divisions in the Hürtgen, Hodges and Collins elected to take the forest. Bradley agreed to the decision. Ibid., 191, and Weigley, *Eisenhower's Lieutenants,* 2:633.

61. Bradley, *A General's Life,* 343.

62. As early as the 1930s, Polish intelligence had been working to break the German ciphers used in military and diplomatic traffic. Much of their work found its way to Britain's Government Code and Cipher School at Bletchley when German armies overran Poland in September 1939. The British eventually did succeed in deciphering much of the German code system used to deploy German ground and some naval forces. Code-named Ultra, this capacity frequently tipped Allied intelligence to German plans. At the time of the Ardennes offensive, German units assigned to the attack were placed on radio silence, which somewhat mitigated the usefulness of Ultra. See John Keegan, *The Second World War* (New York: Viking Press, 1989), 497.

63. The German plan changed in the first days of the offensive. Sixth Army proved unequal to the task assigned and came to have its hands full holding the northern flank of the penetration. American resistance by the 2nd and 99th Infantry divisions on Elsenborn Ridge largely accounted for Sixth Army's failure. Fifth Army became the main attack. Hitler called off Fifteenth Army's supporting attack.

64. Known as Operation Liège-Aachen or the Small Solution, the plan called for a German drive from northern Luxembourg penetrating the Ardennes and then turning northward to link with a secondary attack originating near Aachen. Both Rundstedt and Model considered this option within their capability. Neither favored the larger concept Hitler demanded. See Charles V. P. von Luttichau, "The German Counteroffensive in the Ardennes," in *Command Decisions,* ed. Kent Roberts Greenfield (Washington, D.C.: Center of Military History, 1987), 453.

65. Adams, *The Battle for Western Europe,* 273.

66. Charles B. MacDonald, *A Time for Trumpets: The Untold Story of the Battle of the Bulge* (New York: Morrow, 1984), 298.

67. Allied intelligence, Forrest Pogue argues, should have detected the Ardennes offensive well before it was launched. Although little in the way of Ultra traffic suggested an offensive, human intelligence, as well as aerial reconnaissance, had nonetheless largely located and identified most of the units in the panzer armies. See Pogue, *The Supreme Command,* 371.

68. Bradley, *A General's Life,* 356.

69. MacDonald, *A Time for Trumpets,* 262.

70. The withdrawal of 7th Armored Division came by way of Montgomery, who had assumed command of both the U.S. First and Ninth armies by this time. Montgomery's intention was to gather together a counterattack force. The problem was that First Army was not only extended but lacking a reserve. In part to create a reserve but also to save 7th Armored from being overwhelmed, he pulled the division out of St. Vith. To better allow for the creation of a reserve, he ordered Simpson to extend Ninth Army's frontage to permit First Army to employ its VII Corps as a counterattack force. See Robin Neillands, *Battle for the Rhine: The Battle of the Bulge and the Ardennes Campaign, 1944* (Woodstock, N.Y.: Overlook Press, 2007), 294–95.

71. Pogue, *The Supreme Command,* 359.

72. Eisenhower directed that Devers expand his Army group front to take over that of Third Army.

73. Eisenhower had asked Bradley and Patton how soon Third Army could ready a counteroffensive into the southern flank of the German penetration. Patton, who had seen the opportunity well before Ike's request, had already directed his staff to prepare plans for just such a contingency. Patton's response was three days with four divisions. In disbelief, Eisenhower responded, "Don't be fatuous." Patton attacked in three days as promised. Pogue, *The Supreme Command,* 359.

74. The Army's official history lists German casualties as approximating 100,000. Neillands claims the numbers were closer to 81,000 and still other sources go as low as 67,000. See Luttichau, "The German

Counteroffensive in the Ardennes," 458, and Neillands, *Battle for the Rhine*, 300.

75. Neillands, *Battle for the Rhine*, 299.

76. German reconnaissance elements from 2nd Panzer Division of Fifth Panzer Army fought their way to within four kilometers of the Meuse at Dinant but could go no farther. Opposition from the U.S. 2nd Armored Division as well as shortages of fuel and ammunition brought the drive to a halt. Furthermore, clearing skies had brought American airpower fully into play, and, as Manteuffel noted, "the activity of the enemy air force was decisive." General der Panzertruppen Hasso von Manteuffel, "The Fifth Panzer Army during the Ardennes Offensive," in *Hitler's Ardennes Offensive: The German View of the Battle of the Bulge*, ed. Danny S. Parker (Mechanicsburg, Pa.: Stackpole Books, 1997), 115–17, 144, and Neillands, *Battle for the Rhine*, 295.

77. Bradley, *A General's Story*, 453.

78. Ibid., 451.

79. Ibid., 483.

80. Ibid., 482.

81. Ibid., 483.

82. Ibid., 485.

83. NSC-81 authorized MacArthur to go north of the 38th parallel as well as to effect the unification of all of Korea for free elections. As for the North Korean army, Bradley admits that it was the unanimous belief of the Joint Chiefs that it was destroyed. Ibid., 559–60.

84. Ibid., 577.

85. Ed Cray, *General of the Army George C. Marshall: Soldier and Statesman* (New York: W. W. Norton, 1990), 707.

86. Matthew B. Ridgway, *The Korean War* (New York: Da Capo Press, 1967), 145–47.

87. The idea of employing the bomb did not in fairness begin with MacArthur. Navy Secretary Francis P. Matthews proposed its use on August 25, 1950, at a commemoration for the Boston Navy Yard. His suggestion was that the United States employ it as part of a preemptive strike against the Soviet Union. When Truman heard of the speech, he all but relieved Matthews of his job. The following month Major General Orville A. Anderson, commandant of the Air War College, found himself suspended from his duties when he elected to offer a course on preemptive war as part of the school's curriculum. While making public statements denying that the United States intended to employ the bomb, Truman directed the Atomic Energy Commission and the JCS to examine the feasibility of increasing U.S. nuclear capabilities. The earliest discussions were of a more limited tactical use of atomic weapons. The problem was how to employ them so that the target

was appropriate to the weapon and limited to North Korean forces and supporting infrastructure. See Stanley Weintraub, *MacArthur's War: Korea and the Undoing of an American Hero* (New York: Free Press, 2000), 253–58.

References

Adams, John A. *The Battle for Western Europe, Fall 1944: An Operational Assessment.* Bloomington: Indiana University Press, 2010.

Blumenson, Martin. *Breakout and Pursuit,* Washington, D.C.: Center of Military History, 1961.

Bradley, Omar N. *A General's Life: An Autobiography.* New York: Simon and Schuster, 1983.

———. *A Soldier's Story.* New York: Henry Holt, 1951.

DeFelice, Jim. *Omar Bradley: General at War.* Washington, D.C.: Regnery, 2011.

Garland, Albert N., and Howard McGaw Smyth. *Sicily and the Surrender of Italy.* U.S. Army in World War II. Washington, D.C.: Center of Military History, 2002.

Harrison, Gordon A. *Cross-Channel Attack.* U.S. Army in World War II: The European Theater of Operations. Washington, D.C.: Center of Military History, 2007.

Luttichau, Charles V. P. von. "The German Counteroffensive in the Ardennes." In *Command Decisions.* Edited by Kent Roberts Greenfield. Washington, D.C.: Center of Military History, 1987.

MacDonald, Charles B. *A Time for Trumpets: The Untold Story of the Battle of the Bulge.* New York: Morrow, 1984.

Neillands, Robin. *Battle for the Rhine: The Battle of the Bulge and the Ardennes Campaign, 1944.* Woodstock, N.Y.: Overlook Press, 2007.

Perret, Geoffrey. *There's a War to Be Won: The United States Army in World War II.* New York: Random House, 1991.

Pogue, Forrest. *The Supreme Command.* U.S. Army in World War II. Washington, D.C.: Center of Military History, 1954.

Sullivan, John J. "The Botched Air Support of Operation Cobra." *Parameters* 18 (March 1988): 97–110.

Veranov, Michael, ed. *The Mammoth Book of the Third Reich at War.* London: Constable and Robinson, 1997.

Weigley, Russell. *Eisenhower's Lieutenants: The Campaigns of France and Germany, 1944–1945.* 2 vols. Bloomington: Indiana University Press, 1981.

Afterword

Ethan S. Rafuse

In the seventy years since World War II, Fort Leavenworth has remained the crossroads for the officer corps of the United States Army, the place where field-grade officers receive an educational experience designed to prepare them for the rest of their careers. The challenges that the United States has faced during that period have been formidable. Though no officer has been appointed to five-star rank since Omar Bradley's promotion in 1950, the list of accomplished officers who have passed through the course at the U.S. Army Command and General Staff College (CGSC) and the contributions of graduates of that institution to the Army and American national security is an impressive one.

For more than four decades the Cold War divided the world, and the officers educated at the CGSC played critical roles in the efforts of the U.S. military to contribute to the cause of containing and ultimately defeating Communism. It was Matthew Ridgway, a 1935 CGSC graduate, whose skilled and determined leadership helped turn the tide of battle in Korea after the entry of massive numbers of Chinese troops sparked fears of the total defeat of United Nations forces. Ridgway's determined leadership of the Army in the years after Korea, supported by such officers as James Gavin (a 1942 graduate of CGSC) and Maxwell Taylor (a 1935 graduate), proved to be a key factor in sustaining the Army and its ability to continue playing a significant role in the defense of the free world from Communist aggression.

After the Vietnam War, in which the high command of the U.S. Army was dominated by William Westmoreland, a former CGSC instructor, and Creighton Abrams, a graduate, CGSC was at the heart of the effort to revitalize the Army and prepare it for the future. As chief of staff of the Army, it was Abrams (CGSC Class of 1949) who in the early 1970s began driving what would be a successful, generation-long process of reforming the Army and provided the vision that would guide it to fruition. Playing critical roles in carrying Abrams's vision forward were officers such as William DePuy (a 1946 CGSC graduate), who as the first commander of Training and Doctrine Command initiated an intense debate over doctrine, out of which would come the development of what became known as AirLand Battle doctrine. To support the development of doctrine and ensure the officer corps possessed the intellectual and leadership skills necessary to execute it successfully, the staff college underwent its own period of reform.

Under the direction of CGSC graduates and leaders like Donn Starry, William Richardson, Dave Palmer, Frederick Franks, Robert Arter, and Carl Vuono, the curriculum and methods of instruction at CGSC underwent a profound transformation during the 1980s. The School for Advanced Military Studies (SAMS) was created in 1983, giving officers an opportunity to continue their studies after completing the one-year Command and General Staff Officers Course (CGSOC); SAMS was headed by one of the officers who had developed AirLand Battle. At both SAMS and CGSOC the study of military history became an especially important component of the instructional program because of its unmatched value in fostering the critical and creative thinking skills the CGSC experience is designed to develop in field-grade officers. It was this foundation that provided much of the intellectual firepower that made possible the stunning battlefield victory in the Gulf War, in which several CGSC graduates—including Colin Powell, H. Norman Schwarzkopf, and Barry McCaffrey—participated prominently.

When the Soviet Union collapsed and the Cold War came to an end, the U.S. military entered an era in which the challenges to American national security became more complex. The clarity that the Cold War had provided to American strategy was replaced by ambiguity in terms of the threat Army leaders were to prepare for, while public expectations for a "peace dividend" led to limits on the resources with which the Army would have to operate. The Army and the junior officers who went on to wear five stars in World War II had encountered a similar situation in the aftermath of the Great War. In the 1920s and 1930s, when funding for the military was limited and popular enthusiasm for the nation's participation in another great land war was low, they were nonetheless able to prepare successfully for the challenge of a global conflict of unprecedented scale. That has been no less true in recent times. CGSC has continued to play an important role in the development of the Army's most senior leaders. Most former Army chiefs of staff, as well as the current one, General Ray Odierno, and most of the Army generals who have served as chairmen of the Joint Chiefs of Staff, including the current chairman, General Martin Dempsey, have also been molded by the Leavenworth experience. It is also true for those officers who have guided the Army in the recent wars in Iraq and Afghanistan from the most senior levels, like General David Petraeus, down to the battalion level.

Indeed, in 2006 General Petraeus commented:

> For 125 years, Fort Leavenworth has been the crossroads for the officer corps of the United States Army. It is at the Command and General Staff College that field grade officers receive an educational experience that prepares them for the rest of their careers of service to the Army and the nation. . . . The College has superbly prepared thousands of officers for duty as field grade commanders and staff officers, as well as advanced the professional development of officers from the Army's sister services and nations throughout the world. It has also played a central role in shaping the doctrines and procedures the Army employs to defend the nation. Today we are seeing CGSC go above and beyond its motto, Ad bellum pace parati—"In peace, prepare for war"—in line with a recognition that . . . it is not just during the relative calm of peace that intellectual preparation for war should take place.[1]

To prepare for war in time of peace is one of the greatest challenges that a military organization must confront. Since 1881 the schools of Leavenworth have accepted that mission on behalf of the United States Army. The graduates of those schools guided the Army and the nation through the tumultuous twentieth century and stand ready to face the twenty-first. The five-star generals of Leavenworth stand in the front rank of the legion of officers who have passed through this post and gone on to serve their nation in conflicts great and small around the globe.

Note

1. David H. Petraeus, foreword to *On the Frontier—Preparing Leaders . . . Yesterday, Today, and Tomorrow: CGSC, 1981–2006,* by Ethan Rafuse (Fort Leavenworth, Kans.: U.S. Army Command and General Staff College, 2006), iii.

Acknowledgments

We would like to thank Bob Ulin of the Command and General Staff College Foundation, who played a key role in the genesis of this project. A special thanks to Foundation trustee Richard Brown and his wife, Christine, for financial support that made this project possible. We would also like to thank Stephen Wrinn of the University Press of Kentucky and Roger Cirillo of the Association of the United States Army for their support during the preparation of this book. For photos and archival material, special thanks go to the National Archives, Library of Congress, U.S. Army Center of Military History, National Museum of the Air Force, Dwight D. Eisenhower Presidential Library, Eisenhower National Historic Site, George C. Marshall International Center, George C. Marshall Research Library, Naval History and Heritage Command, and Virginia Military Institute Archives. We are particularly indebted to the Combined Arms Research Library and the Frontier Army Museum, both at Fort Leavenworth, Kansas, for material and photos from the early days of the Command and General Staff College.

Contributors

John M. Curatola is an associate history professor at the U.S. Army Command and General Staff College at Fort Leavenworth, Kansas. Before holding this position he was an active-duty Marine Corps officer; he retired in 2009 after twenty-two years of service, including deployments to Somalia in 1992 and Operation Iraqi Freedom in 2003. Curatola received a B.A. in political science from the University of Nebraska. He holds a master's degree in U.S. history from George Mason University and a master of military arts and science in military history from the Army Command and General Staff College. He received his doctorate in U.S. history from the University of Kansas.

Joseph R. Fischer serves as a professor in the Department of Military History, U.S. Army Command and General Staff College, Fort Leavenworth, Kansas. He received a B.A. in history in 1975 from the Pennsylvania State University and was commissioned a second lieutenant in the Infantry. In 1979 he returned to civilian life, earning a B.S. in secondary education and a master's degree in history from Penn State. Soon after graduation, he reentered the Army and served as a company commander in 3rd Armored Division and later as an assistant professor of military history at the U.S. Military Academy at West Point. Shortly after leaving West Point, he entered a Ph.D. program in American history at Penn State and received that degree in 1993. His last government assignment before joining the faculty at CGSC was as a command historian at U.S. Army Special Operations Command at Fort Bragg, North Carolina. In 2005 the Army recalled him to active duty, assigning him to serve as a historian in support of U.S. Special Operations Command for Operation Iraqi Freedom. Fischer is the author of *A Well-Executed Failure: The Sullivan Campaign against the Iroquois, July–September 1779* (1997) and is the coauthor of a number of other works on the early republic and special operations.

Christopher R. Gabel received his doctorate from the Ohio State University. Since 1983 he has served on the faculty of the U.S. Army

Command and General Staff College, Fort Leavenworth, Kansas, where he is currently a professor in the Department of Military History, specializing in the World War II era. His publications include *The U.S. Army GHQ Maneuvers of 1941* (1991); *Seek, Strike, and Destroy: U.S. Army Tank Destroyer Doctrine in World War II* (1986); and *Staff Ride Handbook for the Vicksburg Campaign, December 1862–July 1863* (2001).

Jonathan M. House is the William A. Stofft Professor of Military History at the U.S. Army Command and General Staff College. A graduate of Hamilton College, he received both his doctorate in French military history and his commission in the U.S. Army at the University of Michigan. As a career army officer, House served several tours as an intelligence analyst for the Joint Chiefs of Staff. After leaving active duty, he became the chairman of social sciences at Gordon College in Barnesville, Georgia, before returning to Fort Leavenworth to teach as a civilian. He is the author of *Military Intelligence, 1870–1991* (1993) and *Combined Arms Warfare in the Twentieth Century* (2001), as well as several articles about the growth of the U.S. Army in the early twentieth century. He is also the coauthor, with David Glantz, of numerous studies of the Soviet-German conflict, most notably *When Titans Clashed: How the Red Army Stopped Hitler* (1995).

Sean N. Kalic is a professor in the Department of Military History at the U.S. Army Command and General Staff College in Fort Leavenworth, Kansas. He holds a B.A. in political science from the University of Denver and received his doctorate in history from Kansas State University. Kalic is the author of a study of the development of U.S. national space policy entitled *U.S. Presidents and the Militarization of Space, 1946–1967* (2012). He has also written *Combating a Modern Hydra: Al Qaeda and the Global War on Terrorism* (2005).

Tony R. Mullis is an associate professor with the Department of Military History at the U.S. Army Command and General Staff College at Fort Leavenworth, Kansas. He served twenty-three years in the U.S. Air Force as an intelligence officer and retired in 2005. He holds a Ph.D. in history from the University of Kansas. His major fields include the history of the United States and military history. His secondary field is indigenous nations studies. He has taught history at the U.S. Air Force Academy and the Air Command and Staff College at Maxwell Air Force Base, Alabama. Mullis has also taught various U.S., Kansas, and diplomatic history courses as an adjunct with the University of Maryland in Korea and Scotland and with Troy University, Benedictine College, Tiffin University, and Auburn University at Montgomery. His has published various journal articles associated with Kansas and military history. His book, *Peacekeeping on the Plains: Army Operations in Bleeding Kansas*, was published in 2004.

Ethan S. Rafuse is a professor of military history at the U.S. Army Command and General Staff College at Fort Leavenworth, Kansas. He holds a B.A. and an M.A. in history from George Mason University and received his doctorate in history and political science from the University of Missouri–Kansas City. He is the author, editor, or coeditor of eight books, including *McClellan's War: The Failure of Moderation in the Struggle for the Union* (2005) and *Robert E. Lee and the Fall of the Confederacy, 1863–1865* (2008).

James H. Willbanks is the General of the Army George C. Marshall Chair of Military History and director of the Department of Military History at the U.S. Army Command and General Staff College at Fort Leavenworth, Kansas. He has been on the faculty since 1992, when he retired from the Army as a lieutenant colonel with twenty-three years service as an Infantry officer in various assignments, including a tour as an adviser with a South Vietnamese regiment during the 1972 North Vietnamese Easter Offensive. He holds a B.A. in history from Texas A&M University, and an M.A. and Ph.D. in history from the University of Kansas. He is the author of *Abandoning Vietnam* (2004), *The Battle of An Loc* (2005), *The Tet Offensive: A Concise History* (2007), and *Vietnam War Almanac* (2009), and the editor of *America's Heroes: Medal of Honor Recipients from the Civil War to Afghanistan* (2011) and *The Vietnam War*, a volume in the International Library of Essays on Military History (2006).

Index

Page references given in *italics* indicate illustrations or material contained in their captions. Names of military units are alphabetized as spelled rather than by numerical order. For example, the 19th Infantry Division will appear before the 9th Infantry Division.